The New American State

To Janet,
who manages
author o[...]
wi[...]
bureaucracies the Eise[...]
Project encounters.

THE JOHNS HOPKINS SYMPOSIA IN COMPARATIVE HISTORY

The Johns Hopkins Symposia in Comparative History are occasional volumes sponsored by the Department of History at the Johns Hopkins University and the Johns Hopkins University Press comprising original essays by leading scholars in the United States and other countries. Each volume considers, from a comparative perspective, an important topic of current historical interest. The present volume is the fourteenth. Its preparation has been assisted by the James S. Schouler Lecture Fund.

THE NEW AMERICAN STATE

Bureaucracies and Policies since World War II

edited by
LOUIS GALAMBOS

The Johns Hopkins University Press

BALTIMORE AND LONDON

© 1987 The Johns Hopkins University Press
All rights reserved
Printed in the United States of America

The Johns Hopkins University Press
701 West 40th Street
Baltimore, Maryland 21211
The Johns Hopkins Press Ltd., London

The paper used in this publication meets
the minimum requirements of American
National Standard for Information Sciences —
Permanence of Paper for Printed Library
Materials, ANSI Z39.48-1984.

Library of Congress Cataloging-in-Publication
Data

The New American state.

(The Johns Hopkins Symposia in
comparative history; 14th)
Includes index.
1. Administrative agencies — United States.
2. Bureaucracy — United States. 3. United
States — Politics and government — 1945–
I. Galambos, Louis. II. Series
JK421.N44 1987   353′.01   87-4146
ISBN 0-8010-3485-6 (alk. paper)
ISBN 0-8018-3490-2 (pbk. : alk. paper)

Contents

THE NEW AMERICAN STATE

Louis Galambos

By Way of Introduction

Who's running the new and formidable American state? Most of us are uncertain. Most of us would like to know, if only because we send significant amounts of our money to Washington, D.C., and would like to know who is deciding how to spend all those dollars (as well as the billions that have to be borrowed) and who is determining whether they are being spent wisely. We would also like to know what we can do when we are not satisfied with the way things are going. To whom should we look for different policies or for a better effort in existing programs? Our government is now so large and so complex that it frequently seems beyond our influence and all too often beyond the control of our elected or appointed representatives. That's why we wonder who, exactly, is running America.

Every four years we convince ourselves that our presidents are in charge, that they actually run the American government. This is comforting. The president is of course the primary symbol of our national authority in this country and abroad. He commands our massive military establishment and ostensibly directs the great array of administrative agencies that impinge either directly or indirectly on the lives of most Americans every day. If we are dissatisfied with the way things are running, we can always put a new man or woman in the White House. But whenever we do, they seem to develop doubts about who is in charge, who can reshape policy, who is responsible for what our government is doing.

The White House frequently points to the federal bureaucracy as the dominant force in our national government. Most of our recent presidents, including Ronald Reagan, have lamented their inability to control the administrative institutions we think they direct. Government officials immune from political control have acquired so much power, we hear, that neither the chief executive, nor the legislature, nor the courts can break their hold on public policy.

1

Admittedly, the president's grip on the executive branch is weaker than most Americans think. He can place his own political appointees in departments and agencies, but where well-entrenched administrative officers are in charge of programs specifically authorized by statute, even the president can do little to influence their performance.[1] Moreover, the bureaucracies have in some instances acquired a virtual monopoly on expertise, on knowledge about their specific programs and their implementation. In an effort to correct that situation, both the White House and Congress have developed elaborate staffs to generate their own expertise and the sort of information that would enable them to oversee the operation of the federal administration. Interest groups, too, bring experts to bear on policy issues, and consulting firms now make talented professionals available to advise anyone who can afford their services. As a result monopolies have been almost impossible to maintain over the long term. But still problems in the system persist. Bureaucratic decisions have in many cases replaced legislative or executive decisions as the key factor shaping the specific content of our national policies. During this century power has clearly drifted toward bureaucratic hands, and one result appears to be a leaderless style of government.

Concern in Washington, D.C., about the operations of our federal bureaucracy has in the years since World War II prompted the organization of a series of formidable commissions, councils, and task forces to analyze the nation's administrative problems and to present solutions. The first of these was the Hoover Commission, a bipartisan effort in 1947–49 directed by former president Herbert C. Hoover. This well-publicized foray into the operations of the American government produced a ream of hearings, specialized staff studies, and proposals for the reorganization of the executive branch. In the years that followed, many of the Hoover Commission proposals were actually implemented: most obvious of the accomplishments were the changes that strengthened civilian authority in the Department of Defense and that shifted power to department heads and away from subordinates in several vital areas of the executive branch;[2] of more general import was the bipartisan impetus the commission gave to the basic concept of the managerial presidency.[3]

But even those formidable innovations could not keep bureaucratic reform from becoming an American will-o'-the-wisp, a goal that beckoned but seemed always just beyond the government's grasp. Of course that called for new studies: a second Hoover Commission, as well as PACGO (the President's Advisory Committee on Government Organization) in the 1950s, and the Heineman Task Force in the next decade, followed by the Ash Council of the Nixon administration.[4]

No recent president has been more concerned about this problem than was Richard Milhous Nixon. His plans were, he said, thwarted by a bureaucracy peopled with civil servants out of sympathy with his efforts to make the government more efficient and less intrusive in American life. His response was to push political authority down further into the body of the bureaucracy; political appointees such as the PADs (program associate directors) at the Office of Management and Budget, were charged with implementing a Republican program in what the White House considered a Democratic bureaucracy. Following the Ash Council's directives, Nixon also proposed in 1971 a thoroughgoing realignment of the federal departments and agencies, a regrouping that would, he hoped, enable him and his trusted lieutenant John Erlichman at last to bring the bureaucracy to heel. To no avail. Congressional suspicion derailed the Nixon foray into administrative politics.[5] Watergate ensured that his reorganization plan would not be resuscitated.

But the issue would not go away. Jimmy Carter and his successor also thought there were problems in the bureaucracy. Carter's sunset plan — which would have automatically terminated agencies that were not periodically reauthorized by a new statute — was quickly killed in Congress, but Carter was successful in promoting a measure that aimed to update the civil service. One of the most significant changes introduced by the Civil Service Reform Act of 1979 was the creation of a new layer of top-level administrators (Senior Executive Service) who were supposed to constitute a higher civil service that would improve performance by breaking out of the normal, narrow bureaucratic careers and ranging wider and higher in the government. This new layer of officials was designed to improve administrative performance at the crucial interface between political control and the civil service.[6] But this did not satisfy Ronald Reagan, who mounted his own inquiry into the problems of bureaucratic performance. The Grace Commission was certainly as earnest as its predecessors, and it too produced a bookshelf of hearings, studies, and recommendations. It is too early in the commission's history to render a judgment about its impact on our government, but it appears unlikely that changes in either structure or performance comparable to those achieved by the first Hoover Commission will result from this most recent of a long string of ad hoc bodies created to reform the bureaucracy.

About one thing, however, we can be fairly certain. It seems highly unlikely that the findings of the Grace Commission will do any more to educate the American public about the specific nature of their federal bureaucracy than have all of the previous commissions, task forces, and councils. Certainly the bureaucracy is the part of American government about which most of us know the least. Raised as we were to understand the Constitution and the balance of powers it carefully specifies, tutored in the politics of party campaigns and intrigued by dominant political personalities, we have not been particularly interested in or knowledgeable about administrative behavior.

On the whole administrators are not a very exciting lot. They have not fared particularly well in the history of our country. The great personalities we associate with the most important political movements in United States history have generally not been good administrators. Nor has their performance in an administrative capacity been the measure of their careers. In fact, the reputations of those who have had administrative experience and ability have suffered as a result; this was certainly the case with Dwight Eisenhower.

When bureaucracy in our federal government does come to the attention of Americans, it is usually seen in an exceedingly negative light. In this century the bureaucracy has apparently inherited most of the animosity Americans have traditionally felt toward federal authority as such. Although the programs we like are perforce implemented by career officials, we seldom credit these bureaucrats for their accomplishments. We become interested in bureaucracy only when something does not get done, when red tape tangles the wheels of government, when seemingly mindless regulations impinge on our activities. Then the bureaucracy comes in for a brand of universal criticism that we seldom levy on even the worst of our elected officials. Bureaucracy arouses Americans to a level of intensity that some societies can achieve only when attacking religious opponents.

Indeed, so intense have the charges become in recent years that our federal bureaucratic institutions are threatening to become the mysterious "other" that societies sometimes invoke to explain their difficulties in periods of great stress. Like the Protocols of Zion or the Money Power, the Bureaucracy of these diatribes is a hazy, ill-defined entity. It consists not so much of specific officials performing specific tasks as of the entire complex of bureaucratic institutions that provide us with government products and services. No one would deny that the boundaries of that complex have become vague and that there are problems of bureaucratic performance that warrant our attention. But still, it is difficult to avoid the conclusion that the attacks on bureaucracy have acquired a force and an all-pervasive nature that seem out of proportion to the actual problems that exist.

These attacks and the lack of understanding they reflect are one reason for publishing this volume and its exploration of the role of bureaucracy in our federal government in the years since World War

II. Our focus is on an era — and forty years is long enough to be tagged an era — that falls in the scholarly seam between political history and behavioral science. While social scientists today are concentrating largely on developments in the 1980s, professional historians have just begun to inch into the postwar years. The main focus of attention in historical scholarship is still the period before 1945; those historians working on the 1950s and 1960s can hardly help but be aware that they are in a precarious position on the leading edge of their discipline. Some of the records they need to write the history of public policy are not yet available to researchers: some are classified; some are in private hands; some, though in archives, are still restricted or completely closed to scholars.

Even when they have the documentary records they need, historians have been slow to grapple with the emergence of America's bureaucratic state. For the most part they have been no more interested in the intricacies of administrative history than have the American people. Only in recent years have they begun to describe and analyze some aspects of the elaborate bureaucratic structures that have come to characterize our federal government in this century. Behavioral scientists — especially those in economics and political science — have been at that task for some years now and have developed a significant body of research, concepts, and theories related to the political dimensions of bureaucratic behavior.[7] To date, however, these ideas have not had much impact on historical scholarship. This is particularly unfortunate in the case at hand because political history, political economy, and political science are all likely to benefit from an exchange of analyses and research results across disciplinary boundaries. The building of the modern American state is a subject of such magnitude and complexity that we can all use all the help we can get in understanding it better.

Our collection of essays tries to contribute to that understanding by examining in some detail the development of American bureaucracies in selected areas of public policy during the postwar era. The authors are interested in the characteristics of the organizations that have evolved and in how those institutions have influenced policy outcomes. They have asked: What is this new form of administrative entity? What does it do to shape policy? What are the long-run implications of these types of bureaucratic behavior for American politics and the American people?

It would once have been unnecessary even to ask these questions. In nineteenth-century America the organizational landscape — public and private — was less imposing. For the better part of that century Americans could cope effectively with their administrative setting because of the small scale of most organizations. Bureaucratic structures of authority were rare. The individual loomed over the organization, and responsibility could be located with some precision in both public and private life.

It was simple to recognize the boundaries of federal power, in part because it played such a limited role in everyday life in nineteenth-century America. The federal government performed only a narrow range of functions; it collected very little income and employed a miniscule percentage of the work force. Only in wartime did federal authority intrude in a decisive manner on a nation that was still over-whelmingly rural and was dedicated to forms of progress that were largely material and private. Farms and businesses were for the most part family undertakings controlled by an individual or by partners; not until the late nineteenth century did the corporate form of organization become common in the United States. In the private sector responsibility was precisely located: the individual was assumed to be in charge of his own affairs and responsible for his success or failure. The ethos of individualism was a powerful force. Americans were given to collective action in a wide variety of forms, but most were voluntary and a dissenting individual could always withdraw. Americans were quite willing to work together to achieve common goals. It was coercive collective behavior that they resented and resisted.

That was why the Constitution was such a comforting and revered document. It had a relevance to the political system that few Americans today can fully appreciate (any more than they can understand the role the Bible played in everyday life in the previous century). The Constitution defined those boundaries that Americans wanted to believe would never give way: the boundary between federal and state power; the boundary between public and private authority; the boundary that defined the extent to which institutions of any sort could impinge upon the individual. The Constitution ensured that state and local governments would perform all but a specified set of functions that were granted to the central government. Changes in the narrow purview of federal authority were resisted with great rigor. This was true even in the latter part of the century after technological and economic advances had made state boundaries less important than they had been before the Civil War and had left state governments poorly situated to cope with some of the nation's central problems of political economy.

Insofar as the federal government was concerned, there was little need to ask who was running America. Congress kept a tight leash on the rudimentary federal agencies that existed, and within the legislature the major political parties exercised substantial control over the behavior of most members of Congress. Party power and patronage were crucial to the operation of the federal government—a situation that might have produced some serious problems had the government had more functions to perform than it normally did. But there was virtually no bureaucracy to direct; it was, as Stephen Skowronek has observed, essentially a government of courts and parties.[8]

Near the end of the century, however, the underlying structure of American society and of the federal polity began to shift in significant ways. Initially the most substantial and obvious changes took place in the private sector. There an economy of small units—family farms and businesses, individual enterprises and partnerships—began to give way to a new system of large corporate organizations. At the same time many of the nation's existing private institutions—in education and religion and the professions, for example—started to experience a series of substantial reorganizations.[9] One result of these developments was a significant increase in the scale of organized activity in the United States. Along with that went increasing functional specialization. The Renaissance man, the handyman, the dilettante scholar, the general practitioner, the all-purpose businessman—all began to give way to the specialist who, as a popular saying went, knew more and more about less and less.

Functional specialization was most obvious in the professions, where each new sub-division normally broke away to form its own organization, establish its own publications, and develop its own elite. But the organized professions were only the tip of the occupational iceberg; the same process of specialization—though without benefit of the socio-political trappings of the professions—was taking place in almost every line of work and in every facet of American life: in the factory, where both workers and managers increasingly concentrated on performing a relatively narrow range of functions; in education, where both students and teachers began to shift their attention from developing the whole person to developing expertise; in the country's welfare institutions, its churches, and even its leisure-time activities, functional specialization was the handmaiden of social change.[10]

Specialization fragmented the social order, and the founders, the first generation of organization builders, discovered they had to devise entirely new means of coordinating and controlling the activities of those who worked in the large national institutions they were developing. The careers of the founders were normally dominated by the problems of developing new means of ordering social behavior in highly organized, hierarchical settings. From our vantage point, the committee systems, the standardized forms of reporting information, the quantitative measures of performance, and the carefully defined channels of authority that businessmen like John D. Rockefeller developed seem commonplace. But to the first generation of organization builders in America the process of centralizing authority in a setting characterized by increasing functional specialization was a difficult undertaking. This was as true in a university or church as it was on the business frontier. History has preserved and sometimes enshrined the names of those who were successful; we recognize the names of labor leader Samuel Gompers, suffragist Carrie Chapman Catt, and university president William Rainey Harper. But many thousands more failed and disappeared from our written record of the past.

In the first great pulse of organization building that began in the 1880s and climaxed at the turn of the century, one of the most common sources of failure was the inability to consolidate an administration — whether public or private — so that it achieved an adequate measure of efficiency. The activities of functionally specialized individuals and units had to be coordinated. Large numbers of persons with a variety of orientations and self-interests had to be brought together so they could work in unison (if not in true harmony). The founders had formidable problems to solve at a time when each decision had to be made ad hoc, when there were few examples of successful organization building that could be looked to, when administration was just beginning to be understood as a separate and meaningful undertaking.

Moreover, these internal problems had to be solved while many of the new private organizations were engaged in heavy combat along their frontiers. Organization building was seldom a peaceful enterprise. Reorganization involved shifting wealth and income, changing status relationships, and creating new power alignments. The changes were not always a zero-sum game, but there were usually losers and winners in the process. When local unions formed a national, for example, some part of the power of the local had to be surrendered to the new national organization.[11] When a new discipline emerged within a university, resources had to be redistributed and existing departments had good cause to fear that they would be short-changed.[12]

From our perspective today the rise of large national organizations such as the trade union or the modern corporation may appear to have been an inevitable or even "rational" response to a changing society; but those who experienced these developments accurately perceived the conflict and suffering normally involved in this sort of social change. Small businessmen and consumers feared corporate power and lashed out at the trusts through state and federal government. Unions and businesses fought violent battles over control of the production process and the conditions of labor. Suffragists won their struggle for the vote only after years of intense political combat. Late nineteenth- and early twentieth-century America was a tumultuous, strife-laden society in large part because of the conflicts—many of which had a class dimension—on the organizational frontier. Every new form of organization experienced some brand of tension as it developed, and one of the tasks of the organization builders was to negotiate new and relatively stable relationships along their frontiers. When they failed, as many of them did, the conflicts sometimes escalated until they had to be solved either in the courts or by a state or federal legislature. Private-sector organization building thus created a new demand for public action. It also generated a new demand for liaison services, for organizational brokers who could move across institutional frontiers and arrange the compromises that would restore peace in the private sector or between private bureaucracies and public authority.

Representation of organizational interests became a crucial, specialized function in the private sector. During the second great pulse of organization building during World War I and the 1920s, public relations emerged as a semi-profession; so too in the early part of this century did the task of dealing on a continuous, systematic basis with state and federal regulatory agencies. A complex array of interest groups—many of them organized along functional lines as was the American Medical Association—developed and came to occupy a substantial role in our national political system. The interest groups cut across the party, place, and ethnic boundaries that had long been crucial determinants of political behavior; they created new political fault lines and alignments that changed forever the fundamental nature of politics in this country.

By the 1940s, when a third surge of organizational change began in the private realm, the United States had been transformed. Large national organizations structured along bureaucratic lines had become the centerpiece of the economy and a basic feature of most aspects of American society.[13] The way most of the nation's citizens were educated, employed, and provided with services ranging from religion to entertainment had been reorganized. Functional specialization, combination along national lines, and bureaucratization had brought America into the age of the corporation and the expert.

During these same decades, the public sector had experienced a similar transformation. Historians have for the most part dealt with the two phenomena separately, on the assumption that they sprang from different sources and had different outcomes. But in reality the larger outlines of organizational change in the public and private sectors were very much the same. There were new demands for national organizations that would perform functions (usually aimed at providing some economically and politically effective group with greater security) that had heretofore been the province of local or state governments or had not been performed at all. The desire to bring under control aspects of America's fast-growing urban, industrial society prompted some to look to corporations and others to look to a more active state. The nation's new and more demanding role in international affairs also encouraged the growth of government.

In the public as in the private sector, there was a series of pulses of rapid institutional change when clusters of new policies and such new organizations as the Federal Reserve Board and the Federal Trade Commission were developed; the pulses took place against a backdrop of a long secular drift toward new patterns of collective action (as reflected in the steadily increasing number of employees in state, local, and federal government). The pulses have usually been the stuff of political history in America: the Populist Era of the late nineteenth century; the Progressive period from the 1890s through the beginning of World War I; the New Deal of the 1930s; and the War on Poverty in the 1960s.[14] Lately some distinguished scholars have explored to good effect the significant changes that took place between pulses – in the 1920s and the 1950s, for instance – when liberal reform elements were not in the ascendency.[15] But for the most part historians have been more interested in the dramatic political struggles of the titans of reform than in the entire process of state building. They have also been far more concerned about legislative enactment than about the development of public administration.

Nevertheless, we can see outlined in the nation's political history the general pattern of public sector growth, with its first dramatic period of expansion taking place at the turn of the century. In those years the scale of government in the United States began to increase despite the general predilection of Americans for private rather than public activity.[16] By the time the expansion of government began in a decisive manner, private bureaucracies were already well established, and indeed, the rise of big business prompted many populist and progressive reformers to look to a more active state as a means of controlling or eliminating concentrations of private power.[17] To many Americans in the Progressive years there appeared to be no tension between democracy and public bureaucracy: government organizations were simply the means of achieving the ends sought by the people. The possibility that the administrators might develop their own objectives was not a subject that provoked much debate.

At the federal level, the Progressive Era was a particularly important period of experimentation with new forms of administration. Then the foundations of our national regulatory system were laid, as were the underpinnings of our modern military establishment. Along with expansion came functional specialization and a related enthusiasm for the contributions experts could make in the policy realm. The independent regulatory agency was an especially important innovation during this era. The independent agency was seen as the proper means of bringing scientific expertise to bear on problems and of shielding the experts from partisan — hence self-seeking — influence.[18] As this particular movement suggested, Americans were most supportive of democracy when the state had very little to do; when they began to entrust their government with important functions in shaping the nation's political economy, they were distrustful of the vigorous party system that characterized the participatory democracy of that age. Hence they looked to experts for protection from partisanship, much as the authors of *The Federalist Papers* had depended upon the Constitution and the balance of powers to shield the nation from the shifting winds of democratic impulse.

As it turned out, the experts had some strong impulses of their own, and they became in the public arena, as in the private, some of the most dynamic of the country's organization builders. As the modern state began to take form, they helped to shape and reshape the way it was organized and provided the new services Americans wanted from their government.

Public administrators had to solve the same sorts of internal problems that plagued organization men and women in the private sector. For the most part they used much the same line-staff style of hierarchy that characterized private bureaucracies. They had to coordinate the activities of the specialists; they had to create lines of communication along with a structure of bureaucratic authority. Before the passage of the Pendleton Act in 1883 and the subsequent development of the civil service, Congress and the political parties had exercised direct, almost minute control of the federal administration; but gradually in the twentieth century the modern bureaucracy freed itself to operate in a more independent fashion. The architects of the federal state shaped a series of hierarchies that were highly centralized and below their top levels relatively impervious to short-term political pressures. Typical of this line of development were the Army Corps of Engineers and the Federal Bureau of Investigation under J. Edgar Hoover.

Public agencies — again, like private organizations — gravitated toward functional specialization. In the federal government power tended to concentrate at the bureau level, where the functional orientation was strongest. The first Hoover Commission had tried to change this balance of power, but the departments were still like holding companies that combined bureaus that operated day to day in a relatively autonomous manner.[19] Civil service careers were usually conducted within a single bureau; moving across functional lines was dangerous, if only because the official who did so would be losing some part of the value of his accumulated functional knowledge and of his network of personal associations. It was this situation that the Civil Service Reform Act of 1979 sought to change by creating a class of top-level administrators who would be more attentive to national needs than to the needs of the particular bureaus in which they had built their careers.[20]

Public as well as private institutions generated tensions and had to develop means of preserving a measure of stability in their external affairs. Public relations in the public realm became a well-developed art. The relevant environment for the federal agencies included the rest of the government as well as private individuals and organizations. But the first concern normally had to be the agency's source of funding: Congress and the congressional committees and subcommittees. Presidential and public support could be heartening, but without legislative backing a bureaucracy could look forward to a lean future — or possibly no future at all. The successful public official had to be a diplomat as well as an administrator if he was going to protect — and perhaps enlarge — his domain.[21]

One important source of support for most agencies turned out to be the interest groups with a stake in the government's programs. Their backing was vital because they in turn could bring their influence and that of their members to bear on the congressmen who could decide the agency's future. Thus three-sided alliances — iron triangles or, as I prefer, triocracies — took shape in many areas of public policy and became, in fact, one of the crucial features of our modern federal government.[22] Over time the system became ever more specialized: the specialized bureaus were linked to functionally specialized interest groups, and both were tied tightly to specialized congressional committees and even more specialized subcommittees that exercised oversight and sponsored enabling legislation. So important to bureaucracy in this setting was interest group backing that government officials actually encouraged the formation of new groups where none existed to support their policies. Over the years these three-sided alliances became deeply entrenched, almost impervious to assault, prompting one political scientist to ask, Are government organizations immortal? The answer was, as I interpret it, almost, but not entirely.[23] At least not yet, one might add.

In these regards the public bureaucracies functioned in a manner far different from that of their private counterparts. Business bureaucrats confronted markets with price signals that gave relatively quick responses to their organizations' performance. Government administrators faced not a market but a series of publics — legislators, federal executives, interest groups, media, clients, rival agencies — whose conflicting objectives were sometimes hard to discern and usually difficult to incorporate in a compromise policy. When corporate leaders journeyed to Washington to take part in one of the ad hoc committees or councils aimed at reforming the executive branch, they generally ignored these crucial differences between public and private organizations and sought to impose on the government the practices they were familiar with in business. But the public administrative process is inherently different, as the best of the businessmen learned if they accepted a regular political appointment and stayed in Washington to direct a federal agency or department.

As the general business perception of public bureaucracy indicates, however, the cultural and political environment in the United States has traditionally been hostile to the growth of the federal government. When the process of growth began, American democratic values were firmly oriented to localism, regionalism, individualism, and privatism. There was no strong tradition of public service of any sort, state or federal. The Constitution firmly limited federal activities and ensured that every effort to expand the role of the national government would have to fight its way through hedgerows of judicial as well as legislative resistance. Throughout the nineteenth century the balance of power in the United States had strongly favored the states. What the national government acquired, the states lost. There were also private material interests involved. Those who stood to lose from an increase in federal power fought hard to preserve the existing system.

This resistance, deeply grounded in values, interests, and ideology, helps explain why the increase in federal bureaucracy was so slow before the 1940s. In 1901 there were only 239,476 civilian employees in the entire federal government. The federal budget that year was only $524 million. By 1940 the number of employees had increased to just slightly over a million. Even the New Deal, the effective leadership of President Franklin D. Roosevelt, and the crisis of the Great Depression had been unable to break in a truly decisive manner the hold of nineteenth-century political concepts in American society.

But what the New Deal could not achieve, World War II and the Cold War did. Insofar as the role of federal bureaucracy is concerned, the 1940s were a distinct watershed in American life. In the years that followed Pearl Harbor, federal authority grew rapidly, as did the federal budget and the federal bureaucracy. By 1962 there were over 2.5 million persons working for the national government, and the federal budget constituted about 19.5 percent of the gross national product. By 1970 the comparable figures were over 3 million employees and 20.2 percent of the GNP. The pace of bureaucratization had increased sharply, and with it the sorts of concerns that give rise to this book.

In those years the clearly marked boundaries Americans had been accustomed to began to blur. As private and public bureaucracies secured their positions and in many cases established close working relationships, the boundary between what was public and what was private behavior frequently became indistinct. Triocracies were particularly hard to untangle, especially when they had been active over a long period.

Moreover, the number of interest groups with a stake in any particular policy tended to increase over the years, complicating the task of drafting appropriate legislation and implementing a program. This was the case in agriculture, for instance, where the various commodities, processors, consumers, and environmentalists — all organized, funded, and knowledgeable — monitored federal farm policy so closely that they virtually became a part of the governing process. Within the government, too, the boundary between federal, state, and local authority was often hard to see, especially when the federal government began to finance activities at the state and local level through transfer of funds.[24] Even in the federal government the distinctions between legislating, executing, and judicially interpreting policy became obscure. Some agencies performed quasi-judicial functions.[25] Some legislative committees exercised so much oversight that they in effect preempted the executive branch. The executive branch itself sought to preempt the Congress by means of executive orders and departmental reorganizations. To a nation long accustomed to the simple lines of authority spelled out in the Constitution, this was disconcerting.

Compounding the problem was the emergence in the 1960s and 1970s of "issue networks" that came to exert substantial influence on particular areas of public policy. The networks, as defined by Hugh Heclo, consisted of specialists, consultants, former and present staff members from Congress and the executive branch, and interest group experts — all knowledgeable about one public policy issue, whether it was nuclear power, telecommunications, or conservation.[26] In the absence of a dominant triocracy or iron triangle, a network like this could exert a significant influence upon bureaucratic behavior. The networks supplied personnel for political appointments, staff members for committees, and expert witnesses for hearings or trials. They were interlaced with the bureaucracy and Congress through personal and professional ties, and to the outsider they constituted an element of government that was new and especially difficult to understand.

Where the issue networks thrived, political stalemates frequently developed. In part this was because issue-oriented officials tended to be dedicated to particular outcomes and opposed to the compromises necessary to gather support for positive action. In part such stalemates were a product of a very large, complex system in which there were many opportunities to block action.[27] Add that to normal bureaucratic inertia and you have a system of government that has in recent years seldom been guilty of undue haste.[28]

So disturbing were these developments and the sheer size and complexity of the federal establishment that Americans frequently tended to forget what had been accomplished. In the decades I have been discussing, our very large, complex, and wealthy nation assumed a great range of new responsibilities at home and abroad. For the most part, Americans seemed to be relatively pleased that these responsibilities were being met. Internally many of the developmental services the government had traditionally performed — for instance, the improvement of waterways and harbors — were still being provided. But in addition, the government had undertaken a variety of new services, many of which involved welfare activities and the provision of benefits to middle-class Americans. Protection of the environment, for instance, was a new activity with a largely middle-class clientele. Where we have successfully cleaned up our air or water and provided increased security for our citizens, these activities have been conducted by bureaucratic institutions, many of very recent origin. The bureaucracies we have created do not always work the way we want them to. They have obviously gained power in the government in recent years, and in some areas of policy they may indeed have become dominant. But we continue to want the goods and services the government provides, and as long as that is true we will have to learn how to live with our federal bureaucracy.

The first step toward a better understanding of our federal administration consists of recognizing that bureaucracies, like people, are highly varied. From the great sociologist Max Weber we acquired a theory of bureaucracy that stresses its universal properties.[29] But we now know that there are many bureaucratic styles. Some bureaucracies are extremely aggressive in reaching out for new functions, powers, and incomes (the Department of Defense). Others are more cautious (the Social Security Administration). Some are so conservative that they flirt with paralysis rather than seek to expand any aspect of their operations (the State Department in the postwar era). But all of them continue to change, seldom making front-page news if they can help it, but changing nonetheless. There is thus no single, permanent style of federal bureaucracy in the United States and no single set of problems that we can solve if we are interested in improving the performance of our public sector.[30]

The complexity and variability of the federal bureaucracy help explain the organization of this book. Each of the authors has selected a different area of public policy in which to examine the bureaucratic role: Samuel P. Hays, environmental policy; Carolyn L. Weaver, social security policy; Charles E. Neu, foreign policy; and Heywood Fleisig, fiscal and monetary policy. Matthew A. Crenson and Francis E. Rourke have provided a concluding overview designed to help the reader fit the particular concepts developed in the case studies into a general analytical and historical context. The book embodies not one but several approaches to a common subject — again, a tribute to the complexity of the problems and the fact that thus far several academic disciplines have mounted separate analyses of the bureaucratic phenomenon in the United States.

Two of the authors write in the historical tradition, and one of them, Samuel P. Hays, looks at his subject from the bottom up. His richly textured analysis, "The Politics of Environmental Administration," helps us see how the complex institutions associated with this particular set of policies evolved and how they in turn shaped the choices made at all levels of government. The agencies that embodied the traditional interests in economic development did not give way easily when new demands for environmental control arose. Instead, the United States created a new institutional structure that overlapped the old one, generating long-term struggles that occupied the attention of Congress and became the central concern of the agencies involved. Expert opinion became one of the weapons in these struggles. Interagency disputes sometimes led to government reorganization aimed not at improving efficiency but at shaping policy outcomes by administrative fiat. Control of information became in some cases as important as the control of resources. The administrative politics that Hays describes sometimes generated public hostility; as the author says: "It is not government per se that generates cynicism, but the processes by which public objectives realized through legislation become markedly changed through administration."

Although Charles E. Neu is also a historian, he looks at our nation's foreign policy institutions from the top down. His essay, "The Rise of the National Security Bureaucracy," tells us how the role of the State Department diminished as new, more aggressive institutions took over its functions in the post–World War II era. In foreign affairs (unlike domestic policy) the sorts of interest groups Hays describes were less important than were the predilections of our presidents and the pressures of our hot and cold wars. Impatient with bureaucracy, the presidents turned to the Central Intelligence Agency, the military services, and the National Security Council; later the White House staff began to play a leading part in the development of our policies abroad. Neu is highly critical of these choices and of the failure of our postwar presidents (except Eisenhower) to master the national security apparatus. As he points out, the White House can quickly change policy by operating in this way, but it cannot institutionalize the programs it adopts: "This suggests that the time has come for our presidents to turn inward and to confront the prosaic task of understanding and managing the foreign policy bureaucracy."

Economist Heywood Fleisig approaches his subject, "Bureaucracy and the Political Process: The Monetary and Fiscal Balance," from an entirely different perspective. Using a simple model of the political process, he comes to the rather surprising conclusion that in the realm of fiscal and monetary affairs, bureaucracy as such plays hardly any role in shaping policy. Accustomed as we are to seeing in prominent places the latest pronouncements of the chairman of the Federal Reserve Board and noticing that the stock market responds every time the board twitches, most readers will be startled by Fleisig's analysis. But as the author carefully demonstrates, monetary and fiscal policies are in fact of such overwhelming importance to the distribution of wealth and income in this country that our elected officials carefully constrain the bureaucratic role in determining what types of programs should be adopted. To those who fear the rise of the bureaucratic state in America, Fleisig's broad-ranging essay should be reassuring.

Not so with economist Carolyn L. Weaver's chapter, "The Social Security Bureaucracy in Triumph and in Crisis." Weaver's perspective is that of the public-choice economist. Unlike Hays and Neu, she finds the roots of our modern government institutions not solely in new demands; she looks also to supply-side changes — to pressures from the bureaucrats themselves, who behaved very much as private monopolists do. Social security, she demonstrates, started out as a modest program funded on a conservative basis. But program advocates from within the bureaucracy relentlessly promoted expansion of the program and deferral of costs. Congress and the presidents went long with these politically appealing initiatives, hence the "triumph" of the bureaucracy. But these decisions eventually had to be paid for, hence the "crisis" of the 1970s and 1980s. Locked in by a system of indexing that sharply increased costs and unable to bring in new groups of citizens to pay the price for present benefits, social security in the United States was on the brink of bankruptcy. The bureaucracy maneuvered skillfully to protect itself from harm, but as Weaver points out, these tactics could "do little more than delay the day of reckoning" for this crucial part of the nation's welfare system.

Less pessimistic about the nature of our modern administrative state are political scientists Matthew A. Crenson and Francis E. Rourke. Their essay, "By Way of Conclusion: American Bureaucracy since World War II," charts the general patterns of administrative consolidation that characterized the years 1945–60 and reminds us that these changes took place within a democratic context that imposed significant restraints upon even the national security system (a point Charles Neu makes as well). They point out that "to build cathedrals, it was first necessary to have a religion." Where there was no "harmony of political belief," the government could not build "grand, executive-centered organization[s]." Hence countertrends of bureaucratic disaggregation and enhanced citizen participation developed in the 1950s and 1960s; while the income of the federal government continued to grow, more and more of its functions were performed by state and local governments or private organizations, a trend that became even more pronounced in the 1970s. During the latter part of that decade, liberals and conservatives joined hands in mounting a new critique of America's bureaucratic institutions. Deregulation became a major theme in national politics. The market was proclaimed by many to be preferable to the visible hand of administrative control. A century after the passage of the Pendleton Act (which first created our national civil service), Crenson and Rourke conclude that America's federal bureaucracy is still on a short political leash. The bureaucracy continues to grow as the people demand new government services, but it remains a distinctly American hybrid, shaped throughout by a democratic political system and vibrant antibureaucratic ideologies.

After reading that conclusion and the four case studies written by six authors from three different disciplines, we hope our readers will be closer to their own answer to the question, Who's running the modern American state? The answer will not pop up automatically like your morning toast, if only because the various authors approach the subject from different perspectives and reach different, sometimes contradictory conclusions. Crenson and Rourke, for instance, place far more emphasis than the other authors on the distinctive changes that took place in American federal administrations in the 1970s. They stress the innovative manner in which public bureaucracies went about marshaling constituent support, a practice that made for citizen participation in bureaucratic decision making. Hays, however, presents a different and less optimistic view concerning environmental policy. Weaver is even more pessimistic, though she does grant that the crisis in social security has begun of late to generate political correctives to the welfare system's deep-seated problems. Tensions like these between the several essays will complicate the process of summing up, but they should not prevent any reader from reaching unequivocal conclusions about the central questions raised by the book.

My personal, editor's answer is that the United States government has changed decisively in this century and that the bureaucracy has acquired substantial power in our federal system. Clearly the American government can no longer be run the same way it was in the nineteenth century. Our bureaucracy has acquired more power, if only because neither our executives nor our legislators can provide the sort of expertise that is needed in this age of functional specialization. What they can and do still provide is a system of constraints that clearly reins in the administrators of the American state. Neither the White House nor Congress can ordinarily command the bureaucracy in the manner set forth in the classical theory of the hierarchical executive branch. But they retain the power to bypass the administrators, to reorganize their domain, to shift their entire function to another government body, or to deprive them of the resources they need.

To avoid those powerful sanctions, bureaucrats have created elaborate networks of relationships with interest groups, legislators, and other agencies of government — the triocracies or iron triangles. But those networks themselves impose restraints upon the freedom of action of the bureaucrats. The system does not have the happy consequences proposed by the pluralists: only those who are well organized and well positioned in the government system can expect to realize their objectives. Even they may be disappointed, because this elaborate system can be stalemated rather easily by equally well-organized opponents. That, however, ensures that one group in our society — large corporations, for instance — cannot achieve the dominance that some critics of our government have feared. Stasis, not hegemony, is the central problem of the modern administrative state in this country.

But editors should not impose too heavy a hand on either their authors or their readers. The following essays do a good job of speaking for themselves, and I invite the reader to turn to them for answers to the basic questions this book poses.

Samuel P. Hays

The Politics of Environmental Administration

THE EVOLUTION of federal administration since the New Deal years, and especially since World War II, has loomed large in recent American history. Since the mid-1960s, moreover, environmental affairs have become an increasingly important element of that development. They have also played more than an equal role in the debate over the "federal bureaucracy" and the issue of "big government." In this analysis I hope to go beyond the limited scope of that debate to the larger historical question of the role environmental administration has played in recent American politics—especially as an example of institutional development. This constitutes a somewhat limited case study, but I hope it is one that sheds light on the larger growth of recent federal administration as a whole.

Administration is the centerpiece of our modern political system in the United States. It is in administration that the major sustained political choices are now made. For many years it was customary to divide administration from legislation by distinguishing the making of laws from their implementation. Congress decides policy, and the agencies carry it out. But as administrative decision making has been brought under closer scrutiny, its political role has become clearer. As soon as a law is passed the parties at interest shift their attention from Congress to the agency and continue their combat with even greater intensity. The setting is different, but the controversies are the same. Administration is a political context of technical detail, bureaucratic jungles, and professional experts, but it is no less one in which political demands are massive and the adjustment of conflicting interests is central. In the technical apparatus of administration, scientific research and assessment, economic analysis, planning, and management are all devices not for implementing politics in a disinterested manner but for bringing workable agreement out of disagreement.

Administration is the main arena of political combat where environmental political choices of enormous consequence are made.[1]

As a second introductory observation, I shall take with a massive amount of skepticism notions about the centrality of a continuing struggle between government and private enterprise. This is the ideology of political debate. But historians have long understood that government is not something alien to the institutions of corporate enterprise, that large-scale management is quite similar whether conducted under private or public auspices, and that business firms have continually sought an active government to help them achieve ends they could not accomplish by themselves.[2] Not the least example of this was the National Recovery Administration of the New Deal, in which trade association majorities, long frustrated by recalcitrants within their ranks, sought the legal power of government to force trade association minorities to accept their decisions.[3] The issue has been not whether there should be an activist federal government, but who should control it and for what ends. Upon reflection it seems preposterous to believe the ever-larger scales of organization that private corporate institutions have fashioned would not also arise in government. It seems equally clear that organizational development in the private economy not only constituted a model for government to follow[4] but in fact was a major influence in the evolution of large-scale organization in the public economy. As we examine federal administration as an institution rather than an ideology, we become peculiarly aware of the integrative and even symbiotic relationships it embodies between itself and private corporate America.[5]

Finally, I will also be concerned with the significance this common drive for scale has for the larger vertical hierarchy of American economic and political institutions, ranging from the community to the city, the town and township to the county, the county and city to the state, and on to the federal government. We argue, often I fear with little reflection, that the big issues of the day are those of "returning" government power and authority to local levels. So runs the ideological debate. But we can be misled if we do not keep an eagle eye on the more crucial element of institutional development. Often the ideology of a devolution of authority only obscures the practice of its concentration. Today this appears, for example, in the form of federal "preemption" of state authority or state "override" of local action. Environmental politics and administration are shot through with such choices as to the level in the hierarchy of government where decisions are to be made. I shall explore these in some detail.[6]

I shall stress government administration, then, as a set of institutions and their evolution as a case of institution building. My question will be the way environmental administration has evolved as a system of control, and the political options represented by the peculiar substantive choices that have been made. I do not wish to denigrate political ideology, the ideology of administration as a nonpolitical process of implementing choices made elsewhere, the ideology of continuing combat between government and private enterprise, or the ideology of struggle between centralization and decentralization of power and authority. All these play an overarching role in shaping how people understand and explain their political world. But in this effort I wish to concentrate more precisely on the institutions and how they have evolved, on government administration as a phenomenon that has come to play the central role in environmental politics.

Environmental politics reflect major changes in American society and values. People want new services from government stemming from new desires associated with the advanced consumer economy that came into being after World War II. Some of these services pertain to outdoor recreation and the allocation of air, land, and water to natural environment management and use; others pertain to new objectives concerning health and well-being and to the adverse effects of pollution on both biological life and human beings; still others deal with matters such as "least cost" technologies in energy, smaller-scale production, and population-resource balance. Most of these objectives are described by advocates of environmental policies as quality-of-life concerns. All of them reflect new types of demands upon government that leaders in older public institutions have often found strange and difficult to comprehend.[7]

It would be worthwhile to emphasize several aspects of these changes that help one to understand their significance. First, they constitute not temporary but permanent changes in social values; they represent an evolutionary tendency associated with rising standards of living and human expectations. One cannot consider them momentary aberrations any more than one can consider the general desire for new household durables an aberration. Moreover, they reflect desires and values that are widely held, perhaps expressed by only a small segment of society a century ago, but now reflecting a mass phenomenon. Environmental values are perhaps weaker in the top tenth of the social order and the bottom third. But they have a broad middle base that is reflected in a host of attitude studies carried out by both independent agencies and business corporations.[8]

Second, environmental values can be understood historically as a facet in the evolution of consumer desires, as a part of the history of consumption. A century ago necessities such as food, clothing, and shelter were the main items of consumption. By the 1920s a new phase had come onto the scene emphasizing conveniences, taking the form of consumer durables such as the automobile, household appliances, and the radio. This phase continued into the 1930s, reflecting changes in consumer preferences that evolved even during the depression decade.[9] After World War II a third stage of consumption had been reached, that of amenities — goods and services that made life more enjoyable, not just livable and convenient. It encompassed new material goods, new amenity elements of both necessities and conveniences, and a host of new products reflecting purchasing power that came to be called discretionary income. Environmental values and services were a part of this new stage of consumption, not less rooted or firm in the demand side of the economy than were hi-fi sets or the creative art of photography.

Third, the kinds of demands these new consumer wants placed upon politics and government were new. In previous years public economic policy was concerned primarily with matters of production. It grew out of conflicts among producers. Much of what is known as economic regulation by government resulted from the internal politics of the business community in which one sector sought to limit action by another through the coercive power of public law. Conflicts among agriculture, labor, and business emphasized the relative shares each would receive from the surplus of production. The entry of new consumer values into this interplay of political forces represented something quite different. Consumers had played only a minor, extremely weak, and even insignificant role in economic policy during the Progressive Era and the New Deal years. In the 1960s they became more influential, and environmentalists were among them. Hence we should expect tensions between older government arrangements heavily shaped by interaction among producers and the newer demands of environmental consumers.[10]

The transition from the old to the new can be observed in the shift in government regulation. One can distinguish between the older regulatory agencies such as the Interstate Commerce Commission or the Securities and Exchange Commission, which as their major function policed relationships among producers, and the newer regulatory agencies in which consumer objectives were more central. In the older types of regulation a common perspective seemed to arise between the regulator and the regulated that led to persistent cooperation between them.[11] In this consumers had little influence. In the new regulatory system consumers began to develop a capacity to inject a new force into the relationships between the regulators and the regulated. They argued in favor of relaxing older-style regulation on the grounds that the freer market would benefit consumers; at the same time they argued for more regulation of the newer type to benefit consumers.[12]

Environmental administration is part of a new stage in the evolution of government agencies. New values, widely shared, reflecting a significant challenge to an older order of government policy now are on the scene. I will have occasion at several points to contrast the new and the old in order to refer back to the historical context. It is well to keep that sense of evolution, that marked difference between the old and new and the tension between them, clearly in mind in order to comprehend the evolution of environmental administration over the past several decades.

The various sectors of environmental administration can be distinguished in terms of their relation to these new values and political demands. First of all there are those agencies concerned with land resources that long had maintained a mission for commodity development. These include the U.S. Forest Service in the Department of Agriculture, in charge of the national forests;[13] the Soil Conservation Service, which since the early New Deal had been preoccupied with preventing soil erosion but which in the 1950s became more involved in land development;[14] and the Bureau of Land Management, which had arisen out of the decision in the Taylor Grazing Act of 1934 to stabilize grazing on the western public lands and reverse a persistent decline in forage capacity.[15]

Each of these agencies sought to promote the development of material resources: wood, farm products, and forage. Each had taken a stance, described as "conservation," that stressed applied science in order to increase production efficiency.[16] Scientific, technical, and professional leaders in those fields fashioned a common approach to their tasks of resource management. And each in turn found that the new environmental thrust was quite different from its traditional mission. Upon each of them now there were demands to take up new management objectives, called environmental, which in each case involved lower levels of development and more management of lands as natural environment areas. The Forest Service faced demands for wilderness areas where no future development, such as roads or wood harvest, would occur.[17] The Soil Conservation Service was roundly condemned for destroying valuable natural wildlife habitat with its channelization and drainage projects.[18] The Bureau of Land Management found itself faced with competitors for grazing land from among those interested in enhancing wildlife on the western range and those who found western drylands to have amenity and aesthetic value.[19]

The Bureau of Reclamation and the Federal Power Commission

were deeply involved with water development. For many years their objective had been to harness rivers that flowed unused, as the argument went, to the sea. The U.S. Army Corps of Engineers was engaged in a similar task. Together they shared the view that engineered rivers could provide varied commodity benefits such as irrigation, navigation, hydroelectric power, and flood control. The culmination of these ambitions came with the Tennessee Valley Authority. But as the environmental movement advanced, an increasing number of people asserted that rivers were more valuable in their natural free-flowing state.[20] The issue was dramatically sharpened by a Supreme Court decision in 1968 concerning a dispute over who should build a dam on the Snake River in Hell's Canyon, Idaho. In reviewing a Federal Power Commission decision, the Court argued that the agency had failed to consider one alternative — no dam at all — remanded the case for further consideration, and set off a series of steps that led to congressional action over a decade later to manage that part of the Snake as a natural river.[21]

All these were straightforward cases. Agencies with older missions now were faced with new environmental demands that had widespread public support. The conflicts were intense. Each agency was administered by technical professionals who were committed to commodity development, had been trained in disciplines with that orientation, and shared deeply the similar values of those in private institutions — forestry, agriculture, livestock raising, navigation, electric power, manufacturing industry — that the primary objective of public policy should be material development. They could hardly understand, let alone accept, the new environmental thrust that emphasized intangible values in the surroundings of one's home and places of recreation. There was little if any common ground, and what concessions were made by the old to the new were made grudgingly as a result of political constraints from Congress and the courts. Change did not come internally through modified attitudes and values in line with those of the wider public.[22]

This, then, is one context in which to examine the larger role of environmental administration. A second consists of those agencies that accepted environmental values more readily as part of their agency mission. Several of these had been established in the past but received new impetus in the environmental era: the National Park Service, formed in 1916 both to protect scenic resources and to encourage visits to them[23] and the U.S. Fish and Wildlife Service, which first took shape in 1936. Others came later in the 1960s and 1970s. There was the Bureau of Outdoor Recreation, established in 1964 to promote outdoor recreational activities, but especially important in supervising the distribution of federal moneys from the Land and Water Conservation Fund and in planning a system of national hiking trails and wild and scenic rivers. These agencies served as spearheads of newer environmental values, often clashed with commodity agencies, and became involved in a series of controversies among the administrative bodies of each presidency. While they tended to advance environmental objectives in their own missions, to the commodity agencies they also tended to constitute a subversive influence.

The environmental era also spawned a number of new agencies with environmental missions, reflecting especially the new concern for pollution from chemical residuals of industrial and agricultural production. These included air and water pollution agencies that were established in the Department of Health, Education, and Welfare and via different routes ended up with the Environmental Protection Agency when it came into being in 1970.[24] Among them also were the two bodies responsible for industrial health, closely related to community air problems — the National Institute for Occupational Safety and Health, which made scientific assessments and was located in HEW, and the Occupational Safety and Health Administration, which set standards and carried out enforcement in the Department of Labor.[25] Finally, they included the Consumer Product Safety Commission, which had its own legislative mandate to protect consumers from dangers from manufactured products. All these shared a common perspective, the use of scientific and technical assessments to gauge the adverse effect of products and residuals on human health and biological life and then to set standards of acceptable exposure and effects and enforce them. Hence they had a common set of relationships with varied clientele groups, producers of harm on the one hand and victims on the other, which generated a pattern of political interplay somewhat different from that of those who managed land and water resources. There arose the distinction between "resource management" and "environmental protection" as the two arms of environmental administration.

Two specialized problems of land use gave rise to two new laws and hence two new federal agencies. One concerned the coastal zone. After a seven-year debate, in 1972 Congress adopted a Coastal Zone Management Act to try to iron out competing uses. These involved a range of conflicts between development on the one hand, such as energy facility siting, and environmental uses on the other, such as aesthetic and amenity use and ecological protection. The Office of Coastal Zone Management, established to administer the act, began with a brave mission to enhance environmental values, but save for a few states it soon became heavily burdened by the political weight of developmental concerns.[26]

Even less successful in establishing an environmental mission was the Office of Surface Mining, growing out of the Surface Mining Act of 1977. A product of an equally lengthy debate, that act sought to establish firm control of surface mining, to restore the contour of land through reclamation, to reduce water pollution and restore premining levels of water quality, and to prohibit mining in places of particular environmental concern. Passage of the act reflected a persistent and apparently irreconcilable conflict between coal producers and environmentalists. Immediately after passage those opposing forces transferred their battleground to the new agency. Slowly but steadily the environmental objectives that had been crafted into the law lost ground in the process of administration, as the mining industry was able to influence heavily the policies of the new office.[27]

Environmental factors played a significant role in a variety of other agencies. The Department of Energy dealt with alternative energy programs, especially solar energy; this became a special interest of environmentalists.[28] The Department of Agriculture made a few efforts to foster organic farming during the Carter administration under agriculture secretary Robert Berglund.[29] The State Department maintained some activity in international environmental affairs, such as the export of toxic materials,[30] and the Natural Resources Division of the Department of Justice could well play a crucial role in advancing or retarding environmental goals through litigation strategies. Finally, the most explicitly environmental agency of all, the Council on Environmental Quality, identified the advancement of environmental objectives as its major mission. This was reflected most widely in its annual reports on the state of the environment, which became standard reference material.[31]

This brief review of agencies with environmental components underlines the wide range of government administration that arose from the new values and attitudes. They represent the remarkable pervasiveness of those changes. One can often trace the nation's preoccupations through the evolution of government agencies: the concern in the late eighteenth-century with foreign affairs as reflected in the Departments of War, Navy, State, and Treasury; to concerns with internal economic development in the nineteenth- and early twentieth-centuries with Interior, Agriculture, Commerce, and Labor; to the post–World War II years in which the Departments of Health, Education, and Welfare, Transportation, and Housing and Urban Development stressed national problems that had first emerged in the 1930s;

and then the new consumer and environmental bodies such as the Environmental Protection Agency and the Council on Environmental Quality, which reflected still newer concerns. Thus, the pervasiveness of the new objectives in many agencies is just as striking as the far more long-standing pervasiveness of producer objectives.

The range and extent of these innovations provide an especially useful opportunity to examine some major features of government administration. I will explore four of these: the relationships between agencies and the public reflecting both environmental and developmental interests; the relationships of agency to agency and, as a whole, to the Congress, the courts, and the Executive Office; the relationships of federal to state and local administration; and running through them all, the new scientific and technical context of public decision making as a whole. Each of these provides an opportunity to observe distinctive features of the role of environmental administration in American society and politics.

Administrative agencies live and work amid constant interest in their affairs by many groups that have a stake in the outcome of decisions.[32] Hence one beginning point of analysis is the relationship of an agency to the active public. When bureaucracies become controversial this often stems from the dissatisfaction of someone with the impact of action upon them. If we are to understand what that is all about we should go far beyond the general notion of a "meddlesome bureaucracy" to this larger setting of the relationship between agency and public.

In the environmental case the initial impact lay in the strategy of environmentalists to establish new federal agencies and shape existing ones to implement their objectives. We have already identified those agencies and the impact of environmental values on them. But several attempts to shape decisions cut across specific agencies and had a more general import. There was, for example, the environmental impact statement, which sought to bring environmental objectives more fully into decision-making by requiring agencies to identify them and to assess effects upon them.[33] There were the new approaches to planning that it was hoped would bring environmental values into agency actions as objectives on a par with developmental goals.[34] There were changes in administrative procedures that required agency decisions to be open and on the record so that they would be subject to greater influence by those with environmental purposes.[35] There was the Freedom of Information Act, which enabled environmentalists, among others, to obtain information to press their cause when otherwise it would not be available.[36] And there were the courts, which permitted environmentalists to mount legal challenges to administrative decisions.[37]

All of these provided agencies with a new and continuous environmental presence that established limits to their actions if they had a developmental mission and facilitated those actions if their missions were environmental. Environmental political action became transformed from a sporadic social movement into a persistent and permanent political force that the agencies continually had to take into account. Environmentalists transformed their political strength from "after the fact" actions external to the agency to "before the fact" anticipations to which the agency constantly had to be attuned. In shaping this influence environmentalists were developing the same kind of anticipatory power that producer groups had long been able to forge. When agencies made choices they now had to take into account the possible consequences from the side of environmentalists as well as developmentalists. They no longer were confronted by claims from producer groups alone but now found that almost all those groups were being challenged by a new environmental consumer force.

The developmental agencies were none too happy with this state of affairs and resisted it mightily. They objected to the environmental impact statement, adopted it slowly, and continually sought to restrict its role. Over the years they succeeded in transforming the EIS to their advantage, both by using it to focus on economic as well as environmental impact and emphasizing trade-offs between them and by making it a political radar device that helped identify opposition to their proposals.[38] They sought, but with less success, to modify the Freedom of Information provisions by limiting the information that could be obtained; perhaps their failure to get far on this score stemmed from the fact that FOI was as useful to the business community in securing information about competitors as it was to environmental and consumer groups. And for much the same reason, administrators were not able to modify demands placed upon them by the courts for open procedures on the record; to the business community that was as vital for exercising their influence as it was to environmentalists.[39]

For environmental agencies the response was more mixed. On the one hand they welcomed public support that environmentalists gave to their missions and hence reached out with public awareness or citizen participation strategies.[40] These ranged from the more traditional public relations ventures to those that gave environmentalists opportunities to influence decisions. They made documents far more readily available to citizens than had been the case in the past.[41] Yet they found that public involvement could work both ways; it could raise up constraints on agency policy as well as provide support.

Hence even agencies such as the Environmental Protection Agency did not take the initiative to advance such procedures but instead worked to keep them—for example, citizen suits—under control.[42] A significant bit of nomenclature indicated, however, that they differed from development agencies in their relationship to the environmental public. Whereas they described environmentalists as "citizen groups," the developmental agencies described them as "special interests."

The political history of these varied forms of administration seemed to follow a common pattern. Each one was established by legislation that private developers had opposed. They had been able to neutralize some laws in the process of passage, but with others they had been less successful. Hence they faced new agencies and new branches of old ones that displayed missions they objected to. In the face of clean air and clean water legislation, private industry responded with disbelief that it had come onto the statute books. Environmental impact statements and citizen suits seemed to give all the edge to the opposition. And they were shocked at the environmentally oriented appointments that came with the Carter administration and the choices of technical advisers who gave the benefit of the doubt to victims instead of to sources of pollution.[43]

Yet the regulated industries regrouped rather quickly and fought back through new strategies. They sought especially to control the procedures by which administrative choices were made. In earlier years their main device for doing this was the Administrative Procedures Act of 1946, which enabled them to avoid surprise in regulatory action and to check decisions early in the process by injecting their own expertise into the action. But these "fair" administrative procedures, supervised by the courts, had come to be used also by consumers and environmentalists. Hence they were far less useful to the regulated industries than they had been earlier. A new strategy developed. The court-mandated requirement that regulations had to be based on the written record could be avoided by shifting action to the Executive Office of the President and especially the Office of Management and Budget. Here presidential authority instead of agency authority gave scope to communication and influence that were personal rather than "on the record." The industries perfected this strategy during the Carter years, and by the time of the Reagan administration it was firmly in place.[44]

Other strategies came into being as devices to bring the environmental agencies more toward the developmental side. One was to restrict the range of scientific and technical expertise the agency relied on to those more friendly to a high level of direct evidence as a standard of proof in making judgments.[45] Another was to demand that the agency make increasingly elaborate cost-benefit analyses; this became as important an instrument for slowing up environmental action as environmental impact statements were for slowing up developmental action.[46] Another strategy was to restrict steps to identify positive environmental objectives such as high-quality land and water[47] or health objectives beyond death and irreversible disease so as to weaken the positive benchmarks for environmental action.[48] Still another technique was to restrict the environmental information base by limiting research and monitoring so that the absence of information would open more options for leaving environmental problems relatively unattended.[49] Finally, a significant strategy was to transfer general standards of environmental objectives into specific application so detailed as to render agency action burdensome.[50] One variant of this was the pervasive issue of "burden of proof." Would it fall on the regulating agency or the regulated? When in the pesticide program EPA succeeded in shifting the burden of proof to the chemical companies, they responded by submitting such masses of evidence that the regulatory proceedings almost came to a standstill.[51]

By the mid-1970s, therefore, environmental agencies faced both environmental mandates and an increasingly capable set of political groups that sought to implement them, and also developmental groups that had long since learned to use new procedural devices in their own behalf. Environmental agencies found themselves checked and double checked. Their momentum on behalf of environmental goals slowed down. They began to accept demands from industry to be "neutral" rather than to serve as "advocates."[52] Hence agencies that were mandated by legislation to carry out one set of objectives were mesmerized into temporizing and inaction. Many now could not act at all, even within the requirements of legislation, without clear and recurring political crises that might again highlight the urgency of an environmental problem.[53]

Often it was argued that federal environmental agencies exceeded their authority as defined by statute; they took unwarranted initiative beyond the meaning of the law. I am far more impressed by the opposite—by administrative lethargy and inaction, by the degree to which agencies' freedom and will to act on behalf of environmental objectives was limited and restrained. An example might illustrate the point. Under the Clean Air Act of 1967 the National Air Pollution Control Administration was mandated to develop standards for six air pollutants and, in addition, for others for which its investigations might indicate this was desirable. In 1968 the agency announced that standards were in process for some two dozen pollutants beyond the six and that assessments of their harm and guidelines for regulation would appear in the future.[54] But none did appear. The initial assessment of sulfur oxides issued early in 1967 had aroused such intense opposition from the coal industry that the agency became extremely wary of taking on too many political opponents from the industry side.[55] Thereafter only one additional pollutant, lead, came under regulation, and that was a result of continual litigation from citizen environmental groups and a series of court orders—all over strenuous opposition from EPA.[56]

This was a characteristic case. Environmental bureaucracies are cautious and conservative, tend toward inertia, and must continually be prodded into action by external influences. After the lead issue had been resolved, the deputy administrator of EPA made it clear that without the litigation hanging over its head the agency could not have acted.[57] Administrative action generates forces and counterforces galore. The problem is not to keep environmental bureaucracies from excesses but to find some way to enable them to act in behalf of environmental goals.

The new administration of Ronald Reagan in 1981 resolved this deadlock, at least temporarily, by insulating agencies from environmental political influences and thereby enabling administrators to act more forthrightly on behalf of the regulated industries. This was done primarily through the power of appointment, in which environmental agencies were led by new administrators committed to reducing the level of regulation upon industry and giving it a freer hand. They proceeded to shift agency decisions in a marked antienvironmental direction and to reverse environmental policies of two decades, whether of Republican or Democratic vintage. This was facilitated by the administration's conviction that public environmental values were held only lightly—that there was little popular support for organizations active on the political environmental scene and hence that they could be ignored. It took few pains to hide its hostility, even contempt, for the "environmental establishment," creating a climate that closed off communication, let alone influence, from that quarter and left agency leaders free to work out their day-to-day decisions directly with those on the developmental and regulated side of environmental affairs.[58]

The resulting political repercussions indicated both the pervasiveness of public sentiment favorable to environmental objectives and the political liabilities the administration's assault entailed. The Reagan challenge strengthened environmental political support, which under the Carter administration had become somewhat lethargic. Membership increased; financial resources grew; technical capabilities advanced; and cooperation among the various groups in the nation's capital strengthened.[59] Moreover, environmental organizations worked closely with Congress to provide a counterweight to industry influence and served, in some cases, to blunt the force of the administration's mission to turn back environmental gains.[60] The entire exercise was a laboratory experiment in the depth and strength of public environmental values. The short-run effect was to produce considerable chaos in some agencies and some severe political liabilities for the Reagan administration.[61] How far it would work, in the long run, to turn an activist antienvironmental administration back to one more on center remained to be seen.[62]

Environmental agencies also lived within the context of a host of government bodies. There were other administrative agencies with which objectives could conflict; there was Congress, which increasingly kept a watch on agency affairs through its appropriations and oversight functions; and there were the courts, which were prone to consider themselves a special watchdog for preventing agencies from taking arbitrary action not authorized by law or not consistent with the courts' view of "fair procedure." On all sides agencies with environmental responsibilities had to cope with either initiatives or resistance from other branches of government.

Conflicts among agencies over environmental matters constituted one of the initial battlegrounds between environmental and developmental objectives. Citizen concerns as expressed in the 1960s over the adverse effects of development often came to be injected into the political arena most forcefully through action by agencies who felt those effects on their own missions. The most notable of these was the Fish and Wildlife Service.[63] Initial objections to projects by the Army Corps of Engineers, the Atomic Energy Commission, the Tennessee Valley Authority, the Federal Power Commission, and the Bureau of Reclamation were expressed most forcefully within the counsels of government by the Service. Such projects, it argued, destroyed fish and wildlife habitat. The agency, of course, had its own environmental constituents; it served as an important instrument of their action because it shared their views.[64]

The federal highway department was building highways through wildlife refuges that had been purchased with federal funds, much of which had been contributed by citizens through the duck hunting stamp.[65] The Atomic Energy Commission was planning multiple steam-generating plants on Biscayne Bay in Florida that would cause considerable thermal pollution and threaten aquatic life.[66] The Tennessee Valley Authority was planning to build the Tellico Dam on the Little Tennessee River, thereby destroying one of the main cold-water trout streams in eastern Tennessee.[67] The Corps of Engineers was inundating acres of wildlife habitat by building reservoirs. Despite a Fish and Wildlife Coordination Act passed years earlier, the Corps refused to consider, let alone implement, proposals to purchase equivalent lands, called mitigation lands, to replace them. And the Corps was also destroying valuable coastal wetlands in places like Florida by approving dredge-and-fill operations for housing.[68] The Fish and Wildlife Service had many an environmental grievance against other federal agencies.[69]

From this context arose the environmental impact statement.[70] It is often forgotten that the EIS, in its original form, was a device not for citizen review of developmental projects, but for interagency review. It was a procedure for dealing not with citizen objections but with agency objections, meant to facilitate a process by which the Executive Office of the President could resolve differences among its own agencies. When the first EIS documents were in the offing in 1970 officials of the Council on Environmental Quality, which supervised the EIS program, were asked what would be done with them. Would they be shown to the public? The answer was no. They would be circulated within the government and used to assemble the views of other agencies, and only after interagency disputes had been resolved and a decision made would they be released to the public. The device was an instrument to facilitate executive decision making, not to organize public involvement. That came only later.[71]

It is important to identify what the EIS did not do as well as what it did do in interagency relationships. It was confined wholly to agency comment. But some, especially the Fish and Wildlife Service, wanted the procedure also to give its objectives substantive support. An earlier episode had indicated both the possibilities and the pitfalls. In the case of opposition to dredge-and-fill permits issued by the Corps in coastal wetlands, Congressman John Dingell prepared legislation that would have given the Service authority to approve each Corps permit. Perhaps the strategy was only a political weapon to force the Corps to change its policies. At any rate it worked. The Corps agreed to a more effective "consultation" procedure with the Fish and Wildlife Service, and the legislation was withdrawn.[72] In the early days of the EIS the Water Pollution Control Administration, still in the Department of the Interior, tried a similar strategy, this time in the case of thermal pollution from steam generating plants. It asked the Council on Environmental Quality to go beyond supervising the EIS process to the point of throwing its influence behind substantive water quality goals. CEQ declined to become involved in such interagency disputes; it had its hands full merely supervising the new procedure.

Still another way of dealing with interagency conflict was to re-structure government. If environmentalists objected to pesticide policy administered by the Department of Agriculture on the grounds that it favored agriculture and the agricultural chemical industry rather than those harmed by pesticides, it could advocate that administration of the law be moved to an agency that had a protective rather than a developmental mission. And so when the Environmental Protection Agency was created in 1970 pesticide regulation was moved to it. The industry complained that the Department of Agriculture had not made sufficient effort to retain jurisdiction.[73] Or if it was argued that the Atomic Energy Commission was not sufficiently concerned about standards of radiation protection, the task of setting them could be transferred to another agency that had those concerns as a primary mission; that too happened when EPA was established. The formation of the EPA itself involved the transfer of air, water, and other environmental protection programs from Health, Education, and Welfare and Interior, to give more primary mission focus to those objectives. Those were not so clearly moves to defuse immediate interagency conflict as they were to provide a more visible presence for new environmental goals. A host of other environmental-developmental controversies remained as such agencies as EPA, the Park Service, and the Fish and Wildlife Service continued to do battle with Agriculture, Energy, Commerce, and a variety of subdepartmental agencies.[74]

Environmental agencies had to cope with Congress as well. This could cut two ways. On the one hand, congressional committees with developmental missions could thwart environmental action; the appropriations subcommittee in charge of the Department of Agriculture budget was a focal point for the defense of pesticides and could threaten the entire EPA budget, over which it had jurisdiction. The actions of Congressman Jamie Whitten of Mississippi were well known in this regard. More friendly subcommittees, on the other hand, could defend agencies against attack, as was the case with the appropriations subcommittee in charge of the Department of the Interior budget when its chair, Congressman Sidney Yates, successfully challenged attempts by the Reagan administration to reduce and even abolish the Land and Water Conservation Fund in 1981 and 1982.

Quite a different kind of congressional limitation came from the way environmentalists sought to use legislative strategy to force reluctant agencies to act. On a number of occasions the agency lethargy described earlier had arisen as a result of developmental opposition that prompted the agency to temporize. While industry argued that agencies exceeded their powers, environmentalists argued that they avoided using authority that Congress had already given them. To counteract agency inaction, environmentalists demanded more prescriptive legislation, making agency responsibility far more precise and far less avoidable. In place of the general requirement that the agency regulate toxic pollutants it found to be harmful, for example, amendments to the Clean Water Act of 1977 set forth specific chemicals and families of chemicals on which it was mandated to act. In other legislation, polychlorinated biphenyls were specifically identified for action, and in debate over revision of the Clean Air Act in the early 1980s environmentalists sought similar specific mandates for toxic air pollutants.[75] It was relatively easy to argue, and many did so, that to be so prescriptive tied the hands of administrators too tightly. But this depended upon one's views about the substantive wisdom of the action.[76]

Industry equally sought such prescriptive amendments on its behalf. Strategy on this score depended primarily on whether the agency was following one's wishes and hence whether one saw the need for external pressure from Congress to force it to act. On the whole, however, since the major administrative political reality was the ability of industry to frighten agencies with environmental missions into inaction, the most significant use of prescriptive legislation was to force administrators to act on behalf of environmental goals.

An equally significant role of Congress in setting limits on administrative discretion was its investigative powers, which were exercised primarily in oversight functions. Congressional subcommittees could well serve as instruments through which information from within the agency could be leaked both to Congress and to the public. Or more formal investigations could bring information and issues into the open. In the 1960s the industrial water pollution control program was frustrated simply because of the inability of the federal government to collect information about the extent of the problem. Industries refused to divulge that information, and for almost a decade they held up a system of voluntary reporting by blocking agreement on the details of a proposed reporting form. They had considerable influence over this as a result of membership on the relevant committee in the Office of Management and Budget that had to approve the form. Congressman Henry Reuss publicized this recalcitrance through the work of a congressional subcommittee he chaired, and some change resulted in the Water Pollution Control Act of 1972.[77] A decade later a congressional oversight committee publicized private meetings between the EPA and the Formaldehyde Institute, an industry trade association, which led to joint agreement that experiments indicating that formaldehyde caused throat cancer in laboratory animals were not sufficient evidence for curtailing the chemical's use.[78] A variety of settings for controversy over that issue within the Reagan administration is now on the record because of congressional oversight inquiries.

Agencies tended to take refuge in Executive Office devices to shield their activities from legislative attack, and environmentalists tended to use Congress as a device to expose limitations in agency action. The general tightening of executive authority and power that came with the Reagan administration, therefore, was a rather consistent extension of tendencies established earlier. Potential conflict between agencies and the Executive Office of the President that earlier had been in the offing now were reduced as the new Reagan appointees and new authority exercised by the Office of Management and Budget, which sought to change substantive policy though the budget process, subordinated the agencies more fully to the White House.[79] This only enhanced the countervailing tendency of environmentalists to work with Congress to expose, to defend, and on a few occasions to take the initiative against a more unified and disciplined executive branch. Environmental concerns had far more support in Congress than in the Reagan administration. In earlier years the relationships between Congress and the environmental agencies had been more complex, involving both friendly and hostile interaction. The Reagan administration simplified these into a sharper set of patterns more akin to persistent confrontation.

The courts, so far as the agencies were concerned, were quite another matter. They were not so reachable; their mandates were less avoidable; access to them by environmentalists was less controllable. The courts were far more willing than were the agencies to view environmental concerns as reflecting permanent changes in American society and hence as a new and continuing "interest" that should be represented before them. Standing before the courts was now often accorded to those who could demonstrate a clear "environmental interest," as fully as was the case for one who had an interest in property or personal health and safety. At the same time the courts held that environmental matters were as legitimate a part of the "public welfare" and hence as subject to the exercise of the state's police powers as was the case with more traditional realms of public policy. In supervising administrative procedure, as in the Administrative Procedures Act or environmental impact statements, the courts made clear that they recognized substantive environmental values as of considerable merit, fully balanceable in competition with other values.

The major effect of court decisions on agencies was to police procedures of decision making. Although that constituted a burden because of the costs, it only occasionally led to serious modifications of agency action.[80] Whether or not substantive environmental goals obtained any further strength in administrative decisions depended entirely upon the degree to which environmentalists could organize their demands in competition with their opponents. The courts, then, opened the door wider to environmentalists but in no sense guaranteed their influence. Once again such leverage as environmentalists could exercise in this way came more through "anticipatory power," the fear potential litigation might strike in the hearts of administrators, and their need to formulate actions in a way that would make them acceptable to the courts. Agencies were eager to avoid litigation because of the burden of time and cost; and preemptive action was more economical than legal action after the fact. The courts, then, under the influence of new environmental concerns, set limits on agencies' actions and left them to their own devices to find ways and means of protecting themselves against even greater limits.

It should not be thought that environmentalists were the only or even the main users of the courts.[81] A great number of environmental lawsuits were filed by industry. One study found that even those filed under citizen suit provisions, let alone general equity actions, were often instigated by sources other than environmentalists, such as industry and state and local governments.[82] At the same time, it should not be thought that environmental litigation was extensive; on the contrary, it was minimal, a very small fraction of lawsuits, and miniscule compared with the large amount of private contract litigation.[83] Ideological debate and media strategies on the part of antienvironmentalists made the role of litigation appear far larger than it actually was and obscured the degree to which agency action was frustrated by industry as much as by environmentalist litigation.[84] Court decisions were important in some crucial cases and hence did constitute a limitation to action on one side of the agency, as did Congress on the other. In both types of cases, moreover, one must emphasize that the center of day-to-day decisions of consequence was the administrative agency. Despite limitations by Congress and courts, administration played the central role in government decisions; to the actors, influence over those decisions became a crucial element of strategy.[85]

Two conclusions emerge from this examination of the relationships between agencies and the other two branches of the federal government. The first is that the old-fashioned notion that these branches differ according to function — making, executing, and interpreting laws — is more than inadequate in describing their varied roles. Each is a focus of political controversy and hence of political choice. Political initiatives and interests gather around each, and often the political battles are simply transferred from one to the other. When legislation is passed the contestants shift to the administrative agency, and when that goes the wrong way then to the courts. And then back to the agency or Congress. We thus must understand administration as one variant of three sets of political processes in each of the three branches of government. We can distinguish them by their procedures and rules of the game rather than by their contending participants. Administration is the persistent focus of political struggle, and Congress and the courts are more peripheral, entering and leaving the drama at various times and only setting some limits to administrative choice.

Workable public choices, moreover, require that a dispute wend its way through all three sets of institutions and that some degree of compatibility be fashioned in the way each disposes of it. For Congress to approve legislation does not end the matter. Each party to the dispute assumes that the entire issue can be reopened in the process of administration. Hence the history of environmental administration is a case of developmentalists exercising considerable influence in implementing laws that environmentalists have persuaded Congress to enact. Amid all this the administrative process is the ultimate denominator in disputes. If agreement can be fashioned there in the day-to-day relationships among contending parties, it will be far more lasting than with either Congress or the courts. For it means it is an agreement that objectors have accepted or have become resigned to or believe they cannot change. In environmental affairs innovative impulses have come through Congress and the courts. Reaction to these innovations by developmentalists has come largely through administration. Hence administration plays the role of slowing down initiatives from other segments of government and sets the minimal basis for longer-run workable agreements among the contending parties.

I have examined environmental administration in relation to political groups in the wider society and to other branches of government. One should focus also on the hierarchy of government institutions. Traditionally this is thought of as "federalism," with stress on the relative powers of federal and state governments. But there are also important relationships between local governments and the states. With respect to environmental affairs, two sets of controversies arise. There are clashes between federal and state authority in issues of preemption. Shall federal authority be allowed to preempt that of the state? But the same kinds of issues arise as between states and their subdivisions, often described as a problem of "override." Can states "override" decisions of local governments and prevent them from taking action? Preemption is the better-known case; state override is far more obscure but in environmental affairs often more pervasive.

Behind these "constitutional" issues are several substantive realities. One is the politically decentralizing tendency that is inherent in much environmental action. Environmental objectives have a strong grass-roots character. People seek to defend their homes and their places of recreation and leisure from intrusion and degradation. Hence they use local government to avert environmental threats. A typical case might involve a proposal to construct a large-scale facility such as an electric power plant, a synthetic oil plant, an oil tanker terminal, or a chemical plant in the vicinity of one's home. These initiatives seem to come from "out there." Can the local government take action to deflect them? Strategies involve zoning against undesired land use, local referenda to express opposition, or local ordinances that establish higher environmental standards than those provided by state and federal governments.[86]

In response, developers seek action at the state level to override decisions by local government. In some states local air pollution control authorities are prohibited from establishing air quality standards more stringent than those of the state.[87] Most state strip-mining reclamation laws prohibit local municipalities from adopting standards of either land reclamation or water quality that go beyond those of the state.[88] Many a state has enacted laws on hazardous waste facility siting that provide for eventual state action even against the objections of communities.[89] In Wisconsin, state wetland regulations prohibit counties from establishing standards stricter than those of the state.[90] The history of air pollution control in the 1960s is instructive. Many cities and urban counties enacted ordinances to restrict emissions. Objecting industries, in turn, sought to establish state air pollution control commissions that would shift authority from the locality to the state and, they hoped, provide for greater industry influence.[91] For a few years they had considerable success.

This kind of state override did not always work. As environmental interest increased, the accumulation of many local grievances led to a sufficiently large political force that state governments began to take up environmental concerns in ways industry disapproved; in response those industries sought federal laws to override action by the states. An instructive case came in the debate over the 1970 Clean Air Act. Under the previous 1967 law each state had been instructed to adopt air pollution standards, and many had done so. But public enthusiasm, so far as industry was concerned, went much too far; standards were too stringent.[92] In Pennsylvania, for example, the state Air Pollution Control Commission, whose chair was an official of Bethlehem Steel Corporation, recommended a state sulfur dioxide standard of

100 μg/m^3. Well-attended citizen meetings in Pittsburgh and Philadelphia, however, indicated public support for a much stricter standard. The United Steelworkers of American and the congressman from the Pittsburgh steel area, Joseph Gaydos, took the same view and persuaded the governor to join them. The standard was lowered to 60 μg/m^3.[93] Faced with similar action in a number of states, the steel industry testified in Congress that it would not be averse to federal air quality standards that would keep the states in check.[94]

As the 1970s wore on a host of environmental issues involved industry attempts to use federal authority to preempt state environmental action. One of the sharpest had to do with the Coastal Zone Management Act of 1972, in which a "consistency clause" applied.[95] Federal actions such as permits to construct, the statue read, must be "consistent" with coastal zone management plans drawn up by the states. But who should determine whether such actions were "consistent" — the federal agencies alone, who might interpret in favor of development, or a cooperative state-federal action, which would give the states more power to object? Regulatory action during the Carter administration had gone in favor of the states. The oil companies had taken up legal proceedings in the federal courts and in two cases had lost.[96] After the 1980 election they urged the new administration to change the regulations in their favor and provide for a federal preemption. It began to do so. But opposition in Congress made it clear that the contemplated change would meet with congressional disapproval, and the action was dropped.[97]

Actions by the Reagan administration are especially instructive on this score. That administration's ideology was one of transferring power from the federal level to the state; yet it was aligned with corporate business groups who sought to use federal power to override state action.[98] In some cases the administration responded as the business community wished. There was, for example, the case of action by a number of cities to prohibit transport of radioactive materials through their jurisdictions, proposals that prompted the atomic energy industry to push for federal regulations to override such actions. They succeeded during the Carter administration. Final rules were promulgated in the late hours of its tenure, and this was one of the few Carter "midnight regulations" that the Reaganites did not hold up for review.[99] Or there was the case of federal noise regulations that Reagan administrators, on ideological grounds, thought could readily be abolished. Little did they know that those federal standards were in place so that railroads, trucks, and airplanes could use federal authority to override persistent efforts by local governments to establish noise control regulations to which they objected. Soon educated about the issue, the administration reversed field.[100]

On several such proposals the Reagan administration declined to act. One concerned the long-standing desire of the agricultural chemical industry to require that states not issue pesticide regulations more stringent than the federal ones.[101] The immediate issue concerned the insistence of the California government that it have the right to require more technical information about proposed pesticides than was required by the federal government. During debate on the federal act in 1982 the administration declined to back the industry's demand to include a federal preemption provision because it feared compromising its states' rights ideology on an issue on which federal action would be difficult to conceal. In subsequent action on the matter, however, the administration shifted ground.[102]

These relationships between political forces and the levels of government at which action takes place do not follow a neat pattern. One overriding factor is federal ownership of public lands, which leads to federal political action and well-mobilized environmental interest in the four national land systems. Federal agencies are often more responsive to environmental objectives, and developmental interests are allied with local and state governments. Over the years, old-style conservationists and new-style environmentalists fought efforts to transfer federal lands to the states.[103] But in recent years a subtle change has been taking place. As the West has become more densely populated, a considerable number of urban people there have taken up environmental values in public land management. This in turn has led to support within the West for an effective federal presence. Natural environment values are strong in the Rocky Mountain West, often stronger than in most other sections of the nation.[104] This became sharply etched during the first two years of the Reagan administration in controversies over mining and oil drilling in western wilderness areas. It was the West itself that protested these developmental proposals by the Reagan administration and prompted both the president and Secretary James Watt to change political direction.[105]

Another episode, the Sagebrush Rebellion, is equally instructive. This movement, from the West, sought to raise support for transfer of federal lands to the states. But once the western public understood the options, the drive collapsed. The eleven western states manage 35 million acres of state lands, almost all for income-producing purposes in which hunting and fishing and environmental land uses are greatly restricted, often prohibited. Once Rocky Mountain citizens interested in those uses realized that the same restrictive policies would hold for lands acquired from the federal government, they exercised considerable opposition to the proposal.[106] The Sagebrush Rebellion arose out of conflicts within the Rocky Mountain region, in which developmentalists sought to restrain a rising indigenous environmental sentiment by defining the region as developmental, constrained in its ambitions by the environmental East. The effort failed primarily because those with environmental objectives within the West itself were fashioning their own political clout in regional politics.[107]

Environmental air and water quality standards involve a more complex set of circumstances. In the late 1960s and early 1970s environmentalists were convinced that local and state governments were unreliable on that score. Hence they chose to use the federal government for leverage against the states. They worked on behalf of federal standard setting and viewed their actions as devices to force recalcitrant states to act.[108] Industry, on the other hand, sought to shift standard setting to the states, or maintain it there, for precisely the same reason — their belief that now, after federal standards were in place, the states might be more lenient. In some cases federal standards ran headlong into opposition from the general public and state governments on such issues as mandatory inspection and maintenance of motorized vehicles, transport controls, and controls over indirect sources such as shopping centers. All of these backfired on the EPA owing to the protests of automobile owners and organized automobile associations.[109]

In the protection of the highest quality air and water through what were known as the "prevention of significant deterioration" and "antidegradation" programs, environmentalists also sought a federal lead.[110] In both cases the objective was not to clean up dirty areas but to prevent cleaner ones from becoming degraded. Most state governments were reluctant to take up such initiatives because of their implications for land use. But citizen support emerged in some quarters such as Wyoming, where the state took action under the air quality provisions, and Pennsylvania, where the protection of high-quality waters was upgraded because of federal and citizen prodding. Grassroots support for federal air quality programs seemed to increase steadily in the 1970s and often took on an aura of local protection against larger private and public institutions similar to the case of hazardous wastes. But these were only glimmers of change rather than clearly identifiable trends.

Environmentalists especially sought an increasing level of federal action in the scientific and technical aspects of environmental affairs. Few states, aside from the financially stronger ones such as California and New York, could provide the resources necessary to undergird environmental action with scientific and technical data. Research into the health effects of pollutants, alternative energy conversion, or the environmental effects of development all required massive funding, which only the federal government seemed to be able to provide. Program implementation required technical skills (for example in air quality management at state and local levels) and equipment (for example, for monitoring) that most states found they could not afford save at relatively limited levels. Federal agencies alone seemed to be capable of financing the needed science and technology.[111]

Developmentalists, in contrast, sought to reduce such expenditures for the opposite reason, to limit the capabilities of management agencies to act and hence to limit the level of environmental protection. Often it was a contest between research financed by industry to argue against action and research financed by government to bolster it.[112] Industry well understood the political leverage of its own technical capabilities and knew that controversies often turned on the relative ability of the contending parties to apply scientific and technical data to the issue.[113] Hence it sought to scale down federal activities on behalf of environmental aims, such as research concerning indoor air pollution or the monitoring of radiation releases from atomic power plants.

An episode early in the air quality program illustrated the problem. In the early 1960s many communities had sought to restrict pollution emissions and passed ordinances to that effect. When industries challenged them in court on the grounds that existing pollution levels were not harmful, local governments had few if any resources to counter those claims. In contrast to industry's ability to present its case about health effects, the municipalities were woefully weak. Hence in the 1963 Clean Air Act they successfully established a program whereby the U.S. Public Health Service would expand its technical air quality capabilities and use that expertise to assist local government. As this aid developed and was so used, industry objected that this was unwarranted interference by the Public Health Service in local air quality matters. The implications of this episode continued to structure environmental politics. Those who sought environmental protection reached out for technical assistance from many quarters. But on the whole the resources of municipal and state governments were extremely limited and only those of federal agencies seemed equal to the task. Environmentalists sought to advance these technical capabilities, and that drive continued with some success until it was severely blunted by the Reagan administration.[114]

Administrative environmental decision making was heavily influenced by technical considerations. Hardly an environmental question failed to require ever-increasing amounts of empirical data and analysis. This was the case with the full range of environmental effects issues, problems of the balance between natural and developed resources, and larger questions of the balance between population and resources. Cutting across all such issues were questions of economic analysis and planning that seemed to involve the application of empirical detail in ever greater quantity and refinement. Environmental administration became heavily infused with technical experts — scientists and engineers, economists and planners.

Most of these technical activities conveyed the aura of being value free, of constituting what were called rational processes, of seeking "objective" solutions to contentious political disputes. None, so the self-perceptions went, were steered by personal value judgment; instead all constituted modes of action that submerged such values in the face of facts and analyses derived from more objective circumstances. And so it was that as administration brought together these technical disciplines to apply knowledge in the service of public policy, it too thought of itself and described itself to others as being above day-to-day political battles. The U.S. Forest Service argued that its decisions carried out an impartial spirit of "wise use," while the U.S. Army Corps of Engineers maintained that it simply carried out the law rather than expressed its own preferences. All sought to give their actions validity at the highest level of discourse by identifying their objectives with the "national interest."

But the details of controversy often revealed that even objective technical questions involved personal judgments and provided an opportunity for particular rather than universal values to prevail. Arguments over the meaning of scientific and technical experiments on the effects of lead on human health turned not so much on the "facts" per se as on the way they were assessed. The patterns of debate over two decades reflected consistently held opinions on the part of individual scientists and individual institutions depending on personal values and agency missions. Scientists in industries that sought to continue the use of lead in gasoline persistently found that lead was not harmful at low levels of exposure, while those who sought to protect the health of children came to the opposite conclusion. Those competing viewpoints continued even though over the same span of years the exposure levels around which the argument raged declined from 10 to 5 and then to 1.5 $\mu g/m^3$ of ambient air and from 80 to 60 to 25 $\mu g/dl$ of blood. Something more than the facts alone shaped the persistent disagreement.[115]

One could make the same observation about economic analysis. The effects of this or that regulation on the "economy" fueled debate from the earliest days of environmental regulation, and in each case exponents of diverse views could develop diversely favorable analyses.[116] Much depended on one's ability to command the computer resources that provided a more "sophisticated" model—that is, with more variables accounted for—than one's opponent's.[117] Often the legislative as well as the administrative debate took the form of last-minute injections into the argument of the "latest" study, which demonstrated conclusively the wisdom of one's previously declared position. Given time the opposition could usually marshal contrary evidence or interpretation, but it was especially convenient, once the hearing record with the agency had closed, to persuade the Executive Office that one's latest economic impact analysis rendered the regulatory effort indefensible.

All this is merely to underline the extensive scientific and technical context of decisions and to serve as the starting point for investigating the "politics of science," "the politics of economic analysis," the "politics of planning," and, running through all of them, the "politics of information," which lay at the root of many a political choice in environmental affairs. The parties to disputes recognized that the new scientific and technical context of administrative choice was all-pervasive, that the most fundamental of all political stakes lay in the ability to shape the information on which decisions were based. This rarely involved overt strategies of control; rather, more subtle ones were used—seeking to discredit the validity of an opponent's information, to protect information as privileged and hence not subject to disclosure, and to overload the decision process with quantities of information that would bog it down or increase its cost. It also involved the political legitimacy of experts, since part of the political game lay in attempts to raise or lower the credibility of individual scientists or economists.[118]

From the developmental side a variety of strategies emerged. One involved devices to prevent information from entering arenas where it could be used by the public. Many a regulatory program was stymied by the argument that such and such information was a "trade secret" and could not be divulged. That claim was made by the chemical companies from the first moves to regulate pesticides; it reached its highest use when the EPA attempted to implement the Toxic Substances Control Act of 1976 and found that companies applying to register chemicals demanded that information about their names, the names of the chemicals in question, and the quantities produced not be released. Environmentalists complained that this made it impossible for them to make their own evaluations of chemical safety.[119]

A variant on this issue was the "right to know," the argument by workers that they should be allowed to know what chemicals they were exposed to. They wanted this for their own purposes, either in order to press claims for liability in the future or to enable their own industrial health scientists to investigate the effects of exposure to chemicals. As the movement for public disclosure grew in the early 1980s, supported by municipal fire departments, which found that lack of knowledge often led to critical dangers for their personnel in chemical fires, several cities and states passed "right to know" ordinances. The companies struck back with a proposal that they would provide for some disclosure, limit it at their own discretion, and so reduce the usefulness of the information to those exposed.[120]

A somewhat different strategy of information control lay in efforts to command the technical resources that generated information. In some cases this involved computerized data. The "allowable cut" in public forest management, for example, that is, the amount of wood that could be cut each year, depended on complex calculations based on annual growth rates over the life of a forest and even over several generations. It also hinged upon the results of "inputs," such as herbicides, fertilizers, or improved seed, that might increase yield in any one generation.[121] All the relevant information was fed into the computer to determine the appropriate level of cut. But if one wished to question such decisions one had to be able to question the assumptions involved in either the data input or the analytical bases of computer programs. Environmentalists who might be critical of Forest Service choices had little opportunity to develop competing computer analyses and hence little basis for challenging Forest Service allowable cut policies.[122]

Still a third focus for the politics of information lay in controversies over the methods to be used in analyzing the effects of pollutants. Was information from experiments on laboratory animals sufficient proof of potential harm to humans to warrant regulation? Was epidemiological evidence essential before regulation could be adopted? And if epidemiological evidence was required, was it sufficient to compare a study group with a norm, or would a matched case control method be mandatory? In the earlier years of environmental protection controversy probable anticipated harm was an acceptable standard of proof, and for this reasoning from animal data, for example, seemed to be widely accepted. But the political stakes involved in the issues led to persistent demands from the regulated industries for higher levels of proof: more direct evidence on human effects, more specific case control methods, and far more extensive procedures for ruling out "confounding variables." Their demands had considerable impact on scientists, who in turn insisted on higher levels of proof and more direct evidence before conclusions were drawn.[123] One can debate the issue as to whether or not changes in scientific approach came through the internal evolution of science alone or as a result of constant exposure to the demands from industry, which in turn gradually sharpened latent tendencies within science. The two seemed to work in tandem. Whatever the cause, it provided a constantly changing context for administrative action; industry and scientists demanding ever higher levels of proof sought to shape the strategies of decision makers concerning the choice of scientist and scientific assessments on which action or inaction concerning environmental harm would be based.[124]

For environmentalists this mobilization of resources to shape and control information constituted one of their most difficult political problems. Their own technical resources were limited. Hence they had to be far more selective in their approach, emphasizing not massive mobilization of expertise, but more critical points of action and analysis. Litigation seemed to be adapted to their limited resources, for in this arena it was not massive overkill that carried the day but crucial and telling argument. Several well-constructed pieces of scientific investigation that were to the point might well outweigh a hundred pieces of technical data that were not directly relevant. Hence environmental strategies lay more in the search, through literature reviews and discussion with scientists, for critical research.[125] Litigation organizations such as the Environmental Defense Fund and the Natural Resources Defense Council brought onto their staffs technical experts who were sufficiently knowledgeable to be able to keep abreast of ongoing work.[126] Most important, they brought frontier as well as more conventional studies into decision making.[127] Hence they played a vital role in science and technology transfer from the world of research to the world of administrative action.

Environmentalists also found that the media were of considerable help. Many a controversial issue, ranging from radiation to lead to pesticides to asbestos, involved a series of controversies in which industry and the agencies carried out a parallel effort to control the flow of technical information to the public and to disparage the significance of information about adverse effects. A sequence of issues generated a pattern in the public mind and the media: information was subject to persistent "management" by private and public authorities so as to minimize public concern. This only led the media to believe there was more to environmental effects than met the eye and to engage in vigorous detective work to get at the bottom of affairs. Often potential victims of pollution, such as toxic waste dumps, found that the media were valuable allies to force action when government agencies held back.[128] The ensuing struggle over publicity about environmental harm came to be one of the major battlegrounds in the politics of information.[129]

In this struggle to control information administrative agencies seemed to be increasingly skeptical about the public's ability to understand or accept the scientific facts and to be convinced that the media greatly exaggerated harm in order to arouse public concern. Hence they sought to establish their own ability as far greater than that of the media or the public to determine the extent of potential harm. Scientific and technical determinations were best made by the "experts." Out of these circumstances grew much mutual distrust. The public readily believed that the agencies were deliberately underestimating harm and were willing to subject the public to higher levels of risk, while the technical experts of the agencies believed that the public was simply misinformed and a victim of manipulation. Agencies spoke of "perceived harm" with the clear meaning that beliefs about harm were not justified, and when they took action to restrict harm they increasingly did so on the grounds that their purpose was to restore "public confidence" rather than solve a "real" problem.

During the Reagan administration the public came to believe that technical decisions were being made behind closed doors and to its detriment. In the 1960s pollution control agencies had often established "liaison committees" between government and industry to take up relevant scientific and technical questions. These inevitably involved the assessment of harm and hence the degree of pollution abatement desired. Early in the 1970s, however, the proceedings of such committees came to be more open and subject to public scrutiny. Hence industry found them to be no longer useful, and often the ventures came to an end. But the assessment of harm as reflected in the criteria documents continued, and over the years the EPA developed a strategy for a rather extensive and far more open process for coming to conclusions about the meaning of the evidence. Under these arrangements industry chafed considerably. At the advent of the Reagan administration it was able to persuade administrators to make such decisions in more "closed door" sessions much akin to the practices of over a decade before. This only encouraged Congress and the media to undertake campaigns to "expose" undue industry influence and served as the major twist in Reagan administration policy to undermine confidence in the EPA and bring about a change in agency leadership.[130]

To the relatively disinterested observer it was tempting to dismiss such disputes as matters of mere "politics," to argue that scientific and technical questions should be above such maneuvering. Such issues were a matter of what was accurate and what was not, of "good" and "bad" science, of facts about a world "out there" that could be discovered and applied by impartial experts. If one's own conception of expertise was heavily laden with self-images of "rationality," it was relatively easy to project that view onto the larger scene of public affairs and imagine that "politics" was the culprit that restricted one's freedom to act. But the details of such disputes make it clear that considerations of personal values, professional commitment, and institutional interest had the capacity to manufacture disagreement out of many an accumulation of objective facts.[131] In the world of technical politics those who had superior resources sought to obscure value choices with a burden of technical overlay, and those who had fewer equally sought to ferret out and expose the value choices as best they could. The problem in political analysis was to identify the value choices embedded in the technical detail. At the least this could provide an understanding of many important issues in environmental administration. At the most it identified variations in the ability to control information as one of the most significant elements of modern political inequality.

We might, at the end of this analysis, focus especially on several general conclusions. First of all, people want government. They want environmental programs and environmental administration because they produce desired benefits. California voters approved Proposition 13, but in the same election they approved a statewide bond issue for water quality programs and a local bond issue in San Diego for purchase of open-spaced land. A recent Harris poll indicates that people want less regulation in general but more regulation on behalf of consumers. There are always mixed reactions to government action, for what benefits one can easily work hardship on another. And this gives rise to hostility to government. But we must not lose sight of the institutional changes beneath the overlay of ideology. The mixture adds up to the fact that government environmental programs rest heavily on the public's desire for them.

There are also implications for the ties between the wider society and government. Usually, it is argued, all this involves a "welfare state" that benefits the lowest third of the socioeconomic order. But social service policies provide more benefits to the middle class and serve to attach that broad stratum of society to government. Since the New Deal, government social programs have created strong bonds between the middle layers of society and an activist federal government. Social security and the financial underpinning of private housing constituted such beginnings in the 1930s. Health and education services added to that. And the more recent social service programs involving consumers, women, environmentalists, and the arts only cemented further the attachment of the middle class to the state.

Environmental administration also involves a major element of equity. Benefits are provided for the middle class that formerly were available only to the very top levels of society, such as enjoyment of wildland natural environments. The starting point for equity in this case was the public lands, where outdoor recreation was available at a low cost. In Europe, where much outdoor recreation could be enjoyed only on sufferance from the landed aristocracy, equity in the form of "access" was and still is a constant political battle.[132] Cleaning up pollution where masses of people lived made available to them what others had earlier enjoyed by being able to travel to cleaner environments or by purchasing urban housing upwind from pollution sources.[133] With limited resources, as was the case with high-quality land, air, and water, the private market of increasing demand amid fixed supply tended toward inequalities of benefits;[134] the public environmental economy provided equalizing influences.

Finally, while the public is positive about government benefits, it often becomes hostile when administrators compromise environmental objectives in the face of opposition. It is not government per se that generates cynicism, but the processes by which public objectives realized through legislation become markedly changed through administration. The environmental movement has sought to expand greatly the use of science and technology for environmental benefits. But the public readily becomes cynical when the development, assessment, and use of information are controlled by antienvironmentalists. According to a recent survey of attitudes toward chemical risk, the public believes that knowledge of effects should be widely disseminated and that the public, not the experts or administrators, should decide the use to which it should be put.[135]

The realm of environmental affairs, and especially environmental administration, can serve as a useful device through which to examine many aspects of the new consumer-information society. It gives special focus to the personal, family, and community context within which values are generated. It also highlights the technical and managerial processes by which resources are organized through private and government administrative systems. Even more, it emphasizes the modes of interaction between these two large sets of social processes. By and large Americans have accepted large-scale organization in the delivery of goods and services, including large corporations and big government, if the resulting benefits respond to their changing values, needs, and wants. In neither realm have they rejected bigness, but they have insisted that delivery systems of all kinds, both private and public, continually justify themselves by performance. Acceptable environmental administration rests upon the realization of environmental benefits as part of Americans' continuing desire for a higher standard of living. These are the grounds on which Americans test the environmental sector of the social service state.

CAROLYN L. WEAVER

The Social Security Bureaucracy in Triumph and in Crisis

THERE IS little consensus among political economists as to who is running the new American state. Economic models of government and politics typically present competing views of the determinants of policy outcomes of an either/or variety. Either citizens and voters, who have perfect control over the bureaucracy and the legislature, are running America; or the legislature, which perfectly controls the bureaucracy, is "out of control" vis-à-vis the citizenry and is running the country for itself and the interest groups; or the bureaucracy is "out of control" and running America.[1]

That none of these views singly is applicable to all or even most government programs or agencies at all points in time seems clear. Policy outcomes are the result of a complex series of choices that are conditioned by the economic and political environment in which they are made. Market conditions change. Bureaucracies mature. Decision-making rules and procedures are modified. Interest groups and constituencies come and go. As the environment changes, thereby changing political incentives and constraints, so do the choices made by political participants, whether as voters, politicians, political executives, judges, or bureaucrats. In each policy arena, different conditions have, it seems, produced different balances of power.

This chapter examines one such area of public policy and attempts to explain the evolution of social security as arising from the interplay of the demand for and the supply of government action. Both sides of the "political market" are explored to determine how the nature of social security — its funding mechanism, its benefit and tax distribution, and its administrative organization — affected political choices. My reexamination of the history of social security suggests that the bureaucracy, working with and fueling the demands of interest groups and politicians, played a decisive role in the evolution of the program in the postwar years. The interests of the citizenry, or even the long-term interest of the elderly, cannot be said to have been governing.[2] As should be clear, however, things are changing. With the aging of social security, underlying forces are at work that are placing new pressures on the bureaucracy (and legislators too) to operate in a more open and competitive political and budgetary environment.

The first section opens with a brief discussion of the economic approach to the study of politics and government. Following sections define "social security" as of 1945, the starting point for this historical review, develop the implications for the incentives and constraints facing the various political participants, and then trace the evolution of social security in the postwar years and pinpoint the economic and political determinants of the current-day crisis.

THE ECONOMIC APPROACH TO THE
STUDY OF GOVERNMENT: ALTERNATIVE VIEWS

The economic approach to the study of government holds that public policies result from the interaction of the demand and the supply of the coercive powers of the state.[3] Much as a shift in the supply or demand conditions facing a firm is seen to induce changes in price, output, or profits in the private sector, shifts in voter demands or public supply are seen to result in changes in government policy.

According to the "broad-based demand-side" view, the evolution of government is traceable to changes in citizen demands. Stemming from various market failures, such demands reflect the desires of citizens to use the coercive powers of the state in the most positive sense — to provide public goods and redistribute income so as to make everyone better off.[4] A growing public sector would, in these models, result singly from demands by citizens for more public goods and service and their acquiescence in paying additional taxes.

Although this view has merit as a conceptual starting point, it has serious limitations because it effectively ignores an important part of the American political landscape — special interest groups. The demands of such groups, of course, may or may not coincide with some broader notion of the public interest or the demands of a broad-based majority. Moreover, these sorts of demand-side models are unable to explain zero-sum income redistribution, that is, policies that transfer income or wealth toward one group at the expense of another (such as some tariff laws and regulatory policies).

A less idealized view of democratic processes is reflected in the interest group models of government, within what might be termed the "narrow-based demand-side" view of government. According to this more recent literature, demands based on considerations of market failure are unlikely to drive government action since they are unlikely to survive the filtering of the political process.[5] The costly nature of political participation and the publicness of the benefits that accrue are likely to cause these demands to be overwhelmed by the more intense and narrowly based demands of special interest groups. In this view, the relevant demands affecting government action are those of interest groups attempting to influence government policy so as to redistribute wealth or income in their favor or to prevent the passage of policies that would adversely affect the interests of the group.

In some of the early presentations of this view dealing with economic regulation, legislators are modeled as brokers who strike bargains with politically effective coalitions of voters to arrange wealth transfers. The resulting administrative agencies and their staff of regulators are modeled, much as they are in the pure demand-side models, as the faithful agents of the legislature in enforcing and carrying out the terms of the bargain.[6] Closely akin to these models are those of more recent vintage wherein the bureaucracy is seen to respond to, and to be perfectly constrained by, the demands of congressional leaders operating within a committee system of decision making. As in the regulation models, any excesses or inefficiencies in government are traced to failures in the legislative process.[7]

Even in these more sophisticated models of government, supply factors are effectively ignored. Whether because of an assumed benevolence on the part of public servants, or the existence of fierce political competition, or constitutional constraints, those who use demand-side models make the critical assumption that the government is staffed by a body of bureaucratic and political representatives — political agents — who respond automatically and efficiently to voter demands. The role and impact of bureaucrats and politicians reduces to the securing of gains for some or all of the citizenry, their political "principals."

An alternative group of models reflecting the "supply-side view" of government attempts to correct the weaknesses of such an approach. The perfectly constrained political agents just described are replaced by an array of self-interested bureaucrats who participate actively and have a measurable impact on the collective choice process.[8] In the words of political scientists Dodd and Schott:

> Protected by civil service tenure, armed with the power to issue orders and rules that have the force of law, supported by strong clientele and interest groups, and possessing a wealth of information, knowledge,

and technical expertise, [the Federal bureaucracy] goes forth to battle its institutional rivals on equal, and sometimes superior, terms. . . . Working through the political appointees that head their departments, or working directly with members of Congress and their staffs, it can mold and constrain the legislative options open to both Congress and the president."[9]

The distinguishing characteristic of supply-side models is the importance attached to the organization of supply. Key differences in the organization of public and private supply are seen to render the competitive firm a poor analogue for understanding the behavior of the public bureau (despite its implicit use in demand-side models).[10] In public supply, for example, the bureau's output is generally produced by a single supplier, financed by a compulsory tax, and "sold" or consumed, on a compulsory basis without individual quantity adjustment. If the public bureau has, through its ability to compel purchase, more independence than a private monopoly, the absence of influence by the bureaucracy is no longer a tenable assumption.

A proper understanding of the evolution of government policy requires an assimilation of these views. Which one is most descriptive for a particular program or agency depends on a variety of factors, not the least of which are the nature of the program at hand, including the method of administration and finance, and the extent of competition from the private sector and within the public sector. These are the factors I consider in applying these viewpoints to the development of social security.

THE HISTORICAL CONTEXT

As a starting point for unraveling social security policymaking in the postwar years, it is first necessary to define "social security" as of 1940 or 1945. The policy was still relatively new at this time (having been adopted in 1935), but it had already undergone important revisions. The original Social Security Act and the amendments adopted in 1939 defined the social security system through the war years and set in place those features most essential for developments since that time.

Originally, social security consisted of one compulsory federal program, old-age insurance, which was simple, was relatively narrow in scope, and possessed some attributes of private insurance. There was only one type of beneficiary, for example: the fully retired worker, who was eligible for benefits (beginning in 1942) at age 65. There were no extra benefits for family members or for delayed retirement, and there were no penalties for early retirement or the receipt of other public pensions. Benefits were based only on the worker's total earnings in covered employment.[11]

The method of computing benefits, which was similar to private insurance, ensured that people with the same earnings history would receive the same monthly benefit.[12] Although the formula was weighted in favor of low-wage workers, the program was primarily designed, in the wake of the Great Depression, to supplement private sources of retirement income in a "safe and systematic way." Poverty among the aged was to be addressed separately, through a means-tested, federally financed program of old-age assistance.

Benefits under the old-age insurance program were restricted to covered workers—those who worked in employment covered by social security and paid social security taxes. Originally, this amounted to 60 percent of the work force, generally concentrated in lower-paid occupations. Government employees, self-employed professionals, and agricultural workers were among those excluded.

The payroll tax was first levied in 1937 at a rate of 1 percent for the employee and employer each, on the first $3,000 of annual earnings. The tax was scheduled to peak at 3 percent each in 1949. It was anticipated that by this time a large reserve fund would have accumulated that, together with interest earnings and tax revenues, would support the system indefinitely.[13] The program was to be administered by a three-member independent agency, the Social Security Board.

Before any retirement benefits had been paid under the new program, social security was altered in a number of significant ways.[14] The 1939 amendments made benefits payable in 1940 rather than 1942 and introduced survivors and dependents benefits. Under the new "old-age and survivors insurance" program, benefits were payable to elderly wives, elderly widows, young widows with children, dependent children, surviving children, and even dependent surviving parents. The benefit rate for dependents was half that payable to the retired worker; the rate for survivors was three-quarters. Also, the benefit formula was weighted more heavily toward low earnings and made applicable to average rather than total earnings. The pattern of returns was thereby made more progressive, and discrimination on the basis of family size and marital status was introduced. Two workers with identical taxes and earnings could now receive benefits that differed by 50 percent or more; people who had paid no taxes at all were now eligible to receive benefits.

On the revenue side, taxes were cut. Despite a significant increase in aggregate benefit costs, the $1.1 billion ($8 billion in 1982 dollars)[15] fund permitted Congress to delay for a decade the first tax increase and to cut the long-term rate from 3 percent to 2 percent. The intention of building up a large reserve fund was thus rejected in favor of a pay-as-you-go type system. [16]

THE SOURCES AND USES OF CONTROL

In what ways did these institutional features of social security condition policymaking? As program advocates were certainly aware, the institutional "details" were of utmost importance to the program's survival and growth. They would determine the ability of the bureaucracy and beneficiary groups to affect fiscal outcomes by defining the degree to which the agency was isolated from competitive processes and workers were removed from a position of control. [17]

Monopoly in Supply

Monopoly in the supply of old-age insurance was the most important source of supply-side control, and it stemmed from two factors: First, the federal government compelled purchase from the public supplier. Second, the public product was noticeably differentiated from insurance attainable privately. The federal agency was immediately set apart from private insurers by the requirement that 60 percent of the work force participate in the system. Most workers would have to pay for government "insurance" even if it would involve sacrificing a private policy or purchasing supplemental protection that was inferior to that available privately (situations that would become more important as the private sector rebounded and social security aged). A government agency thus became the largest single producer of retirement income in the country, and as long as the act survived, its market was guaranteed. That social security was financed by an earmarked tax and thus not subject to the annual appropriations process bolstered this position.

In addition, the pay-as-you-go method of finance allowed social security to provide an output for which there were no close substitutes. Because social security could transfer income between generations—from young to old—and was bound by no legally enforceable requirements to maintain certain reserves, the system could, for at least several decades, pay benefits that were considerably larger than the actuarial equivalent of taxes paid. Whereas private insurers could do little more than provide annuities based on contributions plus interest (albeit on a long-term basis), social security could provide benefits completely independent of past contributions or interest, based instead on the amount of taxes collected from the currently employed. This amount would be enormous relative to the number of elderly people eligible for benefits in the early years. Things were even more favorable for social security in the early decades because reserves could be depleted and coverage could be expanded to provide an unusually large ratio of payout to income during the transition to a universal, mature pay-as-you-go system.

Further serving to differentiate the public output was the ability of social security to transfer income within generations — from high- to low-wage earners, from small to large families, from single to married workers, and from career to part-time employees. The weighted benefit formula and the payment of benefits to noncontributors created subsidies for some groups at the expense of others, subsidies that were not likely to survive in a competitive setting.[18]

Information and Agenda Control

With competition curtailed, the bureaucracy assumed primary control over the production of information relevant to decision making, whether by citizens, interest groups, or legislators.[19] "Customers" could not move their business between rival producers in search of the best buy. The public supplier, among other producers, would not profit or lose in accordance with its ability to attract customers. Even within the public sector, social security would be without competitors in the area of long-range forecasting, so critical for evaluating pension fund performance. As is the case today, all long-range forecasts of the financial condition of the system, and the revenue impact of alternative reform proposals, would be generated internally, without the Congressional Budget Office, the General Accounting Office, the Treasury Department, or the Office of Management and Budget being willing or able to provide competing information.[20] Citizens obviously lost the comparative information necessary for making informed choices and, with it, an important constraint on the performance of the bureaucracy.

Federally funded to undertake research, disseminate information, and initiate and draft legislation, the new social security bureaucracy was in the position of determining not only which issues would be studied internally and which results would be communicated, but also which ones would not be. With only one order from the commissioner or other high-level official, all of the research and policy resources of the agency could be mustered to help sell — or kill — a proposal. With equal ease, proponents or critics, in the White House, on Capitol Hill, and among the lobby groups, could be armed with necessary defenses of policies — and this could be done with or without the consent or knowledge of social security's own political executives. Effects on constituencies could be clarified or obscured; uncertainties could be enhanced or reduced — perhaps best illustrated by the way program costs could be characterized. During congressional hearings in the 1950s, Health, Education, and Welfare secretary Marion Folsom described the cost of a proposal opposed by the administration as "an unscheduled 25% increase in social security taxes on 70 million workers."[21] Social security commissioner Robert Ball, by contrast, when speaking on behalf of program expansion in the 1960s, deemphasized the cost of the addition, telling Senate Finance Committee members that "the benefit increases in the formula, not those that come from the earnings base but from the formula, cost 1.36. These other improvements of our proposals and the improvements in the House bill combined, costing 0.21, for a combined new level of cost of benefits of 9.83. We have the level equivalent of income when you add the income from the new contribution rate of 0.23, giving an equivalent income of 9.73 with a slight deficit of about a tenth of 1 percent over the long range period or a deficit of about 1 percent of the total."[22]

The bureaucracy could not have been expected to use its unique position to provide balanced information on the costs and benefits of social security relative to that actually or potentially available in the private sector. Likewise, proposals to limit the growth of the program would have been uncharacteristic. There was every incentive to use this power to expand the size and scope of social security. As described by Robert Myers, social security's chief actuary for many years, "over the years, most of the American staff engaged in program planning and policy development have had the philosophy — carried out with religious zeal — that what counts above all else is the expansion of the program."[23] In Martha Derthick's words, recounting the history of social security policymaking, "'More is better' could have been the motto of [SSAs] leaders, who were never without a legislative agenda for the moment or ideas for an agenda for the long run."[24] Ever prepared to justify an expansion of social security as "necessary and urgent" for an "admittedly inadequate" program, public executives learned quickly how to communicate the benefits of expansion in terms understandable to the least well informed. Congress would learn, for example, that 2,175,000 people stood to receive an increase in benefits under legislation pending in 1961; that 23 million, or one out of nine Americans, would receive an increase in benefits from legislation pending in 1967; and that nearly everyone would be affected in 1971.[25] On the cost of expansion — who pays the bill and how large it will be — answers like the one Ball provided in 1967 would become commonplace.

This was to be expected. Right from the start, a strongly expansionary staff had been organized.[26] Drawn from the ranks of the Committee on Economic Security (the presidentially appointed committee that wrote the Social Security Act) and from social insurance advocates in government and the universities, the bureaucracy combined individuals who, based on personal values, sought an extensive social insurance system and those who simply found their futures tied to program growth. The bureaucratization and monopolization of research, information, and legislative agendas were sources of control over political outcomes, and growth-oriented advocates were in possession of this control.

Poor Incentives to Monitor Costs

Another important source of power for the bureaucracy and indeed for advocates in general stemmed from the poor incentive for the working aged to monitor social security developments.[27] The very broad distribution of taxes relative to benefits (there were about forty taxpayers per beneficiary in 1945) reduced taxpayers' incentive to incur the costs of becoming informed and lobbying for change. The cost of any particular program expansion, or the savings from blocking such a policy, would be shared by literally millions of workers, whereas the benefits could be concentrated on as few as several thousand people. Whereas expansion could make the difference between eligibility and ineligibility for the beneficiary, it could mean only a marginal increase in the worker's tax, perhaps indistinguishable from the incremental cost of all other activities of the federal government. When reserves were large, coverage was being expanded, and economic growth was healthy, expansion could actually be accomplished with no tax increases at all.

The incentives for control by worker-taxpayers were further reduced by a long-standing misconception fostered by the bureaucracy — that social security was, like private insurance, a funded system providing contractual benefits. Describing the new program in 1936, Arthur Altmeyer, social security's chief executive until 1953, said:

> These benefits are best understood if we compare them to insurance . . . men and women will be assured an income for life after age 65 when they are no longer at work. This income will be paid to them by the U.S. Government in monthly checks — like the installments on annuities from an insurance company. Or the cash value will be paid to the worker's family when he dies. Whatever happens, the worker or his family gets back more than he pays in. Like an insurance company policy, the worker's old-age benefit from the government must be paid for in advance.[28]

But social security was clearly not like an annuity, and so important was this sort of misrepresentation that Congressman Carl Curtis, chairman of the House social security subcommittee, issued a report in 1954 identifying the Social Security Administration as a key source of public misunderstanding of the program. To the extent people failed to recognize that an increase in the tax rate was not like a premium increase to which an increase in future benefits was tied — only a payment to finance an increase in current benefits (or to close a deficit) — opposition to expansion was reduced. Expressing this point most clearly, Congressman Carl Curtis said that "by semantics" there had "been removed . . . the restraint that is applied by people who believe that they are paying for a program." "False notions that have been injected into this system," he argued, were creating "illusions about the future." He continued,

> As long as we say, well now, we have planned this so it is going to be self-supporting, we are going to have a tremendous reserve in the year 2025, and the tax won't be more than this, and we are going to give such and such a level of benefit when we get there, the young fellow 25 years old . . . says, "Senator, I am glad you voted for that. I am looking forward to it. I wish you could increase it just a little bit more."
>
> The people who are receiving it, they say, "That is fine. I wish you would just give us a little bit more."
>
> But if it had been in the concept that this 25-year-old fellow or 35-year-old fellow who is educating his family and buying a home and supporting the community chest and carrying all the burdens and paying a considerable portion of the taxes through his withholding, if he realized that whatever social security tax had been imposed on him was to pay grandma's social security, then he would have said, "Senator, I want you to be generous and fair with grandma, but don't overdo it, because I have got my obligations today. I want to educate my children and I want to pay for my home."[29]

For each of these reasons, lobby activities would tend to be dominated by beneficiary groups and other program advocates, and legislators would tend to respond to these pressures. It would only make sense to work to improve the lot of a coalition of actively participating beneficiaries rather than to make marginal improvements in the lot of the vast majority of taxpayers. Indeed, because of the nature of social security's "output" — cash transfers that could be parceled out to particular beneficiary groups (such as workers who retired late, women who were divorced or disabled, people with sporadic work histories, or very old beneficiaries with long work histories) — the program was a ready target for reelection-minded politicians seeking to gain political favor. With no contracts for future benefits or protections from future premium increases, of course, younger workers were easy prey. All rights and protections under the Social Security Act were statutory, having been granted — as they could be rescinded — by Congress.

Pay-as-You-Go Financing and Incentives for Control

All in all, the incentives for expansion were clear. The pay-as-you-go system provided a method of finance that for many years would obscure and defer costs. In the first several decades, reserves (and thus the pool of resources available to spend on current beneficiaries) would be very large. Most workers would be contributing to the system while only a small proportion of the elderly would have become eligible for benefits. In addition, coverage could be expanded and the ceiling on taxable earnings could be increased, thereby producing unusually rapid growth of income and reserves, which in turn could be spent on beneficiaries. All of this obscured the fact that benefit costs had to rise as an increasing proportion of the population gained eligibility, and individual tax costs had to rise as the growth of the covered work force and taxable wage base fell to a sustainable rate. Also obscured was the fact that future generations of retirees would not fare as well.

Beneficiaries could actually profit from an increase in taxes on young people or an increase in the number of people required to participate in the system. Both were mechanisms for transferring wealth to the elderly and transferring costs to young workers and future generations. In the long term, the return payable under social security could be no greater than productivity and labor force growth in the economy — unless, of course, taxes could be increased once more so as to shift costs further. As described by Edwin Witte, executive direction of the Committee on Economic Security, a pay-as-you-go system, "essentially deficit financing," was financed in a "very dangerous" way and was "likely to prove very unfair to present younger workers and to future employers and employees."[30]

In this political environment, the interests of beneficiaries, politicians, and bureaucrats would all become increasingly coincidental and an increasingly potent force — especially as the proportion of the elderly increased and as politicians became more responsive to their demands.

Complexity and Control

Finally, complexity in the social security system — in the benefit computation procedures and in the age and eligibility requirements —

would be both a source and a use of bureaucratic control. To quote Martha Derthick, "between the expert and nonexpert lie a specialized vocabulary and a mountainous barrier of intricate fact, law, and regulation, much of which is imperfectly accessible to anyone who does not have training in law, economics, public finance, or actuarial science."[31] A complex program, the details of which could be mastered only by experts, removed social security from direct voter as well as legislator control. With limited time and expertise, even such groups as citizens' advisory councils would find themselves dependent upon the expertise of the bureaucracy and upon bureau-generated information. Legislators would be placed in the position of voting on key issues — such as across-the-board benefit increases — leaving it to the experts to decipher the array of seemingly technical changes to which they had been tied.

With the bureau actively publicizing the social gains to expansion ("hope and dignity for millions of Americans," for example),[32] while maintaining discretion over institutional redesign, massive wealth transfers could be effected by simply permitting the political process to run its course — a political process dominated by the demands of interest groups. Technical changes in the distribution of benefits bestowed special treatment to deserving beneficiaries, which in turn generated demands for expansion to eliminate apparent inequities. Ultimately, even the lobby groups most powerful in influencing legislation and the representatives who brokered for them found their demands conditioned by the actions of the bureaucracy. This became apparent early in the postwar era.

EXPANSION THROUGH COST DEFERRAL:
SOCIAL SECURITY THROUGH 1960

A 1943 speech delivered by Social Security Board member Ellen Woodward provided an early glimpse of what would be the agency's stance, official or otherwise, for the next three decades: more is better and also essential. In her words, "We all know that the program doesn't go far enough. Our steps toward social security . . . have not yet led into all our homes nor all the situations that breed hazards and insecurity . . . the time has come to extend our present program to fill in the gaps."[33] This view was echoed by the board in its 1943 report to Congress, which called for a "single, comprehensive system of social insurance with provisions for unemployment, sickness and disability, old age, and death, and a considerable part of the expenses of hospital and medical services."[34] For the existing retirement program, the bureaucracy's detailed legislative agenda for the future involved universal coverage, higher benefit levels, and reduced age and eligibility requirements.[35]

The 1940s were not especially conducive to program expansion, however. People had been paying social security taxes for several years, but monthly benefits had just begun. Something less than 1.5 million people, including less than 10 percent of the elderly, were receiving benefits at the onset of World War II, as compared with some 46 million people paying taxes.[36] This was the general situation President Truman faced when he took office in 1945. The army of beneficiaries was not very impressive. Moreover, Truman was greeted by a conservative postwar Congress, captured by the Republicans in 1946 — a Congress that was not inclined to enact costly program changes. The decade closed with only two minor pieces of legislation, the effect of which was actually to restrict the program somewhat.[37]

This decade of congressional inaction alarmed program advocates, since it seemed to threaten the long-term viability of social security.[38] The number of old-age assistance recipients climbed continuously so that by 1949 there were twice as many aged welfare recipients as social security retirees. Old-age assistance payments, moreover, were substantially higher, on average, than retirement benefits.[39] In the private sector, industrial pension plans were flourishing. The proportion of the labor force covered by such plans more than doubled during the 1940s, with the proportion of all nonfarm employees covered reaching 25 percent.[40] As advocates were aware, a healthy rather than withering old-age assistance program and a thriving rather than struggling insurance industry could provide momentum to conservative efforts to revamp or eliminate the prevailing system of social security. In the words of Edwin Witte, in 1950, "At this time we appear to be at a crossroads as regards social security. Growth of social assistance, the spread of private pensions plans, and the rapid development of forms of public medical care, doom social insurance in this country unless it is soon made more extensive."[41]

By the end of the decade, however, the political outlook for expanding the system was considerably improved. Between 1940 and 1950, the number of elderly persons receiving benefits increased dramatically, from 167,000 to 2.6 million, and the total number of beneficiaries reached 3.5 million.[42] Congress found itself in the unique position of being able to finance benefits to this rapidly growing beneficiary population without any tax increases at all. Economic prosperity fueled an eightfold increase in social security revenues, and by 1950 assets reached $12 billion, some twelve times annual outgo[43] (see tables 1 and 2). When Truman was returned to office in 1948, it was on a platform of social insurance expansion. Democrats had re-

TABLE 1 Social Security Beneficiaries, 1940–1980 (in thousands)

Year	Total Beneficiaries	Percentage of Elderly Receiving Benefits	Percentage of Population Receiving Benefits
1940	222	2	—[a]
1950	3,462	21	2
1960	14,811	65	8
1970	26,229	87	13
1980	35,619	91	15

Source: Social Security Administration, *Social Security Bulletin* 46, no. 6 (June 1983): 33; U.S. Department of Commerce, *Historical Statistics of the United States: Colonial Times to 1970*, part I, p. 10; and *1983 Annual Report of the Board of Trustees of the Federal OASDI Trust Funds*, p. 87.
[a]Less than 1%.

TABLE 2 Social Security Financing, 1940–1983 ($ billion)

Year	Outlays	Income	Reserves	Reserves/ Outlays
1940	$ 0.1	$ 0.4	$ 1.7	2,780%
1950	1.0	2.9	11.8	1,180
1960	11.8	12.4	22.0	186
1970	38.2	46.0	36.7	96
1980	148.6	145.8	43.5	29
1981	175.1	178.2	40.2	23
1982	195.6	187.0	43.3	22
1983[a]	$216.3	$206.6	$34.6	16%

Source: Social Security Administration, *Social Security Bulletin: Annual Statistical Supplement, 1981*, pp. 79–82, and *Staff Data and Materials Related to Social Security Financing*, Committee on Finance, U.S. Senate, CP97-19 (December 1982), p. 17.
[a]Before enactment of Social Security Amendments of 1983.

captured Congress, and momentum again built up for program expansion. Beginning in 1950, social security was elevated to a key political issue, with coverage expanded or some form of benefit liberalization enacted in every election year of the decade.

The Politics of Coverage Expansion

By amendments in 1950, 1954, and 1956, some 22 million workers were brought under the social security system, many of them highly paid, self-employed professionals. This had a profound effect on the system. On the one hand, with the proportion of the work force contributing to social security increased more than 40 percent, the market for the public supplier was further secured and its power enhanced.[44] Up to that time, the existence of large groups of uncovered workers who relied on private savings and insurance had permitted the growth of competing sources of supply. There was also the problem that individuals with their own retirement plans could ultimately threaten the acquiescence of covered workers by highlighting the relatively poor return afforded higher income earners and the inevitable deterioration in the "deal" the system offered.[45] Revenues, of course, were vitally influenced by the extent of coverage.

On the other hand, the nature of the program changed as coverage was expanded. Whereas the original program, by objective, limited coverage to that portion of the labor force least able or likely to provide for retirement through the private sector, the emerging system, with universal coverage as its objective, had a greatly expanded ability to redistribute income. To the extent coverage could be expanded to higher-paid professionals, larger benefits could be financed and a more progressive distribution of costs achieved.

On what grounds did the board and early advisory councils justify abandoning their position that coverage should be limited? "Ten years experience with incomplete coverage," they said, "revealed the many inequities and anomalies which arise" when workers move between covered and uncovered employment.[46] Owing to the weighting of the benefit formula toward low *average* earnings, people with short periods of covered employment received the same subsidy and thus were as costly to insure as low-income workers. Rather than question the source of the anomaly — the benefit formula — proponents of expansion were content to discredit people who profited from its construction, arguing program expansion as the solution. The existence of people outside the system was argued to be inequitable and inconsistent with the objectives of the program. After the changes adopted in 1939, few had reason to recall that the objectives of the original program had included limited coverage, benefits restricted to taxpayers, and reserve funding.[47]

Coverage expansion, as it turned out, required little selling in the 1950s. It appealed to workers and beneficiaries who were already a part of the system and was sought by many uncovered workers. For each group, it provided a direct means for exploiting the redistributive potential of the pay-as-you-go system.

From the point of view of workers not covered by the system, particularly lower-income and older persons, social security provided an unusually attractive "investment" during the 1950s. In its first years in operation, the system provided retirees a level of benefits well in excess of their actuarial equivalent. According to estimates by Robert Myers, the proportion of benefits that were actuarially purchased by those retiring in the early decades of operation was from "less than 1 percent in some instances to at most about 10 percent."[48] Given the liberal eligibility requirements, moreover, workers and their dependents and survivors could become eligible for benefits in less than five years.

From the point of view of covered workers and beneficiaries, coverage expansion — especially to higher-income workers — was also clearly advantageous. Because of the nature of a pay-as-you-go system, the tax rate necessary to finance a given level of benefits would vary inversely with the number of people subject to the tax. Furthermore, since higher-income workers were relatively cheap to "insure" (i.e., they received a relatively low return on their taxes), the long-term financial condition of the system could be improved by their coverage.[49]

In effect, coverage expansion, when compared with the alternatives of outright tax increases or increases in the taxable earnings base, was the finance scheme of least resistance. With relatively little controversy, coverage was expanded to nine out of ten workers in just seven years, with the first major expansion taking place in 1950.[50] In that year compulsory coverage was extended to regularly employed farm and domestic workers, the nonfarm, nonprofessional self-employed, federal employees not covered by the federal retirement system, and persons in Puerto Rico and the Virgin Islands — nearly 8 million people in all. Voluntary coverage was extended to the 2.5 million employees of nonprofit organizations and state and local governments not already covered by retirement systems. Four years later, compulsory coverage was extended to 10 million more workers, including farm operators and the professional self-employed (except lawyers, dentists, and doctors), and voluntary coverage was extended to employees of state and local governments. In 1956, compulsory coverage was extended to members of the uniformed services, the remaining self-employed professionals (with the exception of doctors), and farm landlords. Literally billions of dollars of new revenues were infused into the system.

Program Proliferation

To what use were the new revenues to be put? The Social Security Administration hinted at the answer in its annual report of 1950: "So long as there are . . . major risks which are not covered, the program falls short of its purpose."[51] Rather than being used for additional investment, as would have been the case with a funded program, the expanded revenue base translated into windfalls for new beneficiary groups and benefit increases for current beneficiaries. Rather than being used to take full advantage of the tax reductions made possible by a pay-as-you-go system, Congress legislated changes in the program that would generate more and larger benefit claims on future generations.

In a series of amendments during the decade, benefits were made payable to elderly husbands and widowers, wives and divorced widows of any age provided they had a child in their care, disabled workers and their dependent spouses, children, and parents, and dependent or surviving disabled children of any age provided their disability began before age eighteen. Age requirements were reduced for women workers, widows, and wives; the benefit computation period (the number of years used for calculating average earnings) was shortened significantly. For those already on the rolls and those coming on in the future, benefit levels were increased across the board by 77 percent in 1950, 12.5 percent in 1952, 13 percent in 1954, and 7 percent in 1958; the retirement-earnings test was liberalized on four occasions. As a result of these changes, millions of social security beneficiaries had their monthly benefits more than doubled, thousands of people became eligible to begin drawing benefits, in some cases on a permanent basis, and thousands were removed from the public assistance rolls.[52]

Adding greatly to the scope and the difficulty of monitoring social security was the enactment in 1956 of disability insurance (DI) — a program designed to respond to one of the remaining "major risks" identified by the Social Security Administration. The difficulty of controlling DI would result, in part, from the same factors operating for the retirement program, including the broad distribution of costs and a set of eligibility requirements that were arbitrary at best. Quite unlike the retirement program, however, DI would be extremely difficult to administer. Individual by individual, a determination would have to be made as to the medical severity of impairment (whether mental or physical), expected duration of impairment, and the extent to which it would preclude gainful activity. Many subjective elements would enter the eligibility decision, as would many third-party (medical, vocational, and psychiatric) players without direct responsibility for uniform or cost-effective determinations. Even the states, charged with administering the program, would have an incentive to grant benefits so as to relieve state assistance rolls. Then too, by providing benefits to people for only as long as they remained unable to work, the DI program would create strong incentives for the working disabled to quit and for those who made it onto the rolls to stay there.

Opponents, including the American Medical Association and the U.S. Chamber of Commerce, were aware of the problems that would come to plague the new system. Disability, they argued, would be difficult to define and costly to determine; payments would discourage rehabilitation and defy accurate cost estimation. According to a then-recent study issued by the Brookings Institution, the "danger of abuse" would be "great," since "political and psychological factors would play a large part in determining the cost" of the program. The study continued: "No country that has ever installed such a system accurately predicted in advance anything approaching actual costs."[53]

The Eisenhower administration opposed federal disability insurance. Secretary Folsom argued the administration's case before Congress, a task made difficult by the many years that the Social Security Administration was on record supporting disability insurance. This was a unique situation, according to Derthick, "the first time in history that the program leaders sought expansion against the express preferences of the political leadership of the executive branch."[54]

The AFL-CIO, Americans for Democratic Action, the United Auto Workers, the National Consumers League, and others who were by now strong social security proponents, by contrast, endorsed disability insurance. Endeavoring to downplay the seriousness of the proposal and drawing on the incremental approach to expansion, proponents played heavily on the idea that disability benefits were simply payments to individuals who had to "retire early" owing to disability. Such benefits, they said, would alleviate a "serious deficiency" in the way payments were currently made.[55] Testifying before Congress in 1950, Arthur Altmeyer had described social security as "admittedly inadequate" in its current form. "Permanent and total disability benefits will," he had said, "introduce a much needed element of flexibility in the present retirement concept."[56] Undoubtedly, Secretary Folsom could attest to the importance of Robert Myers's observation that high-level civil service employees could hardly be expected to produce "vigorous, airtight rebuttals" to administration policies if inconsistent with their own desires as "public advocates."[57]

As passed by a two-vote margin in the Senate, the 1956 amendments made cash benefits payable to workers age fifty and older who were determined to be permanently and totally disabled. Workers had to establish a substantial and recent attachment to the work force as well as to meet a waiting period. There were no provisions for dependents' benefits.[58] These, however, were fleeting limitations. Once DI was enacted, and thus accepted as a legitimate and cost-effective activity of the federal government, each of the rules — the age fifty cutoff, the permanent disability requirement, the six-month waiting period, the recent-work test, and the lack of secondary benefits — would begin to appear arbitrary. In the context of the entire social security system, modification of these details was actively sought by a new and powerful beneficiary constituency of disabled workers and families and the medical/psychiatric and vocational rehabilitation industries they would help underwrite. Great strain would be placed on the financing of a system that combined strong work disincentives with a costly determination process.

As history would reveal, the DI program was seriously and chronically underfinanced. Unlike the retirement program, in which tax rates were expected to rise over time, DI was financed on a level premium basis with a constant tax rate expected to finance the program in the long term. That level premium was exceeded in 1966, doubled in 1970, and tripled in 1978. The program came to be characterized by uncontrolled and unexplained growth in the 1970s.[59]

Senator Russell Long recently reminisced over the birth of DI in 1956 (and medicaid in 1965), saying to his fellow senators: "How could [we] be so irresponsible? . . . Well, it was enacted by well-intentioned people who got poor advice. . . . We were told that by 1980 that program was going to cost . . . $4.9 billion (in 1983 dollars). Adjusting for inflation, that is what we understood the program would cost, $4.9 billion by 1980. What is the program costing us? . . . $20.4 billion. . . . Four times as much as the estimate when we voted to put that program into effect. . . . There were some basic mistakes built into what we did in 1956."[60]

Between the new DI program and a host of benefit liberalizations, social security spending exploded in the 1950s. After taking into account inflation, expenditures increased some 800 percent, more rapidly than in any decade since. By 1960, 14.8 million Americans, more than 8 percent of the nation's population, were beneficiaries.[61]

Rather than having "perfected" the program, the resulting patchwork of beneficiary categories and eligibility requirements simply set the stage for further expansion. Benefits were now payable to disabled children but not to disabled wives, widows, and parents. Benefits were payable at a reduced age to women, but not to men, and among women only certain groups received full benefits. As the evolution of the program illustrated, when special benefits were bestowed on particularly deserving citizens, it created great pressure for a further expansion of the program to eliminate the seeming inequity. The bureaucracy had strong incentives to encourage this type of proliferation; reelection-minded politicians had little incentive to constrain it.[62] And of course there were still unprotected risks (to adopt the vocabulary of the bureaucracy). According to HEW secretary Anthony J. Celebrezze in 1963, there remained a "major threat to the financial security and peace of mind of our older citizens . . . the costs of serious illness in old-age."[63]

What was effectively obscured during this period of expansion was the fact that someone would ultimately have to "pay the piper." Because of the bureaucracy's persistence in painting the program as one with long-run insurance characteristics, and because the system had been financed in so many politically costless ways in the early years, beneficiaries-to-be had expectations about rates of return that simply could not be met without continuously rising taxes.

REDISTRIBUTIVE IMPACT REALIZED: 1960–1972

Following the peak growth period of the 1950s, social security entered a new phase in the 1960s and early 1970s. Increased politicization and more widespread use of the system for redistributive purposes characterized these years. The benefit formula was made more progressive, the minimum benefit was increased, age and eligibility requirements were relaxed, new beneficiary groups were added, and across-the-board benefit increases became commonplace. In addition, medicare was enacted. In all, the system was liberalized nearly every year from 1960 through 1972. After taking inflation into account, benefits for those on the rolls were increased about 30 percent, and total expenditures tripled.

The politics of social security were changing. As the country's age distribution shifted toward elderly persons, there was a sharp increase after the 1950s in the proportion of the elderly receiving transfers from social security. The proportion of elderly people in the overall population was 9.2 percent in 1960 compared with only 5.3 percent in 1935. Whereas 21 percent of the elderly were receiving benefits as recently as 1950, that figure stood at 65 percent in 1960 and 87 percent ten years later. The beneficiary population as a whole more than quadrupled in the 1950s and doubled again in the following ten years. By 1972, 28 million people received a social security check each month (about 13 percent of the total population).[64] Finding an increasing proportion of their incomes supplied by social security, beneficiaries became an important political force and a natural ally of program expansionists. They had a very significant stake in the program's development.

The rapid growth of state welfare costs in the 1960s was another key factor. Fueled by the introduction of disability assistance in 1950 and medical assistance in 1960, real state and local expenditures on welfare increased 3.5-fold between 1960 and 1973, compared with only 16 percent in the preceding decade.[65] A natural outgrowth of this shift was the emergency of bipartisan support for increases in social security for low-wage earners. Increases in the "minimum benefit," financed by a national payroll tax, took hundreds of thousands of elderly persons off state welfare rolls. The tax costs of welfare were thus redistributed geographically and shifted to the federal government.[66]

Then too, with income redistribution an explicit policy goal of both the Kennedy and Johnson administrations, the environment was conducive to demands by pro-government interest groups. Into these administrations were catapulted advocates who had been a part of the social security bureaucracy for years — Wilbur Cohen, appointed assistant secretary of the Department of Health, Education, and Welfare in 1960, and Robert Ball, appointed commissioner of social security in 1962.[67] Two more committed and effective expansionists could not have been found.

Cohen, Ball, and others made good use of the extreme complexity of social security and the absence of clear program objectives. Almost anything was defensible under a program that embraced the conflicting goals of insurance and welfare. Almost anything seemed affordable. In 1960, trust fund reserves were $22 billion, about twice the amount needed to pay a year's benefits. Taxpayers, standing at 73 million, outnumbered beneficiaries by five to one.

What shape did the expansion take?[68] More so than in the early years, the benefits of social security expansion in the 1960s and early 1970s were concentrated on current beneficiaries rather than spread across new beneficiary groups. In a five-year period, across-the-board increases in benefits amounted to 39 percent, more than in the preceding ten years. Three more increases followed in the next four years, amounting to 10, 20, and 11 percent, respectively. By 1975, social security benefits replaced about 64 percent of preretirement earnings for a retired worker and spouse (as compared with about 50 percent just five years earlier).[69] In addition, benefit rates were increased for surviving children, for minimum beneficiaries and very old beneficiaries, and for widows and widowers. For working beneficiaries, the retirement-earnings test was liberalized on five occasions.

Age requirements were relaxed as well, being reduced for adults and raised for children. Early retirement benefits were made payable to men at age sixty-two and to widows and then widowers at age sixty; disability benefits were made payable to workers who became disabled before fifty — first at age thirty-one and then at any age; and children's benefits were made payable until twenty-one and then twenty-two, rather than eighteen. Finally, monthly benefits were extended to divorced wives, to people seventy-two and older with little or no covered earnings, and to disabled widows and widowers age fifty and older.

More significantly, another compulsory federal program was enacted in 1965, one that made benefits available to 19 million elderly people the day it was official launched. Claimed by the administration to have a price tag of just twelve dollars a year for the average worker and to involve not more than a 0.25 percent increase in the employee's payroll tax, the new medicare (or hospital insurance) program covered the cost of a specified number of days of hospital care, posthospital care, outpatient diagnostic services, and home-care visits.[70] Coverage was made available to all social security beneficiaries age sixty-five and older.

Unlike the retirement program, which had as a basic principle benefits related to earnings, the medicare program would provide benefits on an all-or-none basis. Either an elderly individual was eligible for social security benefits and therefore eligible for the full menu of covered services, or he (or she) was not. Yet the program was financed by a regressive, earnings-related tax. The purpose of medicare was not to provide insurance, per se (this could have been purchased privately), but to redistribute costs among the elderly and toward the young. The pattern of redistribution was uncertain at best. The marketing of medicare as prepaid insurance tended to obscure this fact.

Just as DI added a new dimension to cost control, so too would the hospital insurance (HI) program. As a cost reimbursement, rather than a cash benefit, program, medicare costs would be determined predominately by factors outside the direct control of Congress — by hospital-cost inflation, for example. For years the cost of hospital and other medical care had been outpacing the rise in the overall price level. The operation of the program exacerbated this by reducing the incentive for providers to be cost conscious and by subsidizing the demand for medical services.[71] In Congress, policymakers would now have to deal not simply with growth-oriented beneficiaries and advocates, but also with a new and potent constituency of health-care providers and intermediaries.

That the cost of medicare would be difficult to control and that the program failed to deal with the real problems at hand — the high cost of medical care and the relatively high cost of private insurance for low-income people — only slowed somewhat the progress of legislative proposals in the early 1960s. The leaders of the health insurance movement — Ball and Cohen within the administration, Isidore Falk of the UAW and Nelson Cruikshank of the AFL-CIO among major lobbyists, and Congressman Aime Forand on Capitol Hill — responded marginally, adjusting their proposals just enough to allow them to "fly." Early national health insurance proposals were narrowed in scope, were refocused toward hospital insurance, and were tied to the financing and beneficiary population of the popular social security cash benefit programs.[72]

One can easily imagine the reaction to hospital insurance of groups representing the elderly. In a pamphlet entitled "An Explanation of the President's Proposal for Older People — Hospital Insurance through Social Security," the Social Security Administration said that "most older workers will inevitably need medical care and this will cost them more than they can afford. As a result, illness forces most of them into poverty — poverty from which there is no escape."[73] Just as early social insurance advocates reasoned in the 1920s, the answer was compulsory social insurance. The pamphlet continued, "social security hospital insurance would be provided to all people over 65 who are entitled to social security benefits. In addition, people now over 65 as well as those becoming 65 in the next few years who do not qualify for social security benefits would be eligible for hospital benefits."

Endorsed by Presidents Kennedy and Johnson and recommended by the social security advisory council, medicare became law as part of the Social Security Amendments of 1965. With the assistance of the largest democratic majorities since the Roosevelt era, medicare was adopted as part of a comprehensive legislative package which included many sweeteners.[74] Medicare began providing benefits on 1 July 1966. By 1969 the cost of the program was double its original projection and a tax increase had been enacted. By 1970 the medicare trust fund was in critical financial shape, and in 1973 the HI tax exceeded the rate expected to be sufficient to finance the system in the long term. Rather than a $12 annual tax, the average taxpayer now pays $200 annually (employee share only) and has recently been told that projected benefits dwarf available income.[75]

By the time Nixon took office in 1968, social security seems to have been firmly established as an American institution without partisan lines, one whose expansion was perceived as profitable to politicians of all persuasions. Social security spent some $30 billion a year, 17 percent of the federal budget; it was providing benefits to nearly 20 percent of the voting-age population. During Nixon's term of office, the issues became simpler, and there was a frenzy of legislation. By and large the issues reduced to how big and how frequent the next benefit hike should be. With Wilbur Mills, chairman of the House Ways and Means Committee, and Russell Long, chairman of the Senate Finance Committee, joining the fray, even the threat of a presidential veto was to little avail. Amendments were enacted in 1969, 1971, 1972, and 1973, typically in spite of the threat of a veto, by tying politically appealing benefit increases to pending legislation for which passage was all but certain (the federal debt limit, for instance).[76]

By far the most significant expansion to take place under the auspices of Nixon was the enactment of the automatic cost-of-living adjustment (COLA) in 1972, coupled with an across-the-board increase in benefits of 20 percent. Indexing came on the heels of a 15 percent increase in 1970 and a 10 percent increase in 1971, and Nixon apparently saw it as a way to control costs by tying benefit increases to the actual rate of inflation. In his words, indexing would "depoliticize to a certain extent" social security.[77] As a member of the administration put it, indexing "would lead to a substitution of economic determinants for biennial politics" in the setting of benefit levels. The series of ad hoc benefit adjustments since 1965 had already overcompensated the elderly for inflation by about 10 to 15 percent.[78]

As members of Congress who opposed the provision recognized, the automatic adjustment of benefits would have another result. It would shift credit for these increases away from Congress and toward the administration.[79] More time was devoted to this issue than to those which, in retrospect, deserved the most attention. First of all, what was the potential cost of guaranteeing a real level of purchasing power for the elderly? The cost was an "uncontrollable" federal expenditure that would be fully borne by workers. Unless wages and employment grew rapidly, such a guarantee could be made good only by an increasing rate of taxation.[80]

Second, there was the seemingly technical question whether the automatic adjustment met the objectives of indexing — immunizing the system against the effects of inflation. Actually, benefits were "double indexed," as the "technical flaw" became popularly known.[81] In addition to increasing benefits for people on the rolls, inflation — through its impact on nominal earnings (which were not indexed) — also increased the initial benefit to which future beneficiaries were entitled. This method of indexing, crafted within SSA, would be the undoing of social security's long-run financing. The failure to accommodate the possibility that workers' wages (and therefore tax payments) could grow too slowly to support price-indexed payments to the elderly would be the undoing of social security's financing in the short run.

Few knew the damage that had been done. In one swoop, the new indexing provision — adopted as a floor amendment offered by Senator Frank Church — converted a system characterized by ad hoc growth to one of automatic growth; it converted the system from one in which economic growth and reserve accumulation preceded legislated expansion into one in which expansion would necessitate economic growth; and it converted a system that was — for a pay-as-you-go system — financed in a relatively conservative way (in terms of actuarial methodology) into one that would be chronically underfinanced.[82]

Under the new system, benefits would replace an increasing proportion of workers' preretirement earnings during inflationary periods. Replacement rates — the ratio of benefits to gross, preretirement earnings — were stable historically. Double indexing, along with the 20 percent benefit hike, however, led to a continuous rise in replacement rates among middle- and low-wage earners to the point that the average worker retiring in 1981 found nearly 50 percent more of his preretirement earnings replaced by social security than did a similarly situated worker in 1972.[83]

Even before the consequences of this improperly financed expansion were felt, covered workers were beginning to feel the pinch of a maturing pay-as-you-go system. Unlike the 1940s and 1950s, when economic growth and the expansion of coverage allowed for reserve accumulation and a spreading of tax costs, the more recent period was characterized by cost increases that had to be absorbed by a group of covered workers whose ranks and earnings were growing slowly. The typical worker, who paid $76 in taxes (employee's and employer's share combined) to support the system in 1950 and $240 in 1960, was paying $594 in 1970 and $741 in 1972.[84]

For the high-wage earner, tax increases were sharper yet as Congress turned to increasing the amount of earnings subject to the tax in lieu of direct tax increases. In this way costs could be concentrated on the minority of workers earning more than the earnings base and the redistributive impact of the program (from high to low earners) could be enhanced. Having been $90 in 1950 and $288 as late as 1960, the maximum tax payment reached $936 in 1972, a real increase of some 130 percent over the 1960 level.[85] Few were aware that these tax increases were modest compared with those that would ultimately be necessary to finance the expansion of the system that had just taken place.[86] Nevertheless, program advocates from within the bureaucracy relentlessly promoted expansion of the program and deferral of costs, something that was perfectly compatible with the interests of lobby groups representing beneficiaries. Congress and the presidents generally went along with expansion, a policy with powerful political appeal.

Social Security since 1972: A System in Crisis

As even the most casual observer of public affairs is aware, nothing has been quite the same for social security since 1972, in the areas of financing, administration, or politics. In the span of just a decade, the financing of the system deteriorated to the point of insolvency. Reserves in the giant retirement trust fund, which amounted to close to a year's worth of benefits at the start of the decade, fell to less than a month's worth in 1982. Only borrowing from the DI and HI trust funds permitted retirement checks to go out on time between November 1982 and July 1983.[87] The agency, heralded by many in the 1960s as a "model of governmental efficiency and effectiveness," fell subject to charges of inefficiency in the 1970s. In the words of Jack Futterman, assistant commissioner under Robert Ball, "larger and larger numbers of people [are being] overpaid or underpaid [the totals involve vast amounts of money], processing delays have increased in number and duration, and mishandling of actions involving individuals have mounted to the extent that even the present commissioner has described the system as all but about to collapse."[88] Whereas 1972 was the high-water mark for social security expansion, 1982 was certainly the low-water mark, with one of the most popular domestic programs in history having become one of the most divisive.[89] A history of benefit-increasing bills gave way to four bills (in 1977, 1980, 1981, and 1983) that reduced benefits.[90]

The Bureaucracy under Pressure

What changed? Theories abound on the emergent crisis in social security. Some say the problem is internal and organizational. Before 1973, SSA was effectively run by only two people, Arthur Altmeyer (1937–53) and Robert Ball (1962–73). In the following ten years, SSA ran through another nine people — five of whom were full commissioners appointed through the regular process and four of whom were acting commissioners, with the position now vacant. Whereas in 1970 Ball, his deputy commissioner, and four assistant commissioners had 191 years of service at SSA (each having joined SSA in the 1930s), the most recent commissioner (John Svahn, 1980–83) had no prior service in social security, and only one deputy, Robert Myers, had been with SSA since the beginning.[91] By 1983 all of the "founding fathers" and social security leaders such as Myers, Ball, and Cohen had retired from their positions in the agency or administration.

Certainly, by eroding the esprit de corps and the appearance of a single-minded agency committed to the principles of social security, these developments were important. In Futterman's words, the high turnover of commissioners generated high turnover in "organizational values, policies, goals, etc." and greatly diminished the importance of the commissioner "in achieving the mission, purposes, and objectives of the social security program."[92]

The phenomenon of short-term commissioners also contributed to what is now one of SSA's most nagging problems — a seriously outdated computer system.[93] Computer redevelopment, like any major administrative reorganization, constitutes a long-term investment with generally delayed payoff. Not surprisingly, short-term commissioners have generally lacked interest or success in getting such projects on line. Yet with SSA's primary function so well defined and relatively limited — ensuring the prompt and accurate payment of benefits to the system's 36 million beneficiaries (SSA does not even have responsibility for tax collection; IRS does) — an ailing computer system is tantamount to bureaucratic failure in the eyes of the public.[94]

Others would argue that the source of the crisis lies in factors quite external to social security — the budget reforms of the early 1970s and the general tax resistance movement of the late 1970s. In 1974 the Budget Reform Act was passed with the explicit purpose of introducing a degree of discipline to congressional spending and revenue decisions. The Congressional Budget Office was created to provide Congress with an independent source of information on the cost and operations of federal agencies and programs; the House and Senate budget committees were formed. By refocusing congressional attention on *all* government programs, even those previously rendered "sacred" or considered within another committee's jurisdiction, these reforms were certainly important. After all, social security and medicare, accounting for a quarter of the federal budget, grew each year by an amount that exceeded the total funding level of the vast majority of government programs. Letting the payroll tax inch up during the decade as a way of bringing a trust-fund income in line with exploding outlays became politically more costly in the presence of an active and broad-based taxpayer resistance movement.

The Structural Sources of Conflict

But there was clearly more going on in the 1970s than organizational changes within SSA and budgetary pressures from the outside. The key to recent events lies in understanding the implications of the aging of social security. Benefits relative to taxes paid (or the real rate of return) could remain extraordinarily high, and huge reserves could accumulate and persist only when such a system was relatively young or when its revenue base was being expanded by legislation. Neither of these conditions exist today. What social security could and could not do began to clash with what we came to expect of it, and conflict has been the result.[95]

At the root of the conflict is the fact that the original social security program had as its purpose the elimination of financial insecurity in old age. Yet, the system embodied no political or institutional means of accomplishing this end. Short of the power to tax, and therefore the power to put into jeopardy the well-being of future retirees, no guarantees could be provided in regard to either standard of living or return on investment. Through expansionary or contractionary legislation, or through expansionary or contractionary economic or demographic developments, benefits could be granted or increased or reduced or eliminated at any point in the future. Rates of return could be improved or worsened.

That social security, in its first decades of operation, produced huge wealth transfers to most beneficiaries was a unique product of the pay-as-you-go method of finance.[96] All of the revenues collected — during periods of prosperous economic growth and artificially high ratios of taxpayers to beneficiaries — could be paid out rather than stashed away in interest-bearing investments. During a finite and now passing time, social security could help millions of people at a low current cost. The program was, as Ball described it, a "tremendous bargain."[97]

The underlying reality, however, was that social security possessed no "magic money machine" capable of producing "bargains for everyone."[98] Rates of return had to fall. As recently retired couples enjoy a return on their taxes well in excess of that attainable privately and benefits that replace from half to all of their preretirement earnings, the system rapidly approaches maturity; this is the point at which the transitional gains from pay-as-you-go financing have been fully captured. Coverage is now nearly universal. The ceiling on taxable earnings exceeds the earnings of nine out of ten workers. The payroll tax is high. As population growth declines, the real return of social security taxes must fall, approaching the rate of growth of labor productivity, or only about 1–2 percent.[99] Taking into account the redistributive nature of the benefit formula (as well as the new provision to tax benefits), the rate of return for young, higher-income workers will certainly be negative.[100]

Declining returns naturally breed conflict. Young participants will want to leave the system in search of more lucrative investments, while older participants, concerned about the permanence of their benefits, work to perpetuate the system. This conflict is exacerbated by social security's inherent financial instability. There is perforce uncertainty about future returns. As clearly revealed in recent years, there are no automatic pilots that ensure long-term solvency, no linkage between the two sides of the ledger that ensures financial stability. As a result, there is no predictable way the system responds to and accommodates economic and demographic changes.

Before 1970, financial instability went largely unnoticed. Huge reserves tended to buffer changes in income and outgo. Now that the system is on a true pay-as-you-go basis, however, difficult political decisions must regularly be made. Shall financial solvency be maintained by tax- or benefit-side changes? Shall the effects of such changes be concentrated on particular generations or be shared by them all? In effect, how should the costs associated with an unfavorable economic or demographic event, or the benefits of a favorable event, be allocated across the population? Each such decision involves basic questions of intergenerational wealth and equity. The outcome of each decision determines how different generations of workers will fare. That social security is unable to eliminate risk for beneficiaries in retirement and for younger workers planning their retirement — it can only rearrange that risk — does not fit well with the vision fostered over the years by program bureaucrats.

Legislative developments since the mid-1970s suggest that for the first time the intergenerational nature of social security and the potential volatility of the system are coming to be recognized.[101] Long-term reductions in benefits, the effects of which are borne disproportionately by today's young people, are increasingly perceived as a price worth paying for the increased certainty that accompanies a system with a realistic cost burden. Near-term benefit reductions are increasingly perceived as a price worth paying to prevent continual tax increases that could alienate the young workers expected to finance the system.

None of this is intended to suggest that the interests of beneficiaries are being subordinated to the interests of taxpayers. A financing bill that did not increase taxes substantially would require a reversal of the history of social security policymaking. Tax increases — amounting to about $500 billion during the 1980s alone — were a part of each bill.[102] The important point is that basic underlying economic forces are at work that are altering the profitability of social security. Perceptions are, if only slowly and begrudgingly, being brought into line with reality. The unprecedented, adverse condition of the economy since 1970 and the near collapse of social security financing in recent years are disrobing the myths of the system — full funding, individual retirement accounts, and assured income security — and increasing the incentive for workers of all ages to become better informed and to influence policy. Growth is scrutinized as never before.

But Have Things Really Changed So Much?

Are SSA and the programs it administers now being run in a political environment with sufficient competition to ensure broad-based citizen control? Has the power of the bureaucracy been curtailed? Whereas the foregoing discussion focused on long-term underlying forces, the day-to-day operations of the agency and its interactions with congressional leaders, other executive offices, and the public at large still must be assessed realistically.

My own conclusion is that despite the changes that have taken place, the bureaucracy retains much control. Advisory councils, which have long served as conduits for the views of bureaucracy, continue to be staffed by SSA employees, receive all cost estimates from SSA actuaries, and include at least a few old-line advocate-bureaucrats.[103] Even the National Commission on Social Security Reform, created by President Reagan in 1981, could count Robert Ball among its most influential members and Robert Myers as its executive director. Truly different (or as social security advocates would describe them, "radical") proposals for reform—those involving an expanded role for the private sector, for example—are still not carefully considered or given the same thoughtful analysis by staff or the agency as those that accept the present framework.

Short-term commissioners and their array of deputies and associates may come and go, moreover, but the career social security employee goes on and on. During this highly volatile period, there has been a surprising degree of stability in the ranks of the high-level career civil servants at SSA, even among those holding positions in such key policy and information offices as Research and Statistics, Legislative and Regulatory Policy, and Legislative Reference. These offices control virtually all of the information flowing to the top political appointees in SSA as well as to Congress. SSA's Office of the Actuary remains the only organization in government that provides long-range projections.

The "founding fathers," though no longer holding positions in SSA or the department, may now have positions with even more influence. Ball and Cohen, for example, are with the Save Our Security (SOS) organization, maintaining the contacts in the agency necessary to provide them with vital information. Yet they are able to approach Congress in a different way—as an "interest group" able to deliver votes— and are able to bypass entirely the political constraints imposed by the department, OMB, and the White House. In a city where timely access to information and people is everything, these men have suffered little by moving to the "outside." Beneficiary lobbies, of course, are bigger and better organized than in earlier years. The ability to mobilize write-in, call-in, and voting campaigns among the elderly has been good for many years. The financing difficulties of recent years have now raised the stakes for the elderly and encouraged them to become politically active. Their clout on Capitol Hill has been duly noted since 1981.

The Bureaucracy Works to Secure Its Position

How is the bureaucracy responding to the pressures of the 1970s and 1980s? Characteristically, SSA is making efforts to retrench and secure its position. With program expansion infeasible, efforts are being made to immunize the system against the political competition that naturally surrounds a period of transition. Frequently discussed proposals in recent years include removing SSA from the Department of Health and Human Services and making it an independent agency; removing the trust funds from the unified budget and from the budget reconciliation process; preventing the opting out of state and local governments and compelling participation by groups not previously covered (employees of nonprofit organizations and the federal government); applying the payroll tax to nonwage income ("fringe benefits"); and enhancing the power of the SSA actuaries in determining the assumptions underlying financial forecasts. Though few of these proposals were officially embraced by the Reagan administration, all of them had internal support and all were addressed in some way in the Social Security Amendments of 1983.[104]

The theme of these bureaucratic policies is clear. They tend to shield the agency from the intragovernment struggles of the budget process and protect the system from the erosion of the tax base that results when people seek alternatives to social security. They create an illusion of a separate, independent, and apolitical system. In arguing for the removal of the social security trust funds from the unified budget, Robert Ball recently said: "The obligations of social security *should* be 'uncontrollable' because they result from an agreement to furnish certain group insurance and retirement benefits in return for certain specified contributions. . . . People are paying today for social security benefits that may not come due for 45 years or more. . . . The annual budget process is no place to consider social security."[105] Maneuvers such as these, of course, can do little more than delay the day of reckoning — the day when the public comes to recognize that no amount of independence (for the agency or program) from the vagaries of the political process can restore guarantees of income security *and* financial solvency. Unfortunately, the promise of delayed reckoning was just as appealing to policymakers in 1983 as it had been throughout the complex political history of the nation's social security policies.

CHARLES E. NEU

The Rise of the National Security Bureaucracy

THE ORGANIZATIONAL revolution that transformed American life in the twentieth century was slow to leave its imprint on American foreign policy. Although large corporations arose to master national and international markets, the horizons of American political leaders remained more limited and their need for organizational support less pressing.[1] In the four decades stretching from 1900 to 1940, the scale of American diplomacy changed, but far less dramatically than in other areas of American life. Even at the close of this period, political leaders had to contend with only a modest foreign policy bureaucracy and, if they chose to intervene, could always have a decisive impact on policy.[2]

In the early years of the century, the American foreign policy bureaucracy was by our current standards relatively primitive, and the presidents differed in their approach to how much organizational change was needed. Theodore Roosevelt was wary, concerned that a larger bureaucracy would restrain him, whereas William Howard Taft was eager to apply what he viewed as business methods to diplomacy. Regardless of who was president, however, the nation's international involvement was growing, as was the need for reform of the consular and diplomatic services and of the Department of State. These reforms accumulated slowly, coalescing at certain critical points, such as 1908 and 1909, when the Department of State acquired four geographical divisions, and 1924, when the Rodgers Act created the modern American Foreign Service.[3] Gradually the Department acquired a modern administrative system attuned in particular to the nation's commercial interests abroad. Gradually, too, a new generation of diplomats emerged with a strong sense of its own unique skills, and the Department of State became more complex, acquiring enough size and expertise to influence American foreign policy. Its geographical bureaus, staffed by those who had served abroad, became repositories of expert knowledge and dominated the flow of information from the field. During the interwar years the influence of the Department of State varied, depending on the attitudes of presidents and secretaries of state, but State could seldom be ignored. It had achieved a critical mass as an organization, large enough to maintain some continuity in policy from one administration to another.[4] On the eve of World War II, the morale of the Foreign Service was high and the influence of the Department of State was substantial. Its role in American foreign policy was not challenged by any other organization.[5]

But in the late 1930s, as the world crisis mounted, President Franklin D. Roosevelt shifted his attention from domestic to international affairs and assumed a more direct role in the formation of policy. Lacking confidence in most professional diplomats and in Secretary of State Cordell Hull, Roosevelt improvised, turning to other people and organizations for advice. He leaned on prominent New Dealers such as Harry L. Hopkins and Henry Morgenthau, Jr., and on sympathetic millionaires such as W. Averell Harriman and Edward Stettinius, and he created a personal foreign policy staff that shared his goals and assumptions. Unwilling to control the Department of State, Roosevelt ignored it. During the war it stagnated as an organization and at the war's end was unprepared to shoulder the vastly expanded duties that arose as a result of the nation's new position in the world. In contrast, military leaders inspired confidence in the president, and the urgent demands of the war brought into being large staffs and highly complex organizations. Before the war the Army and Navy had exercised little influence on American diplomacy; by the end of the struggle they had acquired new prestige, self-confidence, and organizational strength.[6]

In the foreign policy sphere, Roosevelt's legacy was controversial. Whatever his diplomatic astuteness and sensitivity to public opinion, Roosevelt's mastery of foreign policy was never the equal of his talent in domestic politics. His haphazard approach to foreign policy left too many crucial issues unresolved and gave the public unrealistic expectations about the postwar world.[7] The war had given America new responsibilities, but the administrative response of the president and his associates was piecemeal, as if many of these burdens would fade with the end of the struggle. No permanent institutional adjustments, they seemed to believe, would be necessary. Far from confronting these organizational challenges, Roosevelt's divide and rule tactics, pitting subordinates and agencies against each other, left a legacy of bitterness and confusion. As Dean Acheson concludes, "he was tone deaf to the subtler nuances of civil governmental organization. This was messed up in his administration for the simplest of reasons: he did not know any better."[8]

The postwar years brought a tremendous outburst of creativity in the organization of American foreign policy as government leaders struggled to end the chaos left by the war and to close the gap between the nation's new world responsibilities and its obsolete administrative structures. From 1945 to 1960, Harry S. Truman and Dwight D. Eisenhower presided over a new phase in the evolution of American foreign policy, one marked by the rapid expansion of what became known as the national security bureaucracy. They understood the seriousness of the organizational issues and realized that Roosevelt's ad hoc approach was obsolete. The burdens of the Cold War required a more systematic administrative response.

For Truman, Roosevelt had set a powerful negative example in his approach to foreign policy. Truman was determined to restore regular lines of authority and the primacy of the Department of State. After some initial uncertainty he found the men to carry out his desires, and under George C. Marshall and Dean Acheson the department played a key role in the formulation of early Cold War attitudes and policies. These were strong, effective men, wise in the ways of bureaucracy. They dominated the foreign policy advice that Truman received. Marshall had emerged from the war with great prestige and experience, while Acheson understood Truman well and presented the president with the best information and clear options. Both gave their professional diplomats responsibility and took their advice seriously.[9]

Truman's wartime experience had convinced him of the need for military unification and for coordination of the government's intelligence activities. As early as December 1945, Truman asked Congress for military reorganization, but bitter quarrels among the services delayed the passage of the National Security Act until June 1947. Although Truman received less than he wanted, he still considered the legislation one of his "outstanding achievements"; it improved the nation's intelligence system, integrated the diplomatic and military sides of policymaking, and set up a new command system for the defense establishment. The Central Intelligence Agency, the National Security Council, and the National Military Establishment created, in theory, a new institutional framework for American diplomacy.[10]

In fact, however, these new institutions took time to sink roots within the permanent government. The CIA got off to a slow start, Truman did not use the National Security Council extensively until after the outbreak of the Korean War, and the secretary of defense found himself bogged down in the job of presiding over a federation of autonomous service bureaucracies. Soon Truman was disappointed with the results of unification. Concerned about the domestic economy, he placed a rigid ceiling on military expenditures and directed the secretary of defense and the service chiefs to allocate the available funds. The Army, Air Force, and Navy, however, could not agree on military strategy or on the importance of weapons systems and engaged in open political warfare that pulled the president and his aides into their feuds. In 1949 Congress strengthened the authority of the secretary of defense and reduced the Army, Air Force, and Navy to military departments within a new Department of Defense—but the parochialism of the services remained strong.[11]

Truman and his advisers were not able to solve all the organizational challenges left by the war. Although they restored the secretary of state as the president's principal foreign policy adviser and devised new ways to bring coherence to national security policy, they slighted the internal organizational problems created by the rapid expansion of the Department of State and allowed a further dispersal of responsibility in some areas of American foreign policy. By 1949 twenty-one agencies had representatives abroad and only half of the civilians stationed overseas were Foreign Service officers. The organizational disarray of American foreign policy was too great to be corrected in one administration.[12]

Eisenhower continued Truman's efforts to mold new institutions to deal with the demands of the Cold War. In contrast to the experience of other postwar presidents, Eisenhower's career had drawn him into the organizational revolution that had transformed the American military during World War II, and he had thought long and deeply about the problems of complex, large-scale organizations. Eisenhower accepted them as a reality of modern society, arguing in his memoirs that organization "is not the enemy of imagination or of any other attractive human characteristic. Its purpose is to simplify, clarify, expedite, and coordinate; it is a bulwark against chaos, confusion, delay, and failure." Thus he devoted much attention to assembling his White House staff and to elaborating a foreign policy apparatus that would bring information to him in an orderly way, engage in long-term planning, and provide for the systematic consideration of policies.[13] Eisenhower created the position of special assistant to the president for national security affairs and filled out the skeletal structure of the National Security Council, creating committees to plan its meetings and implement its directives. He attended most of the weekly NSC meetings, participated in vigorous discussions, and in general gave that group a major role in shaping policy. Eisenhower realized, however, that the NSC was not a suitable forum for making operational decisions, especially in time of crisis. He made those decisions in consultation with a few key advisers. The president understood both the formal and the informal uses of organization.[14]

By the late 1950s heated disputes erupted over the effectiveness of Eisenhower's system. Critics saw only the formal organizational facade and applied an activist standard to a president whose record was largely negative. They claimed that the NSC committees muffled dissent, slowed action, and presented the president with bland memoranda that obscured rather than clarified his choices. Eisenhower and his aides argued that the system produced a careful weighing of options and that, whatever the quality of the policy papers, the process of producing them improved communication within the administration and made its assumptions and policies more explicit.[15]

Even Eisenhower, however, was not entirely satisfied with the system he had created. He felt that the NSC discussions often became mired in detail and was especially disturbed by the narrow perspectives of the military establishment, which refused to accept his budget ceilings and forced his secretary of defense to make across-the-board cuts in service budgets. The Joint Chiefs of Staff could not shake Eisenhower's determination to hold down military costs, but they could refuse to cooperate and could carry their case to Congress. By the end of his second term, their insubordination had deeply angered the president. For all his prestige and organizational insight, Eisenhower had been forced to compromise; he could not completely subdue the military bureaucracy.[16]

During the Eisenhower years major shifts occurred in the influence of various agencies within the national security establishment. The president was aware of some of these shifts, such as the growing authority of the military and the CIA, but he seemed insensitive to the decline in the effectiveness of the Department of State. John Foster Dulles's strength as secretary of state obscured the fact that he used the department sparingly and was uninterested in its administrative problems. Throughout the 1950s the secretary of state remained powerful, but the department over which he nominally presided lost much ground. The ascendancy that the Department of State had achieved over American foreign policy in the late 1940s had been ephemeral; it was gradually beset with internal organizational problems and overshadowed by other segments of the mushrooming national security bureaucracy. Adopting a defensive bureaucratic strategy, the Department of State resisted the acquisition of functions in intelligence, propaganda, and economic aid. As a result new agencies emerged, either entirely separate from it or only nominally under its control. The military also expanded into foreign policy, especially through the creation in 1953 of the Office of International Security Affairs. More and more agencies sent representatives abroad. The diffusion of responsibility within the foreign policy bureaucracy continued.[17]

These developments should not have been surprising, since the Department of State had never received much understanding or support from Congress and the public, and the nation's deepening involvement in world affairs after 1945 had not altered these traditional attitudes. The department was the nation's formal link to an outside world that seemed increasingly intractable. It was far easier to focus frustration on American diplomats than to appreciate the limits on the exercise of American power. In the early 1950s suspicion of the Department of State reached new heights, as Senator Joseph R. McCarthy and others claimed that it was riddled with communists who had betrayed the nation's vital interests. As the president and secretary of state passively watched, prominent diplomats were attacked and sometimes subjected to drawn-out loyalty investigations. Many felt victimized, unprotected by their political superiors. Fear and demoralization spread throughout the Foreign Service. When W. Averell Harriman and George F. Kennan returned to government in 1961, they were shocked by its transformation.[18]

While the Department of State thus declined, the CIA prospered. It seemed on the front line of the Cold War, and throughout the 1950s it increased rapidly in size and prestige. The anticommunist tide did not touch the CIA, and its new director, Allen W. Dulles, developed close ties to Eisenhower. The president valued the agency, for it allowed the American government to achieve secretly what it could not attempt openly and to depart from conventional standards of official conduct. He believed that carefully planned covert operations were vital to American foreign policy. So too did Dulles and other leaders within the agency, who were absorbed in the glamor of covert operations and convinced they were the essence of their new organizational mission. Dulles lacked interest in the analytic side of the CIA. He also neglected his role as the unifier of the intelligence community, as the man who would coordinate information for the president and present him with predictions about the behavior of other nations. Eisenhower wanted more evaluation and was at times disappointed with Dulles's performance, but he never tried to replace him or to reshape the CIA's priorities.[19]

Eisenhower was reluctant to meddle with an agency that performed so many essential tasks. The CIA funneled money to noncommunist political parties and organizations in Western Europe and also scored dramatic successes in toppling anti-American regimes in Iran and Guatemala and bringing to power governments that stabilized those two nations. Eisenhower was impressed with these successes, along with other achievements of the agency. During the decade the CIA constructed a network of agents abroad, and its analytic side grew in size and expertise. Its National Intelligence Estimates came to have a real impact on the formation of policy, as did its striking technological breakthroughs. When the Air Force proved skeptical about the development of a photographic reconnaissance plane, the CIA took up the task and, in collaboration with the Lockheed Corporation, developed the U-2 with amazing speed. In 1956, when the first U-2 soared high above the Soviet Union, the United States could photograph any area of that nation and achieve much more precise knowledge of Soviet military strength. Before the end of the decade the CIA was pushing toward the next step, the development of the reconnaissance satellites that became operational in 1961.[20]

By the end of the 1950s, the CIA had become a key agency in both formulating and executing American foreign policy. It was an agency full of zeal and enthusiasm, riding the crest of a wave, impressed with its own successes and sure that more would come. Its star would never rise higher. As William Colby, a future director, remembers, "the Agency had enjoyed a reputation with the public at large not a whit less than golden. After all, we were the derring-do boys who parachuted behind enemy lines, the cream of the academic and social aristocracy, devoted to the nation's service, the point men and women in the fight against totalitarian aggression, matching fire with fire in an endless round of thrilling adventures like those of the scenarios in James Bond films."[21]

But all of this was soon to change. The election of John F. Kennedy brought a new phase in the evolution of American foreign policy, one that has lasted more or less to the present. By the early 1960s the national security establishment was much larger than it had been in the late 1940s, and officials within it had greater power. Conscious of these organizational constraints, Kennedy and his successors turned away from the task of management and reform and began to bypass parts of the national security bureaucracy. As a result it was excluded from more areas of foreign policy and by the 1970s, with the breakdown of the Cold War consensus, it also lost its immunity from public and congressional scrutiny.

Kennedy came into office determined to inject a new dynamism into American foreign policy. He and his advisers wanted to develop new programs and to compete more vigorously with the Soviet Union, especially in the non-Western world. Foreign policy engaged Kennedy's imagination, for it offered endless challenges and the opportunity for presidential decisions that would affect the fate of all mankind.

"Foreign affairs," Theodore Sorenson remembers, "had always interested him far more than domestic. They occupied far more of his time and energy as President."[22] In the domestic arena, presidential power had become sharply circumscribed by the emergence of complex alliances among private groups, public officials, and congressional committees. The growing centrality of the federal government in American life had made it a magnet for ambitious groups, a focus for all their aspirations and discontents, while the decay of traditional political institutions made it more difficult for presidents to respond to these demands. The stalemates and frustrations of domestic politics turned presidents toward the foreign arena, where they possessed exceptional freedom. Far fewer domestic interest groups were engaged. Congress was not inclined to interfere. A solid Cold War consensus ensured agreement on the fundamentals of American diplomacy.[23]

Kennedy accepted the critique of Eisenhower's foreign and defense policies and decision-making system and moved quickly to place his own stamp on the national security bureaucracy. He ordered his new secretary of defense, Robert S. McNamara, to inaugurate drastic changes in military policy and organization, ignoring Eisenhower's warning that rapid reform of the military bureaucracy would not be easy. Kennedy was less concerned about the weaknesses of the Department of State, for he planned to dominate the foreign policy process and deliberately chose a secretary of state, Dean Rusk, who would be content with a modest role. In January 1961 the new president told George F. Kennan that he did not intend to put himself in the position of Truman, who, in Kennedy's judgment, had allowed Dean Acheson to control his foreign policy advice. From the start, Kennedy intended to rely heavily on his White House staff.[24]

Kennedy was convinced that the elaborate structure of the NSC delayed decisions and deprived the president of clear choices. Key NSC committees were abolished, and in their place the president adopted a much more freewheeling bureaucratic style, relying on a series of ad hoc groups and a shifting array of advisers. Relishing a certain amount of contention, Kennedy sometimes dipped down into the lower layers of the bureaucracy and sought to gather more information into his own hands. It was a system that required much time and energy from the president, skillful coordination by the special assistant for national security affairs, and an assertive secretary of state who could break through the inner circle of presidential confidantes. One observer, General Maxwell D. Taylor, who joined the White House staff in June 1961, initially "was shocked at the disorderly and careless ways of the new White House staff." By the end of Kennedy's first year, McGeorge Bundy's staff had settled in and was operating efficiently, but Taylor still found that Kennedy "like his subordinates . . . had little regard for organization and method as such. . . . The President would have little of my feeble effort at regimentation as he found it far more stimulating to acquire information from the give-and-take of impromptu discussions."[25]

This initial disorder was in part responsible for the president's failure to subject the CIA's Bay of Pigs plan to more searching scrutiny. Kennedy's attraction to the Bay of Pigs scheme, however, was more than a temporary aberration; it reflected a determination to overthrow Fidel Castro and an affinity for the organizational style of the operation. Kennedy admired the brilliance and ingenuity of its director, Richard M. Bissell, who had the ability to cut through traditional bureaucratic boundaries. With the permission of Allen Dulles, Bissell had sealed off the Bay of Pigs planning from other areas of the CIA. Dulles and Bissell were deeply committed to the attack on Cuba, and it may well be that they never believed the plan they presented to the president would bring Fidel Castro's collapse. Once the invading force was established at the Bay of Pigs, with a government-in-exile attached to it, they may have reasoned that Kennedy would be forced to abandon official American neutrality and use American forces to finish the job. It was a classic example of the way the CIA, or a portion of it, could generate its own policy and seek to impose it on the president.[26]

After the humiliating failure of the Bay of Pigs, Kennedy was eager for success, impatient with those agencies within the national security establishment that displeased him, and inclined to rely more heavily on his White House foreign policy staff.[27] Graham Allison and Peter Szanton argue that Kennedy's frustration over the inadequacy of the organizational legacy of the late 1940s to deal with the problems of the early 1960s led him and his successors to seek shortcuts. "The resulting mismatch," they conclude, "between the work at hand and the means available for dealing with it is not simply inefficient; it is dangerous. It largely accounts for fifteen years of intermittent White House efforts to govern without government—a circumvention of the cabinet departments and the Congress that has deepened the isolation of the President, demoralized able bureaucracies and embittered executive–congressional relations."[28]

Little evidence suggests, however, that Kennedy's bureaucratic strategy was based on such a sudden turn of thought. After all, Kennedy's senatorial career had not introduced him to the intricacies of modern bureaucracies, and he seemed disinclined to learn—to appreciate their importance in the functioning of American diplomacy. As Sorenson recalls, "he had always been more interested in policy than in administration, and would later admit that 'it is a tremendous change to go from being a Senator to being President. In the first months it is very difficult.'" In fact, Kennedy lacked Eisenhower's sophistication about large-scale organizations. In the aftermath of the Bay of Pigs, Kennedy privately vented his anger at his official advisers, especially the Joint Chiefs of Staff, rather than realizing that he had made poor use of them and the organizations they represented.[29] Although he organized his advisers more effectively in future crises, he never sought to understand the unique histories and peculiarities of the agencies that composed the national security establishment. Instead, he conducted what Gary Wills refers to as "guerrilla raids" against them, convinced that they were not essential for success in diplomacy. He began a tendency — which would persist all the way to the present — for presidents to turn their backs on the complexities of large-scale organizations and to attempt to govern without coming to grips with the necessity for management and administrative reform. In the short run success could sometimes be achieved; in the long run difficult problems became nearly insoluble.[30]

Of all the agencies of the foreign policy establishment they dealt with, the Department of State seemed to cause the president and his associates the most frustration and bewilderment. It was unresponsive to the president's wishes and resistant to efforts to change it. Secretary of State Rusk and his chief subordinates were not interested in administrative reform; Kennedy and his aides became acutely dissatisfied with professional diplomats who were skeptical of new ideas and programs. As a result, the president and his close advisers vilified the department, making it the butt of endless witticisms and disparaging comments. Increasingly, the White House foreign policy staff circumvented the Department of State, taking over those tasks that it was not handling well.[31]

The antiorganizational bias of the president and his advisers made it difficult for them to understand the Department of State's special characteristics. State had always been oriented toward serving American missions abroad; its traditions, personnel system, and organization all reflected this. The department was dominated by Foreign Service officers who were fascinated with life overseas and who sought an ambassadorship as the climax of their careers. They spent some time in Washington but generally disliked these tours, were not interested in administration, and were ineffective in dealing with Congress and other bureaucracies. Their life was far removed from presidential and congressional realities; from the perspective of these field-oriented officers, Washington was a "great bureaucratic sludge."[32] George F. Kennan viewed the American political process as "a sordid, never-ending Donnybrook among pampered and inflated egos." The insinuation of domestic politics into the diplomatic process left him feeling "as I can imagine the surgeon might feel if told to deflect the knife and make the cut in a different and unsuitable place because he might look better, so doing, to people in the seats of the theater."[33]

Because of its history and traditions, the Department of State was insensitive to presidential needs. Often professional diplomats did not wish to help the president make clear-cut decisions that might lessen the leeway of overseas embassies or disrupt long-established policies. The Foreign Service subculture, with its emphasis on overseas assignments, its internal, guild loyalties, and its detachment from national politics, rewarded traits that presidents disliked. It was a subculture that discouraged risk taking or sharp and disruptive debate and that gave most of its officers real responsibility only years after they were ready to exercise it.[34]

The Department of State had the well-deserved reputation in Washington of being poorly run. "In the postwar period," Donald P. Warwick writes, "State acquired the dubious distinction of being almost *the* model of bureaucratization in the U.S. Federal executive system. Caught in an incredible tangle of hierarchy, rules, clearances, interdependencies, internal wars, and external constraints, the department in the 1960s was a constant target of criticism for its rigidity and inaction."[35] Even Foreign Service officers judged its administrative failings harshly. One of its critics, John Franklin Campbell, labeled it the "Foreign Affairs Fudge Factory," or "The Machine That Fails," while older diplomats, who remembered the prewar years, were appalled by its "interminable interiors" and "vast sprawling mass of people." An amateur diplomat, John Kenneth Galbraith, found a day in the department depressing and felt suffocated by the "endless, undirected meetings." Many of these diplomats believed that size was the major problem, forgetting that America's new, worldwide responsibilities inevitably led to the development of far larger organizations in Washington.[36]

More perceptive observers realized that although the scale of the Department of State in Washington and of its overseas missions had gotten out of hand, size was not at the heart of its organizational malaise. An endless series of studies carefully documented the various bureaucratic diseases of the department, both in Washington and in the field.[37]

In the postwar decades most secretaries of state were concerned with questions of high policy, not with the internal operations of their department. Few really ran it or put administrative reforms near the top .of their agenda. As a result, it became both larger and less efficient. The distance between the secretary of state and the country desks widened, until six to eight layers of assistant secretaries, under secretaries, and deputy secretaries separated the secretary of state from officers with a firsthand knowledge of a particular region or country. At the time each new layer of administration was inserted, it seemed reasonable. But the cumulative result was a cumbersome, ponderous organization, with a tendency to dissolve into autonomous fiefdoms. At every level or layer it was necessary to clear a dispatch or memorandum horizontally, with other bureaus and offices, before it could move up the chain of command. This system of horizontal clearance was an extremely cautious way of doing business, one that diffused responsibility, encouraged stalemates and the acceptance of the status quo, and ultimately produced bland policy recommendations. Many decisions were pushed up to the top, burdening the secretary of state with minor matters and a huge volume of communications. Even so seasoned a diplomat as Henry Kissinger, when he became secretary of state, occasionally found himself overwhelmed with the flood of paper.[38]

Thus the Department of State moved slowly both in making decisions and in mastering new areas of knowledge. The Foreign Service resisted new specializations in information, administration, and economic development, insisting that the key aspects of foreign policy were the political ones and emphasizing the traditional functions of negotiation and political reporting. Only gradually did the Foreign Service broaden its vision.[39]

Given these characteristics, the department of course pursued a cautious bureaucratic strategy, taking a particularly narrow view of its interests and accepting a smaller part in the national security establishment. By staking out a limited domain, it hoped to acquire dominance within it and to work out informal nonaggression pacts with other agencies. Sometime it lacked the expertise to challenge the CIA, the military, or the Department of the Treasury, but more important, it rarely did so because it did not want to be challenged in turn.[40]

This defensive strategy failed. The Department of State ended up with the worst of both worlds. Although it limited its own ambitions, other organizations did not reciprocate and gradually built up a foreign affairs capability. The Department of Defense, particularly during the 1960s, strengthened the Office of International Security Affairs, which covered the world with its own geographical-political desks. The CIA also encroached on the Department of State, and often its country station chief had been in a nation longer than the American ambassador and had more money to spend and more influence with local political leaders. In some embassies the CIA, like the military, had more officers than the Foreign Service, and in Washington the CIA duplicated many State Department functions.[41]

The expansion of the CIA, the military, and other agencies into foreign affairs created a huge, fragmented American presence abroad, with highly compartmentalized missions in which each agency's staff enjoyed considerable autonomy. By the late 1960s, of the roughly 23,000 officials attached to American diplomatic missions, only about 20 percent were actually Department of State employees. Increasingly, the Department of State played a support role for other agencies, performing all kinds of housekeeping chores. American ambassadors generally exercised only nominal supervision over their large missions and, though formally heads of the country teams, sometimes were interested primarily in political reporting and did not care to know what the CIA was doing. The organizational sprawl in Washington was duplicated in the field.[42]

By the early 1960s, virtually everyone agreed that the Department of State needed a major reorganization, and in subsequent years a steady flow of recommendations poured forth from special commissions. Many of their findings were partially implemented, and various administrations tried to reduce the size of the department, to accept more noncareer officials, to introduce new management techniques, and to broaden the range of the Foreign Service and encourage more interest in bureaucratic politics in Washington. None of these efforts substantially changed the department, in part because no president or secretary of state was willing to put his full weight behind them, in part because reformers failed to appreciate the powerful pressures from the lower and middle levels for hierarchy and rules. The unique character of the Department of State, like that of other federal agencies, was shaped by many factors other than administrative rationality. Attempts to change the organization, if they were to take root, had to come to terms with this reality.[43]

The ineffectiveness of the Department of State, moreover, was only a small part of a larger problem. In the postwar years the national security bureaucracy became so large that the very nature of the policymaking process changed. These large organizations acquired their own sense of mission, their own subcultures and policies, along with an absorption in bureaucratic politics and a high level of specialization. Reluctant to move in new directions, they slowed down both the formulation and the implementation of policy, forcing a diffusion of responsibility. The distance between a president and those on the operational level was much greater than in earlier years, and the very size of these organizations required standard operating procedures that were likely to fit poorly with a new presidential directive. Occasionally they resisted a presidential order, secure in the knowledge that no president and his staff could monitor the implementation of all his decisions. Sometimes they also sought to manipulate the president, providing him with partial or misleading information or seeking, as was the case with the CIA and the Bay of Pigs, to draw him into a limited operation in the expectation that he would be forced in the end to expand it.[44]

More and more, then, national security policy was centered in the hands of civilian and military bureaucrats, and the power of the president to make and enforce policy was restricted. His power was, to be sure, less dramatically circumscribed than in domestic affairs, but the organizational constraints were increasing.[45] Eisenhower responded to this development by seeking, with limited success, to master the national security bureaucracy. In contrast, Kennedy sought to avoid it. Rather than reconcile himself to the realities of an organizational society, he tried to escape these confines by creating new strategies that would provide the illusion of freedom.

In the early 1960s the tendency arose to enlarge the White House foreign policy staff, or the office of the special assistant for national security affairs, and to make it the center for foreign policy decisions. "For reasons that must be left to students of psychology," Henry Kissinger writes, "every President since Kennedy seems to have trusted his White House aides more than his cabinet." Under Kennedy, McGeorge Bundy assembled a small but aggressive staff that acquired new power, dealing with the substance of policy as well as with its coordination. The process of bypassing the foreign affairs bureaucracy had begun.[46] For a time it looked as if Lyndon B. Johnson would reverse this trend, for he was close to Secretary of State Rusk and gave him the authority to coordinate all aspects of the nation's foreign policy. Rusk, however, was unwilling to exercise this authority or, for that matter, even to administer his own department, and Johnson was not interested in organizational questions. Unlike most postwar presidents, he was more absorbed in domestic than foreign policy, fascinated with all the intricate maneuvering and manipulation of congressional politics, and determined to transform his vision of a Great Society into government programs. As he was forced to focus his attention on foreign policy issues, Johnson came to rely on a small circle of senior advisers, including his assistant for national security affairs. He isolated himself from the permanent government.[47]

In 1969 Richard M. Nixon came into office with firm ideas about power in Washington and the organization of diplomacy. "The behind-the-scenes power structure in Washington," he records in his memoirs, "is . . . a three-sided set of relationships composed of congressional lobbyists, congressional committee and subcommittee members of their staffs, and the bureaucrats in the various federal departments and agencies. These people tend to work with each other. year after year regardless of changes in administrations; they form personal and professional associations and generally act in concert." In domestic policy, Nixon wanted to break the hold of Washington bureaucrats. In foreign policy, he was determined to establish his personal domination and to be certain he achieved credit for his administration's achievements. He believed that "it was in foreign affairs that presidential leadership could really make a difference. 'Whatever legacy we have, hell, it isn't going to be in getting a cesspool for Winnetka,' I told Ehrlichman 'it is going to be there.'"[48]

Suspicious of the Department of State and the CIA (both of which he regarded as filled with liberal Democrats and Ivy League intellectuals), Nixon chose a national security adviser who shared his views and through whom he could implement his ideas. Henry Kissinger met the president's needs, since he combined great knowledge and intellectual respectability with relative obscurity. His skill in bureaucratic infighting, along with his ability to please the president, brought a rapid rise in his influence and a further decline in the authority of the Department of State.[49]

From the start, Nixon and Kissinger believed that the national security bureaucracy would smother initiatives and stifle creativity. They agreed that the management of these large organizations would absorb too much time, making any sharp change of course difficult. As Kissinger puts it in retrospect, "Most great statesmen had been locked in permanent struggle with the experts in their foreign offices, for the scope of a statesman's conceptions challenges the inclination of the expert toward minimum risk." Determined to avoid what they perceived as the mistakes of their predecessors — the excessive informality of Johnson, Kennedy's preoccupation with crisis management, and Eisenhower's "rigorous formalism" — the president and his assistant concentrated power in an enlarged White House staff.[50]

The results of this strategy — the culmination of over a decade of growing hostility toward and frustration with the foreign affairs bureaucracy — were mixed. The great concentration of power allowed Nixon and Kissinger to implement their high-level conceptions without all the tension and compromises that the involvement of large organizations inevitably brought. They were able to dominate a limited range of issues, such as the opening to China, the talks leading to the SALT I agreement, and the Middle Eastern negotiations after the October 1973 war. In these and other areas, they simply left the rest of the bureaucracy in the dark.[51]

The Nixon-Kissinger system worked best in dealing with authoritarian regimes, where power was also highly centralized. It was limited, however, by the fact that a small group could handle only a small range of issues, and that Kissinger's White House staff could not possibly acquire the expertise of the vast national security bureaucracy. Although the permanent government was resistant to change and weak in conceptual thought, it was an unmatched reservoir of knowledge; an institution of its size and capability was essential in dealing with other governments where power was diffuse. Thus the Nixon-Kissinger approach failed on those issues where bureaucracies on both sides had to be engaged. Most of the disputes between the United States and its allies were of this sort, and therefore Nixon and Kissinger's diplomacy often broke down in dealing with Japan and the nations of Western Europe.[52]

Whatever its short-run successes, Nixon and Kissinger's organizational style further demoralized the Department of State and the Foreign Service and ultimately heightened suspicion and hostility in Congress. Those who learned of dramatic diplomatic breakthroughs after the fact were resentful, and a diplomacy of secrecy made it difficult to reestablish a foreign policy consensus among the American people and to reassure Congress that it was a partner in the administration's foreign policy. The late 1960s had brought heated quarrels over the war in Vietnam, ending the Cold War consensus that had provided so many administrations with firm bipartisan support. By prolonging the Vietnam War and by excluding so many groups from the formulation of policy, Nixon and Kissinger embittered the debate over America's role in world affairs. Their spectacular diplomatic triumphs delayed, but in the end could not prevent, growing dissatisfaction with the nation's diplomacy. In Congress, the conviction grew that the powers of the presidency must be curbed, and in foreign affairs Congress became more assertive. Although the president retained the power of initiative in foreign policy, Nixon and Kissinger could no longer count on congressional acquiescence to virtually any foreign policy initiative they undertook. As Kissinger in retrospect realizes, "a President who succumbs to impatience with the ponderous State Department damages the country in the long run. A foreign policy achievement to be truly significant must at some point be institutionalized; it must therefore be embedded in permanent machinery. No government should impose on itself the need to sustain a tour de force based on personalities. A foreign policy to be lasting must be carried by the understanding of those charged with the regular conduct of diplomacy and over time must be implanted in the heart and mind of the nation."[53]

As controversy over the war in Vietnam grew, the military and the

CIA also came under a new, intense scrutiny and found the public's trust in their efficiency and integrity crumbling. From the end of World War II until the late 1960s, the military had occupied a privileged position within the federal government and had enjoyed enormous support from Congress and the public. The military kept or enlarged its wartime functions, dominated the occupations of Germany and Japan, and found that its generals moved easily into key civilian positions. Military leaders such as Omar Bradley, Arthur W. Radford, and Maxwell D. Taylor had a significant impact on policy and were close to the presidents they served. Military planners at middle bureaucratic levels dominated their civilian counterparts. Commanding vast resources, the Department of Defense was action-oriented, accustomed to implementing its operational plans with speed and efficiency. Its extensive domestic involvement made it sensitive to public and congressional opinion. It served presidential needs far better than did the Department of State.[54]

Since the passage of the National Security Act, reformers had sought to end interservice rivalry through a concentration of power in the office of the secretary of defense, and further legislation in 1949, 1953, and 1958 continued these efforts to make unification work. Gradually the Department of Defense became a huge centralized bureaucracy, a new superagency that lessened the role of the services and of the senior military in major defense issues and in the policymaking process in general. These changes accelerated under McNamara, who used his civilian analytic staff to control resource allocation and to cut across the services horizontally by combining various functions and creating defensewide agencies. The Army, Air Force, and Navy became administrative subdivisions of the Department of Defense, although often unruly and insubordinate ones, and found themselves engaged in rivalry not only with each other but also with the civilians who sought to impose their will on the military. In the 1960s interservice rivalry diminished, but tension between the services and the secretary of defense and his staff increased. The services had less power and the secretary of defense more. But the military establishment had become too big to be run entirely from the top down. Somehow a different balance would have to be struck between centralization and service autonomy.[55]

During the Truman and Eisenhower years, the Joint Chiefs of Staff had a strong influence on policy. Both presidents complained, to be sure, about the Joint Chiefs' parochialism, but the chairman of that body was generally one of their most trusted advisers. After 1960, however, the influence of the JCS declined, since Kennedy and Johnson were dissatisfied with the advice they received and critical of the lack of innovation among their military commanders. The JCS, in turn, were often intimidated by political leaders, resentful of their exclusion from the policymaking process, and by 1966 bitter over Johnson and McNamara's refusal to expand the war in Vietnam. Although they remained tied to their individual services, they reacted to the new distrust of the military by working out most differences among themselves and presenting civilian leaders with a united front.[56]

By the early 1970s the military, caught in the backlash of the Vietnam War, confronted powerful demands for cuts in the defense budget. Secretary of Defense Melvin R. Laird responded skillfully to these demands, winning the confidence of his service chiefs and working closely with them in the reduction of expenditures. The military weathered the storm, and late in the decade the tide began to turn as a new consensus formed on the need for larger appropriations. But widespread doubts remained about the efficiency of the nation's armed forces.[57]

During the 1960s presidents continued to rely on the CIA as their chief instrument in the conduct of a secret foreign policy, one that combated instability and anti-Americanism throughout the world. After Eisenhower, however, none understood the careful planning and long preparations that covert operations required, and throughout the decade presidents and their advisers were unhappy with the agency's performance and wary of those who led it. Presidential expectations seemed impossible to satisfy.[58]

Nevertheless, in the 1960s the CIA was active in many areas of the world. It launched a secret war against Fidel Castro, subsidized the Christian Democratic party in Chile, and when Salvadore Allende triumphed there in September 1970, attempted to prevent him from taking office. As the Vietnam War intensified, the agency became deeply engaged, forming a large army of Meo tribesmen in Laos and conducting pacification and nation-building programs in South Vietnam and clandestine operations against North Vietnam. But the CIA was not successful in most of these covert operations, and as the decade progressed the balance within the agency shifted away from covert activities and toward research and analysis, gathering foreign intelligence, and pushing forward technological frontiers. When William Colby returned to Washington from South Vietnam in mid-1971, he was struck with how much the "Covert Action culture" had diminished.[59]

During the 1970s the CIA fell on hard times, suffering a series of unprecedented shocks. In early 1973 its new director, James R. Schlesinger, entered office with a presidential mandate for sweeping reforms. Schlesinger believed that under the dominance of clandestine operators the agency had become complacent and inefficient, over-compartmentalized and full of "dead wood." Determined to end the "clandestine mystique," he fired over two thousand officers. The Watergate scandal, however, was the key to the CIA's decline, for it did what the Bay of Pigs failure had never done, providing outsiders with their first good look into the agency's inner history and ending congressional acquiescence to the special intimacy between the CIA and the president. As the Watergate probes proceeded in 1973 and 1974, the CIA was implicated. Nixon and his White House aides maneuvered to saddle the agency with responsibility for their cover-up, while intelligence professionals sought to insulate it from the scandal. During his few months as director, Schlesinger resolved to learn about the agency's past misdeeds, and his successor, William Colby, continued his policy, compiling a 693-page report about dubious and illegal activities. Colby hoped to clean house quietly, through a process of internal confession. But the intelligence community had become divided and confused, and it was only a matter of time before the so-called family jewels were exposed to the public. As the agency's secret history cracked open, Colby decided to cooperate with congressional investigators, and in 1975 the Pike and Church committees had access to a wide range of CIA files. "The CIA," Thomas Powers writes, "was . . . subjected to the sort of scrutiny usually reserved for the intelligence agencies of nations conquered in war." As revelations of illegal domestic activities and questionable covert operations appeared, many observers were shocked by the agency's free-wheeling style and demanded strict congressional oversight. The CIA was seriously wounded, under attack from without and suffering from low morale within. The prestige it had enjoyed in the 1950s and 1960s was gone. The agency entered a new era in which its role in the conduct of American foreign policy was seriously reduced.[60]

The CIA also suffered from a significant shift of resources within the intelligence community, primarily toward the National Security Agency. Founded in 1952, the NSA was the most secret of the government's intelligence organizations, specializing in breaking codes and in electronic eavesdropping. Its headquarters near Washington housed the largest and most advanced computer system in the world, and its satellites and listening stations revolutionized the nation's intelligence collection system. By the early 1970s CIA director Richard Helms complained that he controlled only about 15 percent of the assets of the American intelligence community, and he and subsequent directors were acutely aware of the CIA's diminishing role. The NSA monitored arms limitation agreements and, as one critic notes, painted "a comprehensive electronic portrait, a kind of wiring diagram, of the Soviet armed forces."[61]

The early 1970s brought a resurgence of congressional interest in foreign policy, ending more than two decades of acquiescence to presidential dominance. Congress rebelled against traditional policies and procedures, in 1973 passing the War Powers Resolution, in 1974 cutting off military aid to Turkey, in 1975 ending funding for covert operations in Angola and refusing to grant further aid to South Vietnam. Through the use of the legislative veto, complex reporting requirements, and new CIA oversight committees, Congress sought to influence many areas of policy, ranging from the president's ability to use force abroad to decisions about the human rights records of those nations receiving American aid. On one level Congress insisted on changes in specific policies; on a deeper level it began long-run institutional changes designed to make its new partnership with the executive a permanent one. Congressional staff had grown slowly in the 1950s and 1960s, but its growth in the 1970s was explosive as personal and committee staffs expanded rapidly along with old support agencies, such as the General Accounting Office, and new ones, such as the Office of Technology Assessment. Congress now had the expertise to deal with the national security bureaucracy on its own terms.[62]

With the assistance of this new staff, the level of congressional knowledge of foreign policy issues increased, as did the ability of individual congressmen to make their voices heard. The revolt against the imperial presidency was accompanied by a revolt against congressional authority, bringing a series of procedural changes that weakened party leadership in both houses. The legislative process was opened up, giving individual members more room for initiative. As a result, Congress became far more active in foreign policy, and the White House, Department of State, and other agencies of the executive branch could no longer deal with a few powerful party leaders and committee chairmen. As agencies were forced to touch base with more senators and representatives, the process of consultation became more time-consuming. Secretary of State Cyrus Vance estimated that he spent one-quarter of his time consulting with Congress.[63]

For all this effort, Congress was still erratic, fragmented, and vulnerable to special interest groups. Although congressional assertiveness had eroded presidential autonomy and produced a more wideranging discussion of foreign policy issues, it had also made the whole process of control and coordination more difficult than before. America's response to world events was less predictable than ever. J. William Fulbright complains that the "resurgent legislature of the late 1970s . . . has gone in the wrong direction, carping and meddling in the service of special interests but scarcely asserting itself through reflective deliberation on basic issues of national interest."[64] By the end of the decade, too, the high tide of congressional assertiveness had receded as the reformers themselves came to realize that Congress was unable to lead and integrate policy abroad. In July 1983, when the Supreme Court struck down the legislative veto, an important legislative weapon was weakened.[65]

Whatever its defects and excesses, however, the role of Congress in American foreign policy was permanently enlarged. Its foreign affairs staff had become the newest element of the national security bureaucracy, an exceedingly large and cumbersome set of institutions.

By the early 1970s, then, noticeable shifts had occurred among the various segments of the national security bureaucracy. The influence of Congress and of the White House foreign policy staff had increased, while that of the military and the CIA had lessened. Kissinger's assumption of leadership of the Department of State in 1973 created, once again, a powerful secretary of state, but he continued his previous style, consulting with only a small group of hand-picked aides and making no attempt to reform the department or to draw systematically on its expertise.[66] In fact, the agencies composing the national security bureaucracy were badly weakened, confronting severe internal problems, and no longer protected by the consensus of the Cold War years.

This organizational disintegration paralleled the concentration of power in the White House foreign policy staff and was in part a result of presidential neglect. Nixon and Kissinger, by carrying this neglect to such extremes, discovered that their approach offered no long-run solution to the problems of foreign policy organization. Their successors, though rejecting the Nixon-Kissinger model, were confused over organizational questions, unable to define the issues or make clear choices. Jimmy Carter and Ronald Reagan saw themselves as outsiders, critics of big government and of the Washington establishment. They exploited popular hostilities, endowing their antibureaucratic stand with a kind of romance. Their uncertainty generated intense rivalries among those they chose for key positions, bringing drift and instability in the organization of American foreign policy.[67]

Although Carter had little experience in foreign policy, he was fascinated by world affairs and determined to dominate the decision-making process. In domestic policy the president was soon mired down among congressional and interest group politics; in foreign policy he found, like so many of his predecessors, that he could make decisions quickly. He immersed himself in the details of policy, dominating, for example, the complex negotiations leading to the Camp

David accords in 1978. Carter's assistant for national security affairs, Zbigniew Brzezinski, complains that the president at times "was like a sculptor who did not know when to throw away his chisel."[68]

During the 1976 presidential campaign, Carter had promised to make government work more efficiently; once in office, however, he seemed uninterested in understanding its machinery and lacked insight into the tensions his approach to foreign policy generated. He assured his secretary of state, Cyrus Vance, that he would be the principal foreign policy spokesman for the administration, but soon found himself disappointed with the Department of State, which was, he records, a "sprawling Washington and worldwide bureaucracy," unable to provide the president with fresh or innovative ideas. Thus Carter gravitated toward Brzezinski, who was eager to move beyond coordination and play a central role in shaping the administration's policies. Carter appreciated his activism and imagination and engaged in wide-ranging discussions with his assistant over history and international relations. As policy disputes between his national security adviser and secretary of state deepened, Carter encouraged Brzezinski to speak out and to assume the dominant advisory position. As Vance's indignation grew, the president tolerated a growing divergence among his advisers and conveyed to the public the image of a leader who was confused and uncertain. In April 1980 the failure of the Iranian rescue mission and Vance's resignation as secretary of state symbolized the disarray of the administration's foreign policy.[69]

Initially Ronald Reagan preferred a more traditional decision-making system, with a dominant secretary of state and a nearly anonymous assistant for national security affairs. Unfamiliar with the substance of diplomacy, Reagan relied heavily on Secretary of State Alexander M. Haig, Jr., who had far more experience than any other figure within the president's inner circle. But Haig was unable to win the president's confidence or even to gain regular access to him. Frustrated by Reagan's bland affability and the interference of his White House staff, Haig resigned in June 1982. Reflecting on his brief term as secretary of state, Haig writes that "the White House was as mysterious as a ghost ship; you heard the creak of the rigging and the groan of the timbers and sometimes even glimpsed the crew on deck. But which of the crew had the helm? . . . It was impossible to know for sure."[70] Before Haig's departure, Reagan had appointed his longtime confident William P. Clark, Jr., as national security adviser. Far more assertive than his predecessor, Clark tipped the balance of power toward his staff, while he and the new secretary of state, George P. Shultz, reduced infighting within the administration and drew the president more deeply into foreign policy formulation. In October

1983 Clark's replacement by Robert C. McFarlane brought a renewed emphasis on the managerial role of the special assistant and a return to the pattern of decision making that the president had originally sought. Throughout all this confusion, Reagan remained absorbed in domestic affairs and seemingly indifferent to organizational questions. He was not inclined to look beyond the near future and to devise a long-term organizational strategy.[71]

Reagan and his intimates were convinced of the need for large increases in the defense budget and for the rebuilding of the CIA. In dealing with the military, they ignored the warnings of General David C. Jones, a former chairman of the Joint Chiefs of Staff, who argues that the Department of Defense has become so large and rigid that "fundamental defense deficiencies cannot be solved with dollars alone—no matter how much they are needed."[72] While pouring funds into the CIA, the administration allowed its new director, William J. Casey, to reemphasize covert operations, calling back hundreds of former agents. Phoenix-like, the CIA was on the rise again, although congressional resistance to its operations against Nicaragua was stubborn and grave doubts remained within the agency over the wisdom of covert activities.[73]

The ebb and flow within the national security bureaucracy continued, as successive administrations favored one agency over another, pursued varying strategies, and, all in all, seemed unconcerned with the larger organizational crisis. From a study of earlier periods, we know that possibilities for positive organizational change had once existed. The decades before 1941 had witnessed the gradual maturation of the Department of State and the Foreign Service, and in the years from 1945 to 1960 Truman and Eisenhower had presided over a period of great organizational creativity—a period when so much of the national security bureaucracy emerged. Looking to these experiences, some observers argue that it is still possible for the president to impose coherence on the sprawling national security establishment, to make it more responsive to presidential purposes while at the same time respecting the distinctiveness of the organizations within it. Others doubt that major reforms can be carried out, suggesting that the problem of bureaucracy is moving beyond the reach of any leader.[74]

In fact the possibilities are obscure, since our nation's leaders, for over two decades, have tried to work around rather than through the agencies of the national security establishment. As Gary Wills writes, "more and more the governmental workings of America have come to reflect the necessities of national size and ambition, while the Presidents express a romantic rejection of that machinery . . . a promise to escape 'back' toward remembered freedom."[75] They have tried to escape backward into the American past and outward into the world, nourishing illusions about unique presidential freedom in foreign affairs. A president is under different constraints in foreign and domestic policy, but sooner or later he has to rely on the agencies of the national security establishment, deal with other nations and an intractable international system, and realize that the possibilities for constructive change in world affairs are far less than at home. This suggests that the time has come for our presidents to turn inward and to confront the prosaic task of understanding and managing the foreign policy bureaucracy. The way our leaders deal with the organizations composing that bureaucracy is one of the most absorbing issues of our era. They cannot do without a large national security bureaucracy; neither have they been able to master it. They will serve the nation poorly if they lose the struggle by default.

HEYWOOD FLEISIG

Bureaucracy and the Political Process:
The Monetary and Fiscal Balance

A T FIRST I found the topic of this volume to be ephemeral; it tended to slip away and become a question about something else. The question of who controls monetary and fiscal policy is not often asked among economists — not, at least, at this level. A mechanical metaphor helped me, and it may help you. Imagine a machine labeled "monetary policy" that has four levers marked "bureaucrat," "politician," "interest group," and "voice of the people." (Be patient — I will define these terms more precisely later.) Suppose, further, that another console, labeled "fiscal policy" has a similar set of levers.

What levers should we pull to make these machines work? This essay proposes the following answers: to change fiscal policy, you would pull only the "politician" lever; to move monetary policy you would pull the "politician" lever and, perhaps, tickle the "bureaucrat" lever. In neither case would you pull the "interest group" or the "voice of the people" lever.

Fiscal and monetary policy may be unusual in this respect. Imagine, for example, a machine labeled "school system of the District of Columbia." Since tenure restrictions largely prevent dismissing employees of the school system and employees largely determine final output, the "bureaucrat" lever mainly moves the system. The Washington, D.C., school system is relatively insensitive to the "politician" lever and impervious to the "interest group" or "voice of the people" levers. Or consider defense policy, where bureaucrats, politicians, and interest groups all have a clearly defined interest in policy; where they can influence outcomes by framing the choices presented to higher-level policymakers and politicians; where politicians have strong interests in which geographic area receives defense spending; and where important, well-funded, and broadly supported organized interest groups, the defense industries, and public groups concerned with defense policy converge to influence both bureaucratic and political decisions.

We lack the machine on which to perform these controlled experiments, so the evidence presented here follows a different course. First, I define a set of terms so that we can distinguish disputes over definitions from disputes over evidence about behavior. Then I set forth the evidence for believing that bureaucrats — individuals relatively independent of political pressure — have no important role in making monetary or fiscal policy. The next section buttresses this direct observational evidence by expressing that evidence in a simple model of political behavior, asserting that monetary and fiscal policy are not bureaucratic because they constitute simple and effective means of changing the distribution of income and wealth and thereby power. Politicians cannot let such instruments slip from their grasp if they are to retain control of the state. I then discuss why it is economically optimal that this situation exist: for an economist, observed facts and a theory are more compelling if they can be shown to be consistent with the material self-interest of society. Economists are trained to believe that individuals homeostatically seek to maximize their material self-interest (we all serve one dogma or another). Having established that bureaucrats do not and should not make fiscal or monetary policy, I then turn to the political forces that do determine monetary and fiscal policy, setting forth several explanations of why interest groups and more generalized popular pressure play so limited a role in such decisions.

Defining Terms

This essay deals with a question of some subtlety. As always when discussing subtle questions, precision commands a higher premium than it ordinarily might. In particular, the discussion employs terms that have, through common use, acquired meanings that vary with their context. So, for example, to discuss whether bureaucrats make monetary policy, we need to agree both on whether the chairman of the Federal Reserve is a bureaucrat *and* on what actions constitute monetary policy. Even two people who agreed on both these definitions might disagree completely about the role of bureaucrats in making monetary policy. Definitions clearly can influence the answer to the second question — the problem cannot be escaped — but I aim here at discussing the question of control. I will use the following definitions in exploring the question surrounding "control."

"Politicians." A politician is any elected government official.

"Bureaucrats." A bureaucrat is any nonelected government em-

ployee. In common usage, though, the word "bureaucracy" also strongly connotes exercising power without immediate accountability outside the bureaucracy. Obviously, however, bureaucrats differ in how insulated they are from such external pressure. This essay, therefore, arranges bureaucrats into several grades:

Type I: Employees who can be hired and fired by a politician at will. Operationally such employees are nearly indistinguishable from their political employers. They have the least insulation from the political process.

Type II: Employees who require political confirmation. Confirmation proceedings redistribute power over appointment between Congress and the administration. Nevertheless, they provide minimal insulation from political pressure, since the appointee can typically be dismissed at will.

Type III: Employees who can be hired *or* be fired by politicians, but not both.

Type IV: Employees hired by politicians for a fixed term.

Type V: Employees hired by politicians for a permanent term.

Type VI: Employees that are neither hired nor fired by politicians.

The type VI bureaucrat, who serves in his job while protected by a tenure system and cannot be dismissed by a political official for dissident views or incompetence, best represents the bureaucrat who is here considered to exercise power independently. A type VI bureaucrat might face the penalty of being transferred to a less interesting position, but the more severe penalty faced by employees in other walks of life — being fired and deprived of livelihood — does not confront him. In such security can lie the ability to exercise power.

Having defined these types of bureaucrats, we can now turn to the task of defining monetary and fiscal policy before proceeding to assess the role of bureaucrats in making these policies.

"Monetary Policy." A "monetary policy" comprises a collection of settings of the instruments of monetary control: the discount rate, the reserve ratio, and the stance of open market operations. A monetary policy is usually directed at aggregate macroeconomic objectives involving inflation, unemployment, and short-term economic growth. Monetary policy may occasionally be directed at other aspects of the economy, though, especially at those for which the Federal Reserve has responsibility, such as the structure of the banking system.[1]

"Fiscal Policy." Defining fiscal policy requires greater care than defining monetary policy. A definition that included the factors entering all government expenditure and tax decisions would make the

scope of this essay unmanageable. Such a lack of restrictiveness would lead, in principle, to including all the topics in the volume. How the government spends crucially determines the content of its policy. For us, therefore, the distinction between the public finance policy of the government and its fiscal policy is critical: first, because it makes the scope of this chapter manageable; second, because a key aspect of making fiscal policy is compromising the government's macroeconomic stabilization goals with its other public finance responsibilities.

Here public finance policy represents the entire set of government decisions about taxes and expenditures. Fiscal policy represents a subset of these public finance decisions: those made primarily with the intention of influencing aggregate demand to achieve macroeconomic targets such as particular rates of inflation, output growth, and unemployment.

Bureaucracy Is Not Important in Making Monetary and Fiscal Policy

In this section, I set forth the evidence that bureaucrats, as defined above, are not important in making monetary and fiscal policy. Later, I will discuss how politicians and interest groups combine to make monetary and fiscal policy and why domination of policy by politicians is economically optimal.

Monetary Policy

Congress and the administration share responsibility for monetary policy. Each has powers that permit it to exercise monetary control. In the present regime they have delegated the making of monetary policy to the Federal Reserve System. I will discuss the delegation process later, when we consider the logic of the relationship between the political process and the monetary policy process, as well as its history in the United States. It suffices now to point out that the Federal Reserve is not a fourth branch of government: Its "independence" is nowhere specified. In most important respects, it is just another regulatory agency.[2]

In a narrow sense, no disagreement exists over who controls monetary policy. Each instrument of monetary control — the discount rate, the reserve ratio, and open market operations — can be changed only by the Federal Reserve System. Moreover, no important instruments of monetary control are in use by any other agency.

In the larger sense, though, these institutional forms determine neither the content of monetary policy nor the identity of the actors who control it. Understanding that requires looking behind the institutional forms. Superficially the Federal Reserve System appears decentralized. It has twelve districts, each possessing a bank, a bank president, and the apparent ability to change the discount rate. The system, however, is run by the Federal Reserve Board in Washington. The Board has veto power over the discount rate changes made by the Federal Reserve Banks. Moreover, those regional discount rate changes — even if allowed to stand — have limited economic effect because of the integration of the nation's capital market. The Board appoints the public directors and the president of each Bank. The Board dominates the Federal Open Market Committee, which contains seven governors but only five Bank presidents. These five are selected on a rotating basis from among the twelve Bank presidents. The Board also controls the budget of each Bank. The Board, furthermore, has veto power over publications by district Banks. No one has seriously suggested for years that anyone else besides the Board runs the Federal Reserve System. The evidence presented here conveys some of the reasons for this.

Although more controversy surrounds the question of who runs the Federal Reserve Board, most observers agree that the chairman does. Most evidently, the chairman is nearly always in the majority on Board votes.[3] But does the majority follow the chairman, or does the chairman follow the majority?[4] Much circumstantial evidence suggests that the chairman typically controls the Board. The chairman controls the Board budget and thereby the access of governors to resources. The chairman determines the agenda of the Federal Open Market Committee.[5] The chairman influences the range of choice of the Federal Open Market Committee by writing the directives among which the committee chooses when it votes. The chairman controls the flow of information from the staff to the governors at the Federal Open Market Committee presentation.

The chairman controls the staff itself not only by controlling the budget of the Board, but by the public authority he has gained from his previous exercise of the chairman's power. Because he dominates the staff, the chairman's positions can always be well supported or "staffed out." Those with a lesser staff find it more difficult to argue successfully against the chairman's position. Indeed, a personally strong chairman possessing substantial intellect can use solid staffing to develop a position from which it is very difficult to dissent. Paradoxically, the appearance of dissent within the Federal Reserve System itself is an indication of the extraordinary power of the Board and the chairman. The Federal Reserve Bank in Saint Louis and the Federal Reserve Bank of Minneapolis have mounted strong attacks on both the way the Federal Reserve System makes monetary policy and the

role of monetary policy in economic policy. These attacks are tolerated by the Board, not suppressed, an outcome consistent with the
conclusion that the Board does not regard such attacks as representing
a serious threat.[6]

No chairman of the Federal Reserve System, in writing about his
tenure, has ever alluded to being a captive of the staff.[7] By contrast,
other important public figures have talked about how their staffs have
limited their access to information and thereby their range of choice.

Finally, that great barometer of power, the United States Congress,
tacitly recognizes that the chairman is supreme. Members of Congress
attend hearings in much greater numbers when the Federal Reserve
chairman testifies than when other members of the Board testify. Press
coverage operates in a similar way.[8]

If the Board controls the Federal Reserve System, and the chairman
controls the Board, is monetary policy controlled by bureaucracy? By
our classification system, the chairman is a bureaucrat whose political
sensitivity is just short of the highest degree. The chairman is appointed by the president of the United States and serves a four-year
term that overlaps by two years the term of the president who appoints him. The chairman cannot be dismissed at will and does require confirmation by Congress. Anyone wishing to be nominated or
reappointed as chairman must espouse a position that the president
and Congress can abide. Even a chairman who does not desire renom-
ination, finding himself serving under a president and a Congress that
did not appoint him and that he is not sympathetic with, must still
reckon with the overall limits on Federal Reserve power that Congress
and the administration can combine to exert. We will turn to these
later. No chairman has ever risen from among the staff of the Federal
Reserve Board. Monetary policy, in short, is controlled by a bureaucrat, but by one who must measure his distance from his political
masters with exquisite caution.

Fiscal Policy

As compared with monetary policy, the institutional forms through
which fiscal policy is created are less clearly defined. The public
finance policy of the government — of which fiscal policy represents a
subset of actions — emerges from the interplay of powers between the
executive and legislative branches of government. Each branch has
some limited ability to introduce tax and spending measures; each
branch has some ability to stop the other from acting. The public
finance policy that emerges represents the result of these forces.

The fiscal policy function of public finance is not always its dominant aspect. In periods such as war time, other public finance needs overwhelm fiscal policy desiderata. Then, the government may not have a coherent fiscal policy reflecting consistent objectives. During such periods, tax and expenditure policy decisions will be made without much emphasis on macroeconomic goals of short-term price stability, employment, or growth. To the extent that a fiscal policy does exist, however, it emerges relatively uninfluenced by bureaucrats in both Congress and the administration.

Does the Bureaucracy Make Fiscal Policy in Congress?

The *Congressional Employment Manual* is absolutely unambiguous on the status of congressional employees: "Congressional employees may be discharged with cause or without." All congressional staff of individual committees serve at the pleasure of a congressman, either on his personal staff or as committee staff reporting to the committee chairman or the ranking minority member. By far the largest number of government employees serving at the pleasure of a politically elected official work for members of Congress. Only a few support agencies have employees for whom some job tenure exists. Those agencies have no responsibility for fiscal policy.

Typical employees of Congress have less job protection than most employees of privately owned firms. Such congressional employees are frequently exempted from general job-security legislation that applies to all workers in the labor force. Congressmen, for example, may discriminate on the basis of sex, race, or religious preference in hiring employees. Nor are congressional employees covered by the occupational health regulations that Congress itself has imposed on the private sector and the administrative branch.

Although these congressional staff members often can influence congressmen by developing well-reasoned positions and by channeling the flow of information, they represent an independent force only in a limited sense. Congressmen need only hire and retain people they agree with. A congressman can be a captive of a staffer only if he so chooses. Congressional staff are thus even less bureaucratic than is the chairman of the Federal Reserve: they have no insulation from the politician.

In dealing with fiscal policy, the Congressional Budget Office is the closest thing to a bureaucracy that exists in Congress. By Washington standards, the Congressional Budget Office is a tiny organization comprising about two hundred people. The head of the Congressional Budget Office is hired by the joint consent of the budget committees of the House and the Senate. The head serves for four years but can be discharged by either the House or the Senate. Employees of the Congressional Budget Office (like the others discussed above) serve at the pleasure of the head of the Budget Office.

Does the Bureaucracy Make Fiscal Policy within the Administration?

Several agencies participate in making fiscal policy within the administration: the Council of Economic Advisors, the Office of Management and Budget, the Office of the Treasury, and the domestic policy staff at the White House. The relative importance of these groups varies with their leaders' closeness to the president and can therefore change quickly.[9]

In these organizations, though, the groups involved in making fiscal policy rarely include individuals who are insulated from the political process in an important way. The relevant individuals will always be those who were appointed by the president in office, can be discharged by him, and serve at his pleasure. In some cases appointment requires congressional approval. Such ratification can restrict the president in his range of appointments, but he will typically not nominate an appointee unless that person is someone the chief executive is fairly certain he can live with. The president's ability to discharge or, more typically, secure the resignation of even a confirmed candidate ensures that political control is maintained as closely as he desires. Such staff reflect the views of the president, or the set of views that he wishes to consider, since he can give himself a new staff at any moment.[10] Even where congressional approval is required, there is little prospect of important opposition.

Often, of course, high-level political appointees can gain dominance over the views of others and even occasionally bend the president to their views through skillful maneuvering with Congress or with interest groups. In some cases the appointee's skill may be so great that a president may find it politically impossible to discharge him. For the purpose of our investigation, though, the appointee's strategy is crucial. In particular, the appointee cannot use the tool of the bureaucrat — legal immunity from being discharged; rather, he must use the tool of any politician — the construction of a winning alliance.

How fiscal policy differs from other government policies in its "bureaucratic" content can be more easily seen by considering the relation between some other government agencies and the political decision-making process. For example, in many departments career bureaucrats maintain close ties with Capitol Hill. They lobby to secure passage of bills that affect their programs, provide vital information to program supporters, obstruct the flow of information to potential opponents, and provide staff support to political allies (see the essays by Samuel P. Hays and Carolyn L. Weaver in this volume for examples; many others could be offered).

Even lower-level bureaucrats can effectively take positions. In some agencies, bureaucrats have years of experience in administering programs and have developed alliances with Capitol Hill staffers after long periods of supplying them with details of programs. These alliances can continue and strengthen irrespective of which party is in power because the administration has no effective ability to discharge the bureaucrat. Nor will a bureaucrat exercising such influence while maintaining a sufficiently low profile normally be transferred or moved.

No comparable set of alliances exists for fiscal policy. Senior-level bureaucrats from the Office of Management and Budget or the Treasury would not confer at length with congressmen or their staffers about the stance to be taken on fiscal policy. Such conferences, were they to take place, would be interesting only if they included the senior political officials in those organizations. Determination of the details of the policy involves the nonpolitical staff, but these details will not determine the fiscal stance. We will turn to these issues later.

WHY MONETARY AND FISCAL POLICY ARE NOT BUREAUCRATIC

If war is too important to be left to generals, monetary and fiscal policy are, for similar reasons, too important to be left to bureaucrats. Monetary and fiscal policy can, potentially, produce immense changes in the distribution of income and wealth through relatively simple changes in policy variables. Because these instruments quickly and obviously change the distribution of income and wealth, politicians have never let them stray far from their own control.

Politicians do delegate those functions in which the complexity of the policy action is great relative to its effect on the distribution of income and wealth. In those areas bureaucrats insulated from political pressures can gain great power, because it takes years to acquire the understanding necessary to execute programs in ways that achieve Congress's intended ends. Therefore a politician could follow this route and achieve the redistributive effects of a policy change, but only at the cost of a huge investment in time and resources to master the details of the program. Moreover, while those mastering the details of the program gain control over an aspect of the program, no individual gains much control over the whole program or, thereby, much control over that program's larger effect on the distribution of wealth and power. A political figure interested in maintaining maximum political influence for a limited time will seek to maintain substantial (though not total) control over monetary and fiscal policy.

Fiscal Policy

Fiscal policy emerges, as discussed above, as one of the ends secured by the public finance function of government. Economics textbooks depict the government as manipulating expenditure policy — represented as G — and tax policy — represented as T — to secure macroeconomic objectives. Even where a macroeconomic change makes everyone potentially better off, however, it is absolutely impossible to change G and T without altering the distribution of income and wealth. If you increase G, someone has to get it; and if you increase T, someone has to pay it. Most good textbooks will note this. To those involved in the process of actually setting G and T, though, the effects of fiscal policy in changing the distribution of income and wealth can take on a political importance that can easily dwarf the political significance of the policy's overall effect on macroeconomic conditions.

The distribution of political power is closely tied to the distribution of income and wealth. Distributions of income and wealth strongly determine distributions of political power; conversely, political power is often used to influence the distribution of income and wealth. Politicians cannot pass those powers on to bureaucrats. The ability to alter the distribution of power in an easy way lies at the heart of the state. By passing that power on to someone else politicians would cease to control the state. Those acquiring the ability to redistribute power would gain control.

The resolution of these issues has a long history reaching back to the roots of this country. Among the grievances listed in the Declaration of Independence was a reference to the Townshend Acts "for imposing taxes on us without our consent." It now appears that the actual economic costs to the colonies of the Townshend Acts were not particularly great. That a revolution could occur in part over issues whose actual costs were low underscores their political sensitivity and the need to handle them with great delicacy. A similar issue arose at the outset of the Civil War. The Republican party did not run on a platform of abolishing slavery; it ran on a platform of limiting its spread to the new territories. The Republicans proposed an increase in G in the form of internal improvements to be received by the northwestern and western territories; they proposed financing it with a T raised with a protective tariff, borne ultimately by the West and

South. From the point of the view of the South, this was the death knell of the slave system. Under the Republican plan, the South would be taxed to pay for internal improvements that would increase the population and political weight of an area that, in turn, would be barred from holding slaves. The arithmetic of this issue was obvious to most Southerners. As time went by, the South would become progressively weaker in Congress: its power would wane in the House of Representatives as the population of the western states increased and in the Senate as the western territories became states. These two effects would combine to reduce the South's influence in electing the president. Many historians regard the Civil War as a preemptive strike by the South aimed at preventing its eventual political extinction as the region of the country possessing its "peculiar institution."

These are only a few well-known examples of attempts to change government expenditures and taxes to achieve certain ends that provoked major upheavals because of their side effects on the distribution of income and wealth and, thereby, on the distribution of power. It is axiomatic: no important political issue in history has failed to involve money.

Politicians, understanding this, have not let this power slip out of their grasp. They do not delegate the power "whole" to a group of relatively insulated bureaucrats, because delegation would turn the state over to them. They do not divide it into small units and diffuse it over a large number of bureaucrats, because division would destroy an instrument of control that politicians wish to use. Such centralization of this power, moreover, keeps power in the hands of a group whose exercise of that power is relatively easy for the population to monitor. The social cost of having politicians rather than experts retain control is relatively low; the social gain is relatively great.

Consider, by contrast to fiscal policy, defense procurement or the administration of welfare programs. Changes in these arrangements also change the distribution of income, wealth, and thereby power. But the global effects of different policies are difficult to predict, so the tool is difficult to use. Moreover, using such policies as a political tool means a tremendous loss of social efficiency. Since the operating decisions are complex, delegation of the immense detail is required in order to make a judgment that is even remotely efficient in a social sense. To attempt to achieve income and wealth redistribution goals in the process would reduce the efficiency of the public finance decision and take too much of the politician's time. But politicians can secure these ends while broadly directing expenditures toward specific ends and taking revenues from various sources.

Monetary Policy

Like changes in fiscal policy, changes in monetary policy will alter the distribution of income and wealth and therefore of power. These issues may at times appear less obvious with monetary policy than they do with fiscal policy. But concern over the effect of monetary policy on the distribution of income, wealth, and power has a long history that explains many of the present institutional arrangements surrounding the making of monetary policy.

The underlying technical issue is simple: the modern state requires fiat money (money without intrinsic worth) because of various inadequacies of commodity money (money with intrinsic worth). Using fiat money, though, requires that someone regulate its issue. Issuing paper money too rapidly raises prices; issuing it too slowly reduces them. Such changes in prices, especially when unpredicted, have social costs. People make contracts that specify performance in money prices. Price uncertainty can make them unwilling to make contracts fixed in nominal prices. Abandoning such contracts can eliminate much of the advantage from economic exchange. Clearly, specialization in trade underpins the modern economy. A government that fails to produce a system conducive to exchange and specialization in trade fails to guarantee the greatest economic welfare of its citizens.

The effect of unanticipated inflation in altering the distribution of wealth has been clearly understood in America since the colonial period. The colonies issued paper currency and had several well-documented experiences with fairly severe inflations in the seventeenth and eighteenth centuries. In 1787, in the most famous example, Daniel Shays led a rebellion against the state of Massachusetts. Shays demanded that paper money be issued at a sufficient rate to depreciate the existing stock of paper debt and prevent foreclosure of farm mortgages. This experience with colonial currency issues formed much of the background of the United States debate in the nineteenth century about the role of paper currency.

Between 1816 and 1836 the Second Bank of the United States issued fiat money in a semiofficial capacity. The Bank was a semipublic institution whose recharter was vetoed by Andrew Jackson in 1832 in a famous political battle. Jackson's reasons for vetoing the recharter are striking even today:

The bank was controlled by private rather than public figures;

It earned monopoly profits because it acted as the bank for the government and yet did not redistribute those monopoly profits back to the citizens;

Its organization permitted potentially excessive influence by foreigners;

It was excessively powerful: Nicholas Biddle defended the Bank he headed by claiming that though it had the power to destroy any bank in America, it had never exercised it; Jackson responded that Congress had no right to create such an institution and set it beyond its own power.

Jackson's veto of the recharter led to the elimination of the Second Bank; thereafter the administration and Congress exercised their monetary control function in a variety of ways. The administration issued small-denomination Treasury bills — as low as five dollars — during the Mexican War and paid infinitesimal amounts of interest on these — as low as one mil. This permitted the Treasury to maintain the fiction that it was issuing bonds and not money. Even this fiction was dropped by Congress and the administration when they issued the greenbacks during the Civil War.

Shortly after issuing the greenbacks, Congress and the administration set up the National Banking System, creating the still existing network of National Banks. These banks were entitled to issue National Bank notes. These notes became the national paper currency, with the help of a federal tax on state bank note issues. The tax extinguished the note proliferation that characterized wildcat banking, but the state banks arose again using the system of demand deposits and checks that we know today. For a variety of reasons, which tended to focus on financial collapse and bank failure, the view gained credence among influential citizens that this monetary system failed to provide an environment conducive to maintaining full employment and price stability. It was replaced in 1913 with the Federal Reserve System.

From the perspective of our investigation, the structure of the Federal Reserve System was striking. The act provided for twelve regional banks in this system, a provision aimed at preventing the control of monetary policy by any single area. The operative fear at the beginning of the twentieth century was of Wall Street domination of national monetary policy. The provision met Jackson's objections (more than eighty years before!) that eastern interests dominated the Second Bank. The Federal Reserve Act limited the earnings of the Federal Reserve to prevent monopoly profits, and today the Federal Reserve System still turns back billions of dollars to the United States Treasury. The act in this way met Jackson's objections to monopoly profits. The act required that Federal Reserve Banks draw directors from different walks of life: one-third of each Bank's directors could be bankers, but the next third comprised public directors appointed by the Federal Reserve Board in Washington. This regional system was capped by the Federal Reserve Board, which included only members nominated by the administration and confirmed by Congress. The act thus took account of Jackson's objection to the lack of public control.

These checks over the exercise of power were placed on a system that was not even originally planned as a system of thoroughgoing monetary control. The Federal Reserve Act envisioned the system as a lender of last resort. The prevention of banking panics was regarded as the major economic stabilization problem facing the economy at that time. It was thought that bank panics produced financial instability, perceived as the major cause of the business cycle. There was certainly no broad support for a monetary policy aimed at stabilizing prices or output. Price and output stability, in the expert view of that time, were taken care of automatically by the operation of the gold standard.

Is This as It Should Be?

From the point of view of economic theory, political considerations should dominate monetary and fiscal policy. An infinite number of efficient macroeconomic policies exist. There is no limit to the number of ways of arranging macroeconomic policies to move the economy closer to noninflationary full employment or to preserve the existing levels of output. The politicians need to choose the path; a unique path cannot be chosen by economic reasoning alone. For that reason economic efficiency cannot be determined without prior and continuing agreement on a satisfactory distribution of income and wealth.

Why is this? Simply put, the market system is economically efficient because prices adjust freely and give signals to individual producers about how much of each kind of good they should produce. That in turn dictates how much of society's scarce resources should be devoted to producing those goods. It maximizes the value of the output produced with limited resources.

But value depends on price, so we must ask what determines prices. Prices, as we all know, depend on supply and demand. But what determines demand? The position of every demand curve depends on the distribution of income and wealth. If you change the distribution of income and wealth, then demand curves will shift and prices will change. Suppose you like cornbread and I like corn liquor: if you have the income, cornbread will be dear and corn liquor will be cheap; if I have the income, the opposite will hold. Which price is right? That depends on the income distribution.

Which income distribution is right? The right income distribution, as close as anyone can reasonably determine it, is the income distribution that the political process sets as being right. These points do not represent, it might be added, a radical and new brand of economics; rather, this is a statement that will be found in the most revered of mainstream competitive equilibrium texts. In particular, see the works of Nobel Prize winners Paul Samuelson and Kenneth Arrow.

Who Does Make Monetary and Fiscal Policy?

This brings us to three types of issues. First, it is necessary to discuss how the institutions that make monetary and fiscal policy balance their responsibilities for macroeconomic control against their other responsibilities. Second, we must consider the balance between monetary and fiscal policy institutions: How do the institutions making monetary and fiscal policy deal with each other? Finally, we need to look at the external pressures on monetary and fiscal policy.

Internal Balance

Monetary Policy

Typically, few internal pressures divert the Federal Reserve from placing macroeconomic considerations at the center of its monetary policy. This general assertion requires two important qualifications. First, the Federal Reserve also supervises private banks, and considerations of bank solvency can influence choices of macroeconomic policies. Such motives may have lain behind the decision to increase discounting to member banks after the Penn Central bankruptcy, or behind the shift toward easier policies in 1982 in the wake of emerging international debt problems. Such episodes represent the Federal Reserve's exercise of the traditional function of preserving the banking system and acting as the lender of last resort. Sometimes, obviously, securing these ends may work at cross purposes to monetary control.

Second, the Federal Reserve conducts its open market operations through the trading desk in New York. The desk is extremely close, of necessity, to the New York financial community. That closeness may permit the community to exert external pressures on Federal Reserve action, a phenomenon I will discuss later.

There is a third possible source of internal pressure on monetary policy: the Federal Reserve, it has been suggested, operates like any bureaucracy to increase its total revenues in order to increase the size of its staff and the perquisites of Federal Reserve managers.[11] Such analytical themes are current in recent models of industrial organization, which depict managers as pursuing their own interests as far as the slack vigilance of shareholders permits. The model is preposterous, though, when applied to the Federal Reserve System. The system turns in a huge operating surplus every year, about which no great fuss is made. The Federal Reserve's control over its expenditures cannot be limited by its operating earnings because the earnings are several times greater than its actual operating budget. Something other than operating earnings, therefore, must restrain Federal Reserve expenditures. Not surprisingly, this rather peculiar view is based on statistical evidence that is not buttressed by any firsthand verification by Federal Reserve decision makers.

Federal Reserve managers appear, on the contrary, to seek to blend in with their bureaucratic surrounding. The Federal Reserve seems to maintain a high degree of comparability between its own conduct and the conduct of institutions around it. The Federal Reserve Board in Washington compensates its employees at about the same rates as other federal agencies; employees of the Federal Reserve System working at Federal Reserve Banks are compensated in a way very similar to those of private banks in the vicinity. If the Board were really operating to maximize managers' utility (as this model indicates), one would expect that the first step would involve raising the salary of the chairman from its present $67,000 to at least the approximate level of the $150,000 salary received by the president of the Federal Reserve Bank of New York.

Fiscal Policy

In contrast to monetary policy, which typically treats macroeconomic stabilization as the most important goal, the macroeconomic purpose of the fiscal policy function is frequently subsumed to other public finance considerations.[12] Fiscal policy is made in historically discrete moves. We can list the important fiscal policy actions over the past twenty years: the tax cut of 1964, the government expenditure reduction act of 1968, and so forth. On many other occasions there simply is no fiscal policy; public finance is dominated by functions besides macroeconomic stabilization. For example, the desire to wage the war in Vietnam or to fund social welfare programs viewed as politically imperative may take precedence over the macroeconomic objectives of fiscal policy.

The Congressional Budget Reform Act of 1974 raised the importance of the fiscal policy function in congressional deliberation. Even that act, however, could not ensure that fiscal policy would become the preeminent function of public finance policy. The procedure set forth in the act did permit using fiscal policy as a better bargaining tool in Congress's negotiations with the administration. The Reform Act originated in President Nixon's impounding funds for certain programs on the grounds that fiscal considerations compelled him to restrict Congress's exercise of the public finance function. Congress responded by increasing the staff devoted to fiscal policy. That increase permitted Congress to make better counterarguments about the budget and to keep track of its own budget process.

Once Congress had achieved more weight in its debate with the executive branch, however, the arena of the debate simply shifted back to public finance issues. There it remained until the latest round of tax cuts produced the present United States budget deficit. Indeed, some observers argue that no measure can permanently make paramount the fiscal policy function. Attempting to do so, as in the present budget debate, creates an irresistible tension between the public finance function and the fiscal policy function, a tension that can be resolved only by eliminating the fiscal policy function.[13] For example, in the current debate the administration brandishes the threat of an unbalanced budget to argue for reduced spending on social welfare programs while Congress uses it to argue for reduced defense spending. If the fiscal policy function were paramount, and if there were general agreement that government spending must be reduced (which is not obvious on economic grounds), then the issues of defense spending and public welfare expenditures would not be raised as sharply as they are at present.

The Balance between Monetary and Fiscal Policy

In the preceding sections we have examined how macroeconomic considerations figure in the internal debates of the institutions that make monetary policy and fiscal policy. We have also discussed how political forces balance against bureaucratic forces within those fiscal and monetary public institutions. Now we need to consider how political and bureaucratic forces create a balance between monetary and fiscal policy. Once again, the key issues are dominated by political considerations and by bureaucrats highly sensitive to the political process.

Monetary Policy

Monetary policy typically takes account of the consequences of the federal budget.[14] The Federal Reserve Board knows what the budget is and has projections of what it will be under different GNP paths, given programmed tax rates.[15] How monetary policy takes account of fiscal policy varies: sometimes the Federal Reserve has accommodated fiscal policy; sometimes it has fought the consequences of fiscal policy;[16] and frequently, it has exhorted Congress. Federal Reserve officials have appeared before Congress to evaluate the fiscal policy that Congress has chosen and to recommend alternatives.[17] Indeed, for the purposes of this essay, if the Federal Reserve were not featured as the maker of monetary policy, we would discuss it later as a special interest group acting on fiscal policy.[18] In many respects the Federal Reserve is the most influential special-interest group acting on fiscal policy.

The Federal Reserve, in formulating monetary policy, must also take account of the political process that has generated the budget. It must respond broadly to the political needs of Congress and the administration for several reasons.[19] First, Congress, and the administration can combine to change the structure of the economy in response to Federal Reserve actions. For example, if the Federal Reserve undertakes a restrictive monetary policy and Congress and the administration wish to offset the consequences of that policy, they may do so by changing the course of fiscal policy. But they may also do so by creating a series of programs that insulate the economy from the consequences of monetary policy, much the way an organism sets up an immune response to a noxious invader. In some cases, and most notably in the Belgrade speech of Chairman Burns, the Federal Reserve has viewed these offsetting actions as damaging to the long-term economic stability of the economy. When the Board views these actions as producing long-term damage exceeding their estimate of the short-term cost of relaxing the current stance of monetary policy, it may change monetary policy.[20] For the Federal Reserve, then, at least from Chairman Burns's perspective, an optimal monetary policy included not just the response of Congress and the administration in changing short-term fiscal policy, but their response in changing the longer-term structure of the economy as well.

Second, Congress and the administration can act in concert to manipulate the Federal Reserve. Most directly, the administration can replace the Federal Reserve chairman.[21] Since the term of office of the chairman overlaps that of the president of the United States by two years, the most a new president need wait to replace the chairman is two years.[22]

Congress and the administration can also combine to change the rules under which the Federal Reserve operates.[23] Contrary to the opinion sometimes expressed in the press, the Federal Reserve is not a fourth branch of the government; nor is its independence written into the Constitution. On the contrary, it is just another regulatory agency constructed by the joint agreement of Congress and the administration.[24]

Congress originally created a Federal Reserve System that would disperse power over several regions. After World War I, though, it found that all the important power in the system lay in the hands of the New York Federal Reserve Bank. In part, this represented only another instance of the capture of a regulatory institution by the groups it was designed to regulate. It also reflected, though, the growth of a national capital market after World War I, itself produced in large part by the need to finance the sale of bonds to fund the domestic government deficit and the war efforts of foreign countries. When a national capital market is primitive and many barriers to geographic mobility exist, some scope remains for regionally dispersed Federal Reserve Banks to produce different credit conditions in different areas. When such barriers break down, though, capital can move freely from one place to another, and differences in interest rates and credit conditions cannot be readily maintained. In such an environment the strongest existing local market tends to dominate the national market.[25] Because the national capital market was concentrated in New York, the Federal Reserve Bank of New York essentially ran the Federal Reserve System.

The collapse of the banking system in 1931, however, showed that the Federal Reserve System had failed to produce the panic-free system it had originally been intended to create. The reaction of Congress and the administration to this failure underlies the limited independence of the Federal Reserve System.

Congress and the administration acted directly to change the money supply, used the public finance function to compensate for the perceived failings of the Federal Reserve, and changed the structure of the Federal Reserve System. For example, the 1933 Thomas Amendment to the Agricultural Adjustment Act authorized printing greenbacks if the Federal Reserve did not increase the money supply faster — Congress, acting in cooperation with the administration, as it often did in the nineteenth century, threatened to act directly on the supply of money. The Banking Act of 1933 created the Federal Deposit Insurance Corporation to insure deposits at banks — Congress and the administration used the public finance function to substitute for the lender of last resort function of the Federal Reserve. Finally, the Banking Act of 1935 changed the administration of the Federal Reserve System in several ways: it increased the influence of Washington on monetary policy by changing the composition of the Federal Open Market Committee to place the majority voting power in the hands of the Board Members (rather than representatives of the Banks); it prohibited any Federal Reserve Bank from conducting open market operations without the consent of the Board, stripping the New York Bank of that power; it prohibited any Federal Reserve Bank from making a treaty with a foreign central bank or government (again stripping the Federal Reserve Bank of New York of an often exercised power). The act capped these substantive changes with the symbolic act of changing the name of a Federal Reserve Bank head from "governor" to "president"; henceforth all governors were to be in Washington.

Structure of the World and Position of the Federal Reserve

The balance between the political forces that affect monetary policy and those that affect fiscal policy depends on the nature of the outside world. Changes in that world can alter the relative effectiveness of policy tools. Politicians may permit a policy to be used freely and without apparent tight control because it appears ineffective. If the effectiveness of that tool changes as the background environment is transformed, politicians are likely to move to exercise more control.

So, for example, when economies are connected by fixed exchange rates and capital and goods move in a relatively free manner internationally, monetary policy will have a limited effect on a national economy. When the monetary authorities attempt to pursue a restrictive policy, any small rise in domestic interest rates attracts offsetting capital inflows, while any small decline in domestic prices is offset by outflows of exports and declines in imports. Interest rates and prices are set in world markets; if each economy is linked to others through fixed exchange rates, and if goods markets and capital markets operate relatively smoothly, a national monetary policy has relatively little domestic effect. Fiscal policy, on the other hand, affects output volumes at given prices and interest rates and can still have an effect on the national economy under fixed exchange rates because its channel of influence is not through prices or interest rates.

The Federal Reserve was permitted increasing independence after World War II. The exercise of that independence was in certain respects illusory: the independent actions of the Fed did not affect much that politicians cared about.

When the United States moved to a flexible exchange rate system, however, the impact of monetary policy on the economy rose considerably. Then monetary actions could have short-term effects on exchange rates that did alter relative national price levels and relative national interest rates. These in turn could affect real output and the price level. Thus the Federal Reserve could influence variables of great concern to Congress. This should lead Congress and the administration to once again reevaluate the amount of Federal Reserve independence it finds desirable.[26]

The Politically Optimal Degree of Federal Reserve Independence

The Federal Reserve is a regulatory agency created by the joint agreement of Congress and the administration, so they jointly determine its independence. What, though, is the optimal degree of Federal Reserve independence from the administration and Congress?[27] It appears Congress and the administration have wanted the Federal Reserve to be sufficiently independent to take policy actions and absorb the public's complaints so long as its actions were close to the political consensus. The Federal Reserve was close enough to the political consensus when opposition groups had insufficient incentive to form a countervailing consensus against its policies.[28]

On major issues, therefore, where Congress and the administration have agreed, they could combine to make the Federal Reserve do what they wanted. Where they disagreed, the Federal Reserve had more freedom to maneuver. The Federal Reserve, as a result, could exercise independence only in a close range around the existing congressional and administrative consensus. To move outside it required great political and rhetorical skill on the part of the chairman — as the recent episode of tight monetary policy indicated.[29]

Outside Interests

It is axiomatic in Washington: when a bill is proposed on a particular expenditure, tax, or regulatory action, the concerned interest groups will descend upon both the agency and the congressional committee in charge of those decisions in order to influence the decision. Observers possessing only the most common political skills, moreover, can predict the names of these groups once they know the nature of the action. So, for example, if the administration were about to announce that it is considering a substantial highway construction bill, it would be possible to compute the economic gains and losses to the affected parties and thereby accurately predict the names of the groups that will ask to testify and that will lobby the key congressmen, congressional aides, and members of the administration. None of this is noteworthy, and nobody finds it very surprising.

Consider, by contrast, the inability to make such a prediction about groups concerned with overall monetary and fiscal policy. For this discussion I separate these outside groups into two types: those that operate directly on the monetary and fiscal policy actions themselves — that have an interest in particular monetary and fiscal policy actions — and those that operate indirectly on monetary and fiscal policy action by stating certain positions concerning the consequences of monetary and fiscal policy. Just as an example, there might be a group that would predictably appear to testify on the consequences of unemployment but would not predictably appear to testify on the connections of monetary and fiscal policy to unemployment.

Outside Interests that Operate Directly on Monetary and Fiscal Policy

Only a few groups operate directly on monetary and fiscal policy: economists; members of the financial community; foreign central bankers and policymakers; and a few domestic interest groups.

Economists and Economic Analysis

Economists probably constitute the largest single group that has operated outside public institutions but attempted to influence monetary and fiscal policies. Appearing in Washington as consultants and as witnesses before congressional committees, they have constructed the larger part of the set of views entertained by policymakers. This collection of views, though, has encompassed a set of analyses that economists at the more prestigious schools would probably not believe is the best state of current scholarly thinking. Keynes twice addressed the issue: First, "Practical men, who believe themselves to be quite exempt from any intellectual influences are usually the slaves of some defunct economists . . . it is ideas, not vested interests, which are dangerous for good or evil" (*General Theory*, 1936). Next, "In the United States, it is almost inconceivable what rubbish a public man has to utter today if he is to keep respectable" (*Atlantic Monthly*, May 1932). Economists have written articles in popular magazines, they testified before Congress, and acted as consultants to the Federal Reserve. They have operated directly on the making of fiscal and monetary policy and also have influenced public opinion.

What is noteworthy about this group, though, is that they lack a strong personal financial interest in the outcome of fiscal policy or monetary policy. They are, of course, frequently paid to testify. In some cases their professional interests coincide with testifying. Their pay is not very much, though, and they gain minimally in prestige or outside income, except for those selling forecasting services. In the latter case their views, when quoted in the press, may create business for their companies.

Financial Community

Employees of a variety of financial institutions have testified before congressional committees and attempted to act directly on the makers of monetary and fiscal policy. The broad interest of the financial sector in monetary and fiscal policy, though, is about the same as the broad interest of any other sector in monetary and fiscal policy: periods of relatively full employment are periods during which bank profits rise. Indeed, in the short run the best environment for bank profits exists when an expansionary fiscal policy or other recovery initiated from the real side produces a combination of rising loan demand and rising interest rates. In the past, government regulation of banks tended to accentuate this profit pattern by controlling the rates banks could pay on deposits.

These interests have not appeared, though, to color especially the testimony of bankers or the macroeconomic policy they have advocated. Broadly, such testimony has typically opposed fiscal expansion, favored monetary restraint, and opposed inflation. Such positions cannot be plausibly linked to the fundamental or narrow economic interest of bankers in certain types of monetary and fiscal policy. More plausibly, it has reflected the existing broad social values of people who tend to choose banking as a career.

In one area, though, the narrow self-interest of the financial community has committed it to a particular monetary rule. A monetary policy rule that stabilizes the quantity of money would make interest rates more unstable and thereby increase the variability of bond values. The interest of the financial community in stable bond prices has been offered as one explanation of why the Federal Reserve was reluctant to consider using monetary aggregates as the measure of targeted monetary posture and instead continued pursuing the policy of "even keeling"—limiting changes in the interest rate in relatively short periods.[30] Given the huge controversy over the desirability of an operating rule that would stabilize the quantity of money, however, it stretches credulity to assume that an important role in the Federal Reserve's decision is played by pressures from the financial community based on such interests.

Foreign and International Influences

Foreign and international influences clearly affect the chairman of the Federal Reserve System. He or the designated governor attends meetings with important foreign policymakers at the Bank for International Settlements and other international arenas. The chairman is sensitive to the degree of responsible control he can exercise over his banking system compared with that exercised by others in a similar position.[31] Their relative independence and responsibility is a frequent topic of discussion among central bankers—as any perusal of their speeches indicates.

Relative to those operating on monetary policy, foreign and international influences appear to have negligible effects on fiscal policy. Policymakers in Congress conduct fact-finding trips to foreign countries and engage in some attempt to discuss the international implications of monetary and fiscal policy. Typically, though, only an international disaster will place international economic considerations at the forefront of congressional deliberations about the budget. The recent discussion of prospects for debt default may come closest to any occurrence in recent history to meeting these requirements. That this situation is so unusual itself underscores how infrequently Congress has taken account of these issues. By contrast, the extraordinary international implications of the currently projected United States government deficit have barely received congressional or administrative notice. That deficit, if financed internationally, could represent an enormous strain on world capital markets as the world economy moves closer to capacity.

The attitude of Congress has typified that of most administrations as well. The administration, as the maker of foreign policy, must be more sensitive than the legislature to the international implications of its fiscal position. Even so, it is difficult to find examples of shifts in fiscal policy occurring as a result of international meetings. It is not impossible, for example, that international influences contributed to the change in fiscal policy recommended by President Carter or that the discussions of President Reagan at the Rambouillet Conference influenced his views; their infrequency, though, bespeaks their relative unimportance.

Other Private Groups

Other private groups have a predictable interest in the stance of monetary and fiscal policy. Preeminently, representatives of the housing and farm sectors have traditionally favored policies that they believed would produce low interest rates.[32] They have favored such policies because of the credit intensiveness of their operations. Such policies might simultaneously produce relatively high rates of interest and inflation. Tempering their concern, one imagines, is the fact that an unexpected jump in the rate of inflation would have increased their net asset positions.

Beyond these groups, it is difficult to find those with a predictable interest in particular monetary and fiscal policy actions. Moreover, their interest in individual monetary and fiscal policy actions need not be a good predictor of their views on the overall stance of policy. In fiscal policy the contrast is stark: individual groups may come to Washington arguing for an increase in government expenditure or a decline in a particular set of taxes, but they might have a completely different position concerning the overall fiscal policy stance. For example, a real estate interest group might argue strenuously for a change in the depreciation allowance that would raise the profit from holding a real estate property by reducing the taxes on it. Such a tax change, by itself, would increase the size of the federal deficit. That same group, though, might have a completely different position on the size of the deficit. They might simultaneously argue that the deficit should be reduced by generally raising other taxes or by reducing government expenditure. Or the group might have no position at all on the general stance of fiscal policy. For monetary policy, individual groups could desire changes in monetary policies that would ease their own credit terms but favor, at the same time, relatively active stands against inflation for the economy as a whole.

Why Do So Few Interest Groups Operate on Monetary and Fiscal Policy?

Few groups operate directly on monetary and fiscal policy for several reasons: the high degree of economic ignorance; the perceptible degree of disagreement among economists; and the changes in the way the world works that have made the old views of effectiveness obsolete. Let me explain.

Economic Ignorance

Economic ignorance contributes to the inability of interest groups to form by making it extremely difficult to understand the connection between a policy action and a desired end. An individual, for example, who can see that he would be better off if he had a larger number of job offers and could change jobs or bargain with his employer more effectively, may not understand the connections between that state of the world and something called the "tight labor market." That individual might also not understand how changes in monetary and fiscal policy would produce such a tight labor market. Moreover, he might not have a clearly developed view of whether the side effects accompanying various policies aimed at producing such a tight labor market were good or bad.

In the face of this situation and the high costs of forming a group to affect any interest in which single individuals do not have a huge stake, interest groups are difficult to form. For much the same reason that consumers rarely band together to fight tariff increases, individual groups seldom form primarily to change monetary and fiscal policy.

In addition, the institutions formulating monetary and fiscal policy take pains to promulgate murk and misinformation along with their policies.[33] The most famous example of this, of course, has been the refusal of the Federal Reserve System to release the minutes of the Federal Open Market Committee until a month has passed. The Federal Reserve claims this prevents profiteering from Federal Reserve decisions; critics claim it benefits the Federal Reserve by diffusing criticism of current Federal Reserve actions because you never actually know what they are.[34] It has created a remarkable industry of Federal Reserve watchers who attempt not only to predict what the Federal Reserve will do but to determine what the Federal Reserve is actually doing right at that moment.[35]

Another remarkable example of the way rhetorical skills have been used to create murk in order to maintain a policy whose consequences were deplored by Congress and the administration was the insistence by the chairman of the Federal Reserve Board, Paul Volcker, that the record-breaking nominal and real interest rates recently witnessed have had nothing to do with monetary policy but rather result from the expectation of a large federal deficit. No studies exist to support the claim that a budget deficit, especially in the face of a high unemployment rate, could produce such interest rates; given the superb quality of the Federal Reserve Board staff, it is apparent that this argument was not generated within the Federal Reserve. Of course, the even more recent collapse of interest rates in the face of exactly the same expected fiscal deficit sufficed by itself to indicate the frivolity of Chairman Volcker's claim (had there been any doubt among professional economists before that). Nonetheless, Chairman Volcker in testimony after testimony said that the major factor keeping interest rates high was the federal deficit. Until the deficit came under control, interest rates would not come down. A more complete statement might have indicated that Chairman Volcker was not going to permit monetary aggregates to expand rapidly enough to reduce interest rates until, among other things, he was satisfied that the federal deficit was under control; in that sense, it was of course correct that the deficits, via the chairman, produced high interest rates.

Completing the logic of the argument, though, does not represent a trivial addition. Had the chairman supplied the essential missing link – the policy reaction of the Federal Reserve to that deficit – Congress and the administration would have been substantially more obstructionist. The elimination of that crucial intermediate step was hardly likely to be accidental – but only the archives will show this. Indeed, the chairman's strategy had all the ingredients of a brilliant policy stroke. The rhetoric permitted him to go far outside the political consensus in reducing the rate of inflation at the cost of increasing unemployment. The key to this strategy lay in delegating blame to Congress and successfully representing to policymakers that the deficit, not monetary policy, produced the high rates of interest. It is a remarkable tribute to his ability to argue that this is the first Congress in years that has been convinced that an expansionary fiscal policy could produce a recession.

Disagreement among Economists

Those individuals attempting to dispel their economic ignorance will find that there is a set of issues on which most economists agree. However, they will also find that economists disagree on many of the issues of greatest importance to them.[36] Even were they to use the measuring rod that many economists themselves use — dismissing the views of those not teaching at the most prestigious universities or employed at the most prestigious policymaking jobs — they will still find substantial disagreement. In many cases the disagreement is so great that every important position in a policy dispute has a prestigious champion. In such cases, how can a noneconomist make up his mind about these issues? The disagreement reflects in part, though not entirely, the difficulty of completely removing values from economic analysis.

Changes in the Way the World Works

The world itself can change in ways that alter the importance of monetary and fiscal policy both absolutely and relative to each other. A set of views that served perfectly well in the world as it was may no longer serve in the world as it is. The most important change in this respect is the shift from fixed to flexible exchange rates. New groups now have a substantial interest in the stance of monetary policy: groups with a large stake in trade and in trading goods now must look to the stance of monetary policy to determine the change in the real exchange rate (which, by itself, can substantially alter their profits). Only recently, it appears, have these groups come to understand this lesson. They are beginning to appear in testimony to complain about the effects of the exchange rate changes, but they have not yet appeared in force.

Groups That Indirectly Operate on Monetary and Fiscal Policy

A number of groups have responded to the general manifestations of monetary and fiscal policy. Groups such as trade labor unions, associations of retired people, and groups representing particular regions have testified about the effects of unemployment, inflation, and slow economic growth. Typically, however, they have not focused on monetary and fiscal policies as remedies to their problems. When they have come to Washington and attempted to influence the political apparatus, they have typically tried to do so through the public finance function of the government. They have attempted to get special grants, programs aimed at affected groups and their areas. They have not typically tried to influence the general monetary and fiscal stance. Even the groups with general interests in the monetary stance—such as housing and farming—have focused more on the need for public finance to redress their injuries than they would have before World War II. If these demands become generally pressing, Congress and the Federal Reserve will respond by changing the general stance of policy. However, that response typically does not result from a specific request from these groups to change the policy stance in a certain way.

CONCLUSION

In brief, then, I have argued that politicians, not bureaucrats, have controlled monetary and fiscal policy. No bureaucrat very far away from being a direct appointee of a politically elected official has any substantial say in making monetary and fiscal policy. Nor, for that matter, do interest groups operate in any particular way on bureaucracies in order to produce a policy stance; to the degree that interest groups operate at all on this policy they operate through the political process, not the bureaucratic process. Politicians cannot surrender control of the tools of monetary and fiscal policy because those instruments affect the distribution of wealth and income in powerful and obvious ways. Exercise of those tools can remain simple and still be powerful; giving up the control of those levers would mean giving up the stuff of which political power is made. As an economic issue, moreover, this is as it should be. An infinite number of satisfactory economic policies exist, and one may choose among them only by using some measure of the political choice of the people. Politicians express that choice.

But of course there are other views of all of this. Some people think that a successful bureaucrat knows that preserving his power requires both denying its possession and delegating blame for its misuse. So, indeed, in this essay I, a bureaucrat by my own definition, may aim only to divert your attention from the bureaucrats who really do make policy. That you must decide for yourself.

Matthew A. Crenson and Francis E. Rourke

By Way of Conclusion:
American Bureaucracy since World War II

At the end of World War II Americans quickly turned away from the discipline of military service and the regulations of a wartime economy only to discover that they had become citizens in an increasingly bureaucratic political order. At the outbreak of the war, James Burnham had gloomily foretold the eventual triumph of this bureaucratic regime when he predicted that the so-called managerial revolution—already victorious in Germany and Russia—would soon sweep toward the United States. In the coming managerial society, he argued, matters of public importance would no longer be left to the free play of the market or the unfettered deliberations of democratically elected representatives. They would be resolved instead by expert administrators and technicians through central planning supported and enforced by the power of the state. We stood, in Burnham's eyes, on the threshold of an age of bureaucratic sovereignty.[1]

By 1945 this new order was by no means fully mature, but it seemed to have sunk deep roots. In the 1930s the need to cope with a catastrophic national depression had resulted in wide-ranging government efforts to manage the domestic economy. In the 1940s the country had become involved in the first truly global war—a conflict from which it emerged with a weighty national security establishment and a position of unparalleled strength in a prostrate world. The courts and Congress had come reluctantly to sanction a large, permanent government organization whose broad authority rested upon neither democratic election nor traditional conceptions of judicial procedure. Bureaucracy seemed firmly established at the center of American government by 1945, ready to provide the American people with a government machinery more powerful than anything they had ever experienced.

The consolidation of this administrative apparatus was the first order of bureaucratic business during the decade and a half that followed America's military victory over the Axis powers. One after another, the administrative legacies of the New Deal and the war were reorganized as their structures were rationalized by national policy. Three interrelated lines of development seemed to define the bureaucratic character of the postwar state. First there was the emergence of the national security system, newly equipped with the central planning capabilities appropriate to a nuclear age and linked by contracts to an enormous industrial establishment. In time the power, autonomy, and magnitude of this military-industrial complex would be regarded with apprehension even by a president like Dwight Eisenhower, whose own career had been closely identified with it.

Paralleling the growth of the national security establishment was a second major bureaucratic trend – the recruitment of science into the public sector. The wartime mobilization of physical scientists had changed the nature of war itself, and now the government moved to establish more permanent and wider-ranging relationships with the scientific community as a whole. Whatever its other effects, the development of the atomic bomb won science enormous deference from the American public and its elected representatives. The incorporation of scientists and scientific advice into the sphere of policymaking was symptomatic of an increasing reliance upon expertise – a distinctively bureaucratic basis for political authority.

Natural scientists were the first among their professional colleagues to play a significant role in government, and their influence was concentrated in the field of defense policy. But social scientists – chiefly economists – would later rise to administrative prominence, and their skill contributed to a third extension of the administrative state. The development of national income accounts provided the means, and Keynesian theory supplied the rationale, for fine-tuning the economy through government fiscal policy. The opportunity for this intervention was afforded by the Employment Act of 1946. This legislation placed only a handful of economic advisers within the orbit of the presidency and added little to the elephantine size of the administrative state. But the presence of economists in the White House signified more than a small addition to the expertise and economic planning capabilities of the national government. By institutionalizing fiscal policy as an instrument for managing the economy, national policymakers had accepted an obvious but unstated premise about the future character of the federal government: it would continue to absorb enormous amounts of revenue in relation to the size of the nation's economy and to generate gigantic expenditures. Even marginal adjustments on either side of the federal budget could thus be expected to produce noticeable differences in consumption, savings, employment, and inflation rates for the country as a whole. Whatever else it might become, the federal government would be big. Bigness in government meant prominence for bureaucracy.

Behind the bigness, however, there were critical sources of uncertainty. It is worth noting, in the first place, that the new administrative state had not emerged by a slow and steady expansion of established institutions. It was a creature of crisis, originating in improvised, often jerry-built responses to national depression and world war. Moreover, administrative improvisation of this kind was nothing new in the United States. Ad hoc arrangements had been just as characteristic of America's managerial reaction to World War I as they had been in World War II. But many of the administrative institutions established during World War I had not survived very long thereafter, and a nation so addicted to impromptu organization was an unlikely setting for the stolid permanence of a bureaucratic state.

It is also important to consider the character of the political environment in which hasty improvisation had so often become an administrative necessity. The country's political experience obviously set it apart from the European nations that had provided American administrative reformers like Woodrow Wilson with models of steady, centralized bureaucratic efficiency. In Europe the modern democratic state had been built up around a core of royal or imperial administration. Representative institutions – legislatures, mass parties, universal suffrage, interest groups – had been added to a bureaucratic foundation. But America had reversed the sequence. Political democracy came first and bureaucracy afterward. In the period following World War II, as in American history before that time, American administration would thus derive its character from developments in American politics.

BUREAUCRATIC CONSOLIDATION, 1945–1960

The consolidating impulse in postwar public administration probably achieved its fullest expression in the work of the first Hoover Commission, but the commission also illustrates the distinctly American protocol by which bureaucracy customarily follows in the train of democratic politics. Created by a newly elected Republican Congress in 1947, the commission was clearly intended to serve its sponsors as an instrument for pummeling a vulnerable Democratic administration. Its original charge from Congress called for an end to wasteful bureaucratic expenditures, the elimination of administrative duplication, the consolidation of agencies with similar responsibilities, and the abolition of public services no longer needed.[2]

Like many other political assaults against bureaucratic government, this one elicited a response that tended to strengthen and extend bureaucratic institutions. The commission's recommendations, submitted to Congress in 1949, were generally designed to solidify the administrative operations of the federal government and to enlarge the scope of executive initiative and control—not to increase the opportunities for congressional oversight and intervention. Congress, in fact, was assessed the major share of the blame for the "chaos of bureaus and divisions" in the executive branch. Congress had multiplied the number of agencies reporting directly to the president; it had attempted to fix by statute the internal organization of departments and agencies; and it had granted independent authority to subordinate officials. The result of this congressional improvidence, combined with the "gigantic and sudden growth of the executive branch" during the depression and the war, was a pervasive confusion both within and among administrative agencies. The commission declared that the "responsibility, the vigor of executive leadership, and the unity of administration of the executive branch as planned by the Constitution must be restored."[3]

Restoring the executive branch to the condition envisioned by the framers of the Constitution apparently required that the haphazard bureaucratic additions of the 1930s and 40s be restructured according to twentieth-century principles of administrative management. The commission's report, observes Harold Seidman, "represents the most categorical formulation of the orthodox or classical organization doctrine derived largely from business administration and identified with the scientific management movement of the early decades of this century. . . . Government organization is seen primarily as a technological problem calling for 'scientific' analysis and the application of fundamental organizational principles: a single rather than a collegiate executive; limited span of control; unity of command (a person cannot serve two masters); a clear distinction between line and staff; and authority commensurate with responsibility."[4]

As applied to the postwar federal bureaucracy, these principles demanded that vast archipelagos of programs cast up by the depression and the war be grouped into a "workable number" of agencies and departments that would not overtax the supervisory capacities of the presidency. The federal employees administering these programs had to be linked by unambiguous and unbroken lines of command to the White House, and the president, along with the members of his cabinet, would need additional staff assistance in order to develop the systems of information and control that were essential for the establishment of a unified executive branch. This consolidation of executive authority, the Hoover Commission argued, would reduce the cost of "disorder in the administrative machine"—not merely the cost of wasted expenditures, but the "lack of national unity that results from useless friction" when the executive branch works at cross-purposes with itself.[5]

The commission's report did not consider the possibility that the lack of national unity might be a source and not the result of conflicting programs and administrative frictions. An executive branch that worked at cross-purposes with itself might simply reflect a political system that was of two minds about a variety of important issues. The commission's recommendations generally presupposed a political system that had made up its mind about matters of policy, so that the administrative machinery could operate at full efficiency to achieve clearly defined and internally consistent objectives. But there is no technical, administrative remedy for a political process that is unable to articulate its purposes without ambiguity, qualification, or contradiction.

Occasionally, it is true, American politics did converge toward the kind of single-mindedness that seemed to be assumed by the commission's proposals for executive unity. World War II, for example, had marked an era of unprecedented national consensus, and national crises in general seemed to bring at least a temporary unity among warring factions. Perhaps this helps explain why crises have so often triggered episodes of administrative development in the United States—because they create the requisite unity for the construction of new bureaucratic institutions. Some observers have noticed similar spurts of administrative innovation and expansiveness in the aftermath of landslide elections: possibly these developments take place for the same reason.[6]

In the postwar era, consensus was more readily achieved in some policy arenas than others. The sense of threat and urgency that accompanied the early stages of the Cold War created especially strong pressures for political unity in the field of national security, and it was here that some of the most important steps toward bureaucratic consolidation were taken—some of them recommended by the first Hoover Commission. As Charles Neu pointed out earlier in this volume, the restructuring of the national security establishment was begun by President Truman only a few months after the Japanese surrender when he asked Congress to create a new Department of Defense that would integrate the separate military services into a single cabinet-level organization. The process of military unification proceeded by degrees through the National Security Act of 1947, its 1949 amendments, and the Defense Reorganization Act of 1950—each of which augmented the formal authority of the secretary of defense to direct the nation's military establishment. Meanwhile, the National Security Council and the Central Intelligence Agency—both created by the 1947 legislation—provided additional elements of an institutional framework designed to facilitate the central direction of American diplomatic and military policies.

But organizational outcomes, as Neu observes, often fell short of this organizational goal. Among the armed forces, intransigence and interservice rivalry helped prompt President Eisenhower's warning about the overpowering and incorrigible strength of the military-industrial complex. Presidents, for their own part, were sometimes reluctant to make full use of the formal administrative machinery for executive leadership. President Truman, for example, was disinclined to employ the National Security Council as a device for shaping and coordinating policy lest the council usurp presidential prerogatives in the fields of national defense and diplomacy. President Eisenhower, on the other hand, made the National Security Council the centerpiece of a comprehensive staff system that probably represented the highwater mark of the postwar progress toward administrative consolidation and rationalization. But the value of this achievement was questioned by critics who charged that endless efforts to coordinate administrative operations through interagency committees and to codify the bureaucratic consensus in policy documents simply diffused responsibility for policy decisions and delayed the decisions themselves. It was not an outcome that would have satisfied the Hoover Commission's demand for executive direction and accountability.

Other organizational developments in the fields of national defense and foreign policy may also have blunted the movement toward bureaucratic consolidation. In diplomacy, the nation's enlarged international role led it to take on new international functions that a traditionalist State Department was not prepared to perform. The Economic Cooperation Administration, the Agency for International Development, and the United States Information Agency were all established outside the boundaries of the diplomatic organization. Meanwhile, the Department of Defense created its own Office for International Security Affairs, which seemed to intrude on territory traditionally reserved to the Department of State. All these bureaucratic developments were clearly inconsistent with the aims of coordination and consolidation implicit in the postwar framework for the management of national security.

But in spite of these departures, the unified administrative framework itself counted for something. At the very least, it established a basis for future efforts to bring national security activities under central direction. The degree of organizational consolidation actually achieved before 1960 is impressive in its own right in view of the pressures toward organizational proliferation and dispersal that had been engendered by the rapid expansion of the nation's international role. It was not simply that new organizations had to be created to handle the increase in the government's international business. At the same time, old agencies discovered that their traditional, domestic business had suddenly acquired an international dimension. The Departments of Treasury, Commerce, Labor and Agriculture all acquired international offices during the postwar period, and as I. M. Destler has pointed out, they "did not establish their own 'foreign offices' just because they yearned to get into the overseas action." Their domestic missions were significantly affected by the country's increasingly ambitious international objectives.[7] It was against the background of these centrifugal tendencies in administration that the government worked to achieve military unification and to construct a comprehensive apparatus for overseeing national security policy.

This movement toward bureaucratic consolidation in the field of national security was followed, at a more halting pace, by parallel efforts to rationalize the management of science and technology in the service of the national defense. During the postwar period, the federal government attempted to institutionalize two kinds of relationships with the American scientific community. One of these had to do with the government's role as an investor in scientific research; the other, with its increasing need to bring scientific knowledge to bear in the formation of public policy — especially national security policy. The wartime Office of Scientific Research and Development had provided a temporary focus for both of these connections between government and science, and its dismantling at the end of the war supplied the occasion for a national debate about the structure of the government's future relationships with scientists and with the academic and research institutions in which most of them worked.

Vannevar Bush, director of the Office of Scientific Research and Development, was one of the first to put forward a plan for organizing the government's support of scientific research. His blueprint envisioned a national foundation financed by the federal government and controlled by a board of civilian scientists who would choose the foundation's director and oversee its support of research projects. The Bush proposal reflected some of the same consolidating tendencies that were evident at other places in the federal bureaucracy; its objective, after all, was to organize the public financing of science under the direction of a single agency. But the distinctive structure of the proposed agency reflected the scientists' suspicion of central direction, especially when it came from politicians and bureaucrats, and it was this attempt to accommodate the independence of the scientific establishment that led, in 1947, to President Truman's veto of the legislation that embodied the Bush plan for a National Science Foundation. Although Truman had previously endorsed the foundation, he objected that its proposed design represented "a marked departure from sound principles for the administration of public affairs."[8] The most serious departures, as Truman saw them, were those that placed the foundation beyond the reach of presidential direction by entrusting it to an independent board of experts.

Not until the Korean War generated new demands for the mobilization of scientific research was there a compromise between the requirements of political accountability and those of scientific independence. A modified National Science Foundation, more accessible to presidential control, finally went into operation in 1950. In the meantime, the Atomic Energy Commission, the Office of Naval Research, and a variety of other agencies handled federal investments in scientific research, most of them aimed at the development of military weapons. But even as the government hesitated to consolidate its support of research, the movement toward administrative unification became evident in another aspect of its relationship with science.

The Korean War helped make the White House aware of its own need for scientific expertise, and in 1950 a study conducted under the auspices of the Bureau of the Budget recommended the appointment of a presidential science adviser who would keep abreast of weapons-related research so that the president might receive up-to-date and comprehensive technical advice in the formation of military policy. An earlier presidential staff report, completed in 1947, had already proposed several administrative mechanisms for coordinating the federal government's own scientific activities, and its chief result had been the creation of the Inter-Departmental Committee on Scientific Research and Development. The new plan reflected the enhanced importance of science in national policy: the presidency itself was now to become the focal point for scientific advice and coordination.

At first the administrative elevation of science was blocked by existing presidential advisers determined to preserve the exclusivity of their access to the chief executive. Instead of appointing his own science adviser, President Truman merely attached a Science Advisory Committee to the Office of Defense Mobilization. Until 1957, a variety of improvised arrangements were used to transmit scientific advice to the president. But the launching of Sputnik by the Soviet Union put an end to makeshift expedients for bringing scientific expertise to bear on presidential decisions. The first response of President Eisenhower was to appoint a special assistant on science; the next step was to upgrade the Science Advisory Committee from an adjunct of the Office of Defense Mobilization to an auxiliary of the presidency itself. The new presidential science adviser became *ex officio* chairman of the President's Science Advisory Committee, and later he also chaired the Federal Council for Science and Technology — a successor to the interdepartmental coordinating committee created during the Truman administration. The culmination of this trend toward the consolidation of scientific advice was not reached until 1962, when the Kennedy administration's science adviser, Jerome Wiesner, combined his various chairmanships with the directorship of a newly created Office of Science and Technology, designed to coordinate science policy for the federal government as a whole.

The comprehensive apparatus created for orchestrating the government's scientific concerns resembled the one that had been constructed earlier to coordinate its national security affairs. Both represented efforts to achieve coherence in public policy through organizational arrangements designed to consolidate the diverse administrative enterprises of the federal government and to place them more surely under presidential control. As exercises in institutional design, they may not have proceeded directly from the managerial maxims of the first Hoover Commission. But they certainly shared the commission's devotion to executive authority and bureaucratic unity.

The resemblance that existed between the new science and national security bureaucracies was not just a matter of shared management principles; it was also a matter of politics. Political unity was the essential prerequisite for bureaucratic consolidation. The foreign policy consensus of the 1950s was the foundation for the style of administrative architecture that achieved its grandest expression in the national security staff system of President Eisenhower. The national fervor aroused by the space race after 1957 helped in a similar way to support the construction of an overarching science bureaucracy. In both instances bureaucratic development and consolidation were a response to an external challenge — the same challenge, in fact — and in both cases the political need for national unity helped to reduce tendencies toward disunity in the bureaucratic structure.

Political consensus may also have contributed to the impression that government organization and administration were merely technical concerns — efforts to discover the most effective instruments for carrying out the will of a nation that knew what it wanted. So long as there was little need to take sides, the appearance of bureaucratic neutrality would not be seriously threatened. Bureaucracy might be portrayed as the province of apolitical expertise, where scientific and military professionals hammered out the technical details for implementing the national interest.⁹ In these circumstances, administration itself might lay claim to scientific status. If that were the case, its fundamental laws were enunciated by the Hoover Commission and demonstrated in the new bureaucratic structures of the Truman and Eisenhower administrations.

But the architectonic designs of government organizations for science and national security were not simply technical achievements of administrative science. To build cathedrals, it was first necessary to have a religion. The tendency toward grand, executive-centered organization in the postwar period depended upon a harmony of political belief whose administrative importance became evident almost as soon as it was lost. The harmony was precarious even while it lasted. President Kennedy, for example, resisted congressional efforts to endow the Office of Science and Technology with statutory responsibility and powers because its director could then be called upon to testify before congressional committees. President Nixon abolished the agency when its purposes seemed to be in conflict with those of the White House. As an agency created by executive order, the office was protected from congressional inquiries by executive privilege, but as James Katz has pointed out, its lack of statutory power seriously limited its ability to carry out its mission of coordinating the scientific activities of the federal bureaucracy at large.¹⁰ In this instance and others, the drive for coordination was constrained by the country's shifting patterns of political power and ideology.

BUREAUCRATIC DISAGGREGATION AND CITIZEN PARTICIPATION

The administrative developments of the postwar period reflected a rather conscious effort to consolidate bureaucratic authority within the executive branch. To many observers, however, the most significant aspect of these changes was their inadvertent contribution to a more general movement toward political concentration in the nation at large. Leonard White, foremost historian of federal administration, warned against the "march of power to Washington" in a series of lectures published in 1953. The centralist tendency, he said, originated in a combination of circumstances, but among its leading ingredients were the federal government's intensified missions in national security and economic management: "The most obvious giant pushing us to the center is the Russian bear. . . . Another powerful influence, equally new in our experience, is the general expectation of Americans that government has a duty to limit the upward and downward movements of the economic cycle."¹¹ As long as these national issues remained prominent and pressing, White observed, it was only natural that the power of the national government would continue to grow. The desire to restore the loose-jointed political arrangements of the past would have to come to terms with the need for political centralization in the present, and defenders of the federal system would have to look in new directions to find opportunities for creating the decentralization essential to American democracy.

President Eisenhower, similarly concerned about the drift of power toward Washington, launched a comprehensive survey of these opportunities when he addressed the annual meeting of the National Governors' Conference in 1957. Like White, he warned against an excessive concentration of public authority, revenue, and functions in Washington. He proposed that the federal and state governments embark on a joint effort to identify those federal programs that might be turned over to the states. The same inquiry was to designate the national revenues that might be reallocated to the states so that they could take on their new responsibilities without assuming unreasonable financial burdens. The result of the president's speech was the so-called Kestnbaum Commission. For two and a half years it discussed a variety of proposals for disaggregating the functions of the federal bureaucracy. Like many earlier efforts aimed at achieving the same goal, the committee failed to discover a formula for restoring federalism that was sufficiently palatable to state officials. Its final report, submitted in 1960, produced no reversal in the march of power to Washington.[12]

In fact, as the 1960s began, the country seemed to be gaining speed in a one-way slide toward bureaucratic centralization. Federal expenditures, slightly over $42 billion in 1950, had more than doubled to $92 billion in 1960, and by 1970 they would more than double again to over $195 billion. Even when these outlays are adjusted to take account of inflation, they reflect a near tripling of national expenditures from 1950 to 1970. More was to come by 1980. The trajectory of central government growth could be traced, not only in absolute levels of expenditure, but in the steadily expanding share of the nation's substance that was channeled through the federal bureaucracy. In 1950 it was 16.1 percent of gross national product; in 1960, 18.5 percent; and by 1970, 20.2 percent.[13]

More than money was involved. As the expenditures of the national government grew, so did the mass of bureaucratic regulations published in the *Federal Register.* Through the 1950s and 1960s, the pages devoted to new administrative rules multiplied at a gradually accelerating pace — a prelude to the regulatory explosion of the 1970s.[14] The federal government's growing appetite for revenue seemed to be explained by an ever greater extension of bureaucratic control across the country.

But the onward march of bureaucratic government was less relent-less and more disjointed than it appeared, and it did not invariably lead toward a greater concentration of bureaucratic power. In the first place, the course of bureaucratic development after 1960 was no mere continuation of the trends established before that time. The most obvious change of direction was a shift in the objects of federal expenditure from defense to domestic programs. In 1960, almost half of the government's outlays were defense related. Ten years later the proportion had dropped by almost a fifth, and it would diminish even more sharply thereafter. This "welfare shift"—so called by Samuel Huntington—was one of the movements that began to reshape the character of the federal bureaucracy during the 1960s.[15]

Another distinctive feature of national administration after 1960 was the administrators themselves. What was notable was the extent to which their numbers remained unchanged. During a period of galloping increases in public expenditures and regulations, the size of the federal civilian work force crept upward at an extremely modest pace. Populist complaints about the proliferation of pointy-headed bureaucrats in Washington during the mid-1960s were, it seems, misdirected—unless they referred to a slight shift in federal employment toward the higher civil service grades where professionals and managers were found. The federal bureaucracy of the 1960s was spending money and writing regulations on a massive scale, but it managed to do so without any corresponding increase in the number of bureaucrats. Later, toward the end of the 1970s, the size of the federal civil service actually shrank slightly.

This peculiar mismatch between money and manpower becomes more comprehensible when bureaucratic developments in the federal government are considered in relation to the growth of the nation's other governments. During the 1960s, for example, when the federal government added only about 400,000 workers to its payroll, state and local governments added almost 4 million—an increase of nearly 40 percent in ten years. Over the course of the same decade, the amount of federal financial aid received by the subnational governments rose more than 230 percent—from $7 billion in 1960 to more than $23 billion in 1969-70—and it would grow even more rapidly in the 1970s. This dramatic broadening of the federal government's fiscal alliance with states and localities explains in part why the expenditures of the federal bureaucracy could increase sharply without a corresponding increase in the number of federal bureaucrats. National funds were helping to pay the salaries for a growing army of state and local bureaucrats. The federal government was performing some of its administrative tasks—especially the ones that were newly acquired—

through a far-flung, twentieth-century version of the putting-out system. Washington provided the resources; states and localities used them to produce goods and services.

Governments were not the only participants in this system. In time it would also include private organizations of many sorts, mobilized through grants or contractual arrangements to do the work of the federal government. Contracts and grants-in-aid were nothing new in Washington, but their systematic use as instruments of national policy came into its own during President Johnson's Great Society in the 1960s. "Creative Federalism" was the optimistic title with which the Johnson administration acknowledged its new reliance on organizational intermediaries. A more descriptive term, recently suggested by Hugh Heclo, is "government by remote control." The federal government would deal with its constituents not directly, but through the intervention of third parties who were expected to accept federal policy objectives along with federal money.[16]

In short, as the government shifted its attention from national security to domestic affairs, it also changed its mode of administration. The bureaucratic consolidation of the 1950s gave way to an era of bureaucratic disaggregation — not because there was any deliberate strategy of decentralization (like the one sought by the Kestnbaum Commission), but largely because disaggregation was an expedient adjustment to political circumstances. Domestic issues, more than matters of national security, tended to arouse heterogeneous collections of organized constituencies, often including the governments of states and localities. Bureaucratic disaggregation provided the means to accommodate many of these organized interests in the administration of national policy. It was also a device for projecting federal policy into new areas without raising troublesome questions about federal power. "Although grants serve many different purposes and have various political and economic rationales," Reagan and Sanzone conclude, "we suspect that the most important single reason for their popularity among both politicians and professionals . . . is the grant device bypasses difficult questions of governmental structure in a federal division of authority."[17] Questions about federalism might not be the only ones avoided. A system that allowed national policy to be administered in different ways in different places could also reduce the necessity of achieving agreement in Washington about just what the policy was in the first place.[18] Grant-in-aid legislation might thus consist of little more than the barest statement of objectives; the details were worked out later through complex negotiations during the process of "implementation."

Bureaucratic consolidation had been dependent on unity of purpose. Bureaucratic disaggregation was a concession to the uncertainty of purpose that arose when unity was difficult to achieve. It did not bring decentralization of the kind sought by the Kestnbaum Commission at the close of the 1950s. Instead of turning power back to the states and localities, the federal government shared power with them. The ambiguity of this relationship was suggested by the fact that the growing role of state and local governments in national policy was accompanied by an expansion of federal regulatory muscle. The connection was not coincidental. Now that the national government was conducting its business through outside parties, matters that might otherwise have been handled within the federal administrative hierarchy by interoffice memo or management directive had to be sent out in full-dress bureaucratic regulations aimed at institutions of the wider society.[19] To make matters more complicated still, sometimes even the drafting of the federal regulations themselves was a product of federal-state cooperation. Preliminary efforts to cope with water and air pollution in the 1960s, for example, relied on states to submit pollution control standards to the federal government for approval.[20] It is difficult to decide whether arrangements like these shifted authority to Washington or toward the states. What they reflected was a general expansion in the scope of public authority and action at all levels of government. The sudden enlargement of the federal budget and the *Federal Register* did not signify that the federal bureaucracy was amassing power in Washington. It heralded the emergence of a sprawling, complex, disjointed administrative apparatus that linked not only national, state, and local governments but also a host of private organizations.

These extended arrangements for delegating the business of the federal government to organizational intermediaries meant that administrative operations were often conducted at some remove from the elected officials who had authorized them. Democratic legitimacy and accountability—almost always sensitive points in American administration—became more troublesome than usual when the linkage between the will of the electorate and the implementation of public policy grew longer and more difficult to trace. Some of the political inconveniences arising from this problem may have been avoided, however, by reason of another administrative innovation of the 1960s—citizen participation. Citizen representatives were incorporated into the administrative process itself so that the will of the people might be invoked to sanctify policies that were being formed and carried out at a great distance from the traditional sources of legitimacy. After its unobtrusive introduction into federal administration in 1964, citizen participation was subsequently adopted as a required feature of one federal aid program after another. The political unrest of the period and the political needs of the national administrative system both helped to transform "maximum feasible participation" from an unnoticed legislative provision to the battle cry of a national movement.

It was not unusual for administrative organizations in the United States to respond to political movements, pressure groups, or constituencies. But there was something new in the explicit adoption of citizen participation as an adjunct to bureaucratic decision making. It signified that administrative agencies were now mobilizing and organizing political constituencies of their own. In this, as in several other respects, the development of public bureaucracy proceeded in distinctly unbureaucratic directions during the postwar period.

The U.S. Office of Economic Opportunity was probably the most complete embodiment of these unbureaucratic movements in national administration during the 1960s. It was hardly a typical agency, but in a decade that saw the initiation of about 150 major federal aid programs for states and localities, no single program could possibly illustrate all of them.[21] What the OEO represented was the leading edge of administrative change — a far-reaching experiment in citizen participation and government by remote control. The agency's flagship in its War on Poverty was the Community Action Program, under which it eventually made grants to almost a thousand "community action agencies" across the country — some of them units of local government, most of them independent private organizations. The functions of these agencies extended beyond mere policy implementation. They were also expected to form policy as they went along. "In the Community Action Program," recalls one of its former deputy directors, "poverty was to be defined, its causes were to be specified, and solutions were to be proposed not by the Federal Government but by local communities throughout the nation."[22] When such important matters were left to so many decision makers, it was difficult to say just what the nation's antipoverty policy was — or whether the nation had any particular policy at all. In practice, the local community action agencies did receive some guidance from national administrators. Instead of devising their own standards of economic deprivation, for example, they could resort to an OEO-approved definition of poverty, and although they were theoretically free to design their own antipoverty programs, there were powerful financial incentives to adopt the "national emphasis programs" endorsed by Congress or the OEO. These concessions to central direction, however, did not substantially alter the basic strategy of fighting the War on Poverty through hundreds of disjointed, local skirmishes.

The approach was disorderly but politically expedient. Taken together, small local skirmishes might be less devastating than one grand battle — and less disruptive to national politics. Poverty and inequality, after all, were issues that might spawn conflict on a societywide scale, and in this case their explosive potential was magnified by the fact that the inequality in question was not simply economic but racial. The civil rights movement, in fact, was probably the chief political stimulus for the War on Poverty.[23]

The idea for a comprehensive antipoverty program seems to have made its first officially sponsored public appearance in the statement that President Kennedy released in August 1963 as a response to Martin Luther King's March on Washington. The subsequent administration of the program would be just as clearly linked to the political and economic aspirations of blacks. Though almost half of the nation's poor lived in rural areas, for example, OEO allocated about three-fourths of its funds to community action agencies in cities, where the poor were disproportionately black. Even the money spent to combat rural poverty tended to be concentrated in areas of the country where blacks made up the bulk of the low-income population.[24]

These commitments carried obvious political risks. In accommodating the political demands of blacks, the federal government was laying itself open to a rapidly intensifying white backlash. The rancorous legislative struggle over the Civil Rights Act of 1964, passed just a few months before the Economic Opportunity Act, provided a foretaste of what might be in store for a national program that was perceived to be pro-black. The architects of antipoverty policy aimed to avoid these dangers. One of them, Daniel Patrick Moynihan, recalls that he and his colleagues shared a general understanding of President Johnson's strategic intentions for the War on Poverty: What the president "wanted in particular," he says, was "to see that Negroes got something fast, without in the process alarming whites."[25] Defining the problem broadly as poverty in general — rather than racial inequality — was certainly consistent with the president's desire to avoid being caught in any interracial crossfire. And if some conflict were unavoidable, it might at least be shifted, as much as possible, from national to local politics. This appears to have been one of the chief consequences of the bureaucratic disaggregation achieved through the Community Action Program. What had begun with the March on Washington subsequently dissolved into countless marches on city halls.

Apart from serving the understandable desire of national officials to minimize national political conflict, the disaggregation of the antipoverty effort was also seen to have certain positive virtues. The sources of poverty were located, by some accounts, in community institutions like school systems or law enforcement agencies that restricted the opportunities of blacks and robbed them of political power. The first step toward the conquest of poverty was to transfer authority from local bureaucratic institutions to their low-income clients, and citizen participation was to be the chief mechanism for achieving this political shift. Although these efforts to mobilize the poor against established local institutions do not seem to have been anticipated by some designers of the Community Action Program, they were to become one of the most visible and controversial aspects of OEO's field operations. They contributed in a substantial way to the localization of the War on Poverty. In practice, full-scale hostilities between community action agencies and municipal authorities were rare; the conflict was more ideological than actual.[26] But the supposed confrontation between the mobilized forces of the poor and the entrenched power of local bureaucracies gave a novel twist to the antipoverty effort. At least since the New Deal, the advocates of social reform had generally found themselves defending social service and welfare bureaucracies against conservative critics of big government. But the Community Action Program helped to crystallize a new ideological alignment in which animosity toward public bureaucracies became almost as common on the reformist left as on the free-market right.[27]

The antibureaucratic suspicions of the left would deepen as the Pentagon pursued the Vietnam War with increasing vigor, but the shift in attitudes toward administrative agencies clearly had domestic origins. The community conflicts prosecuted under the auspices of the War on Poverty were extensions of earlier confrontations in which the aroused supporters of the civil rights movement had been arrayed against town and county officials throughout the South. The new battles were nationwide rather than regional, and they were struggles about deprivation in general, not just the denial of legal rights. But the essential political alignment was the same; it placed bureaucratic organizations on one side and reformers on the other.

The poverty program also exemplified another kind of tension for bureaucratic institutions. It challenged bureaucratic autonomy on the grounds that the existing institutions were obstructing the disparate programs trying to help the poor. One of the missions of the OEO, in fact, was to serve as the coordinator of federal programs in the antipoverty field. That is why it was set up as an independent agency reporting directly to the president, not as a subunit of any existing executive department. Its administrative position was supposed to ensure that its new initiatives would not be stifled by the accumulated weight of bureaucratic inertia; its independence would also enable it to mediate among the established national bureaucracies whose efforts were to be joined in the War on Poverty. The administrative intentions at work here were similar to the ones expressed in the movement toward bureaucratic consolidation during the postwar period. In both cases the object was to integrate administrative activities around some major national purpose. But the resemblance ended there. Postwar bureaucratic consolidation was designed to bring administrative agencies under presidential direction. Coordination was supposed to come from the top. In the poverty program, on the other hand, the aim was to achieve coordination from the bottom. Each of the community action agencies sponsored by OEO was supposed to piece together its own harmonious ensemble of antipoverty programs, tailored to the distinctive circumstances of its own locality.

The limited political authority of local community action agencies made such feats of administrative coordination unlikely, and they became more unlikely still where antipoverty forces were in conflict with the very bureaucratic organizations that were supposed to contribute to the local War on Poverty. But the strategy of coordination from the bottom was not abandoned as a result of these shortcomings. In fact, policymakers began to pursue the approach with more ingenuity and vigor. Soon after the poverty program went into operation, a presidential task force began the deliberations that would lead, in 1966, to the Model Cities proposal, an ambitious federal aid program to be administered by the newly created Department of Housing and Urban Development. The Model Cities effort devoted more attention to the physical facilities of low-income neighborhoods than the War on Poverty had; one of its leading aims was to coordinate programs for the physical rehabilitation of poor neighborhoods with programs for human services. This task was to be accomplished primarily through local Model Cities agencies set up by municipal governments. It was the municipality's responsibility to design a comprehensive plan for reducing deterioration and deprivation within some clearly designated area of the city where residents of low income were concentrated. Some of the money for the execution of these plans would come from the Model Cities program itself. But a substantial portion of the funds to support the efforts of local governments was to come from preexisting federal grant programs that were scattered through the disordered ranks of public agencies in Washington. With the support of the Model Cities program, in other words, local officials were supposed to draw together a collection of federal grants into a coherent program suited to local conditions. There was no particular mechanism for inducing federal agencies to funnel their grants into cities that had qualified for assistance under the Model Cities program. The burden of coordinating federal aid programs fell heavily upon the cities themselves.[28]

By the late 1960s, the burden had become a familiar one. The Model Cities and Community Action agencies were only two in an expanding array of community-level coordinating agencies set up under the auspices of the federal government to overcome the disjointedness and confusion that were perceived to exist among its own aid programs. The Department of Labor had its cooperative area manpower planning systems; the Department of Commerce established economic development districts; the Department of Health, Education, and Welfare had comprehensive area health-planning agencies; and in rural communities the Department of Agriculture had set up its own family of local planning and coordinating committees. The need for local coordinating bodies like these had risen as federal aid programs had multiplied. But by the close of the 1960s some state and local officials were wondering who would coordinate the coordinators.[29]

Local administrative coordination was a substitute, albeit imperfect, for national political consensus. Creative Federalism meant that the national government could launch a poverty program without an agreed-upon conception of poverty, but the corollary was that subnational authorities would have to arrive at such conceptual agreements on their own. Conflicts avoided in Washington would have to be confronted in Milwaukee or Syracuse. Other unfinished national business also surfaced far from the capital. If national leaders sidestepped the task of mobilizing public support for a particular approach to the poverty problem, local organizations had to build political constituencies of their own, usually by promoting citizen participation. Finally, local officials also found it necessary to harmonize disparate federal aid programs, because granting agencies in Washington generally failed to reach agreement among themselves, even with presidential encouragement. Community-level coordination became necessary, in short, partly because the federal government was incapable of coordinating itself.

Managing the inventory of federal aid programs more effectively was one of the declared objectives of President Nixon when he took office in 1969. The Johnson administration's Creative Federalism was to be supplanted by the Nixon administration's New Federalism, which proposed to attack the problems of conflicting federal regulations, bureaucratic delay, and confusion by reducing the impediments that granting agencies in Washington could place in the way of state and local officials. The New Federalism, in other words, called once again for a reversal in the march of power to Washington. Model

Cities was one of the first federal programs to receive its marching orders. It became the vehicle for several experiments designed to reform the federal aid system — innovations that gave local mayors increased influence and discretion in the expenditure of federal funds to upgrade poor urban neighborhoods.[30]

These steps toward the decentralization of authority prefigured more sweeping changes in the grant system. A new approach — revenue sharing — had already been announced at the start of the Nixon administration. It aimed to sever most of the federal strings that accompanied federal money. Revenue sharing would not require states and localities to seek the approval of Washington bureaucrats for each local project or program that might be eligible for support under one of the several hundred grant categories established by Congress. It would not require subnational governments to match federal funds with funds of their own. Instead it would distribute comprehensive grants, to be used as the localities saw fit, for a variety of broadly defined purposes. The money would be allocated not at the discretion of federal administrators, but according to standard formulas based on local population and fiscal characteristics.

Revenue sharing was a simplifying device. It represented a response to the bewildering disarray of federal grant programs. The new arrangements promised to liberate subnational governments from a confusing mass of national guidelines, regulations, and reporting and clearance requirements. States and localities could then use this new freedom — together with federal money — to launch their own coordinated, planned, coherent attacks on the local problems that they claimed to understand far better than distant Washington bureaucrats. Their efforts would no longer be thrown into confusion by irrelevant and frustrating federal restrictions. The national government, once regarded as a leading institution in the country's search for order, was now seen as a source of disorder.[31] Its size had come to be associated with disorganization.

The Nixon administration's revenue sharing plans relied only on the bigness of the federal Treasury. They proposed to distribute some of its funds in two different ways. First, half a dozen "special" revenue sharing programs would consolidate existing federal grants under several public purposes — education, law enforcement, and community development, for example. Second, a general revenue sharing program would distribute money by formula to states and localities for almost any purpose at all. The administration's special revenue sharing proposals were initially rejected because they would have displaced congressionally favored categorical grant programs. But in

1972 Congress passed a general revenue sharing program that would cost the federal treasury about $6 billion a year.[32]

The event was a landmark in the development of national policy. For a decade or more, the disaggregation of administrative business and authority to states, localities, and private contractors had reduced the federal government's responsibility for defining its own independent policy objectives. With general revenue sharing, the substantive objectives of the federal government had finally disappeared almost entirely. The legislation lacked even the perfunctory statement of purpose that customarily served as a preamble for almost all bills introduced in Congress. Later, after several years of operation, the purposes of revenue sharing were still obscure. Social scientists attempting to evaluate the program were stymied by the unusual difficulty of figuring out what revenue sharing was supposed to accomplish. They could not determine whether the policy had been a failure without knowing the mission at which it had been intended to succeed.[33] Nevertheless, the Nixon administration was able to assemble a broad coalition to support the principle that quarterly checks should be sent to the nation's 39,000 subnational governments. There was no comparable consensus concerning the reasons for this generosity. The absence of such a consensus brought about the demise of general revenue sharing under the Reagan administration.

In its day, revenue sharing represented an extension, not an abandonment, of the political logic that had shaped the Johnson administration's New Federalism: When the federal government made large grants of money and discretion to states and localities, it became possible to launch federal programs without clearly articulating federal purposes. National ambiguity might be justified, of course, as a contribution to the cause of local autonomy. But is also represented a response to the difficulty of achieving agreement about national policy objectives. General revenue sharing was the ultimate accommodation to this political inconvenience.

Other elements of the New Federalism did not go quite so far. A few of the Nixon administration's special revenue sharing proposals were modified by Congress and passed, in 1973 and 1974, as "block grant" programs. These consolidations of existing grants-in-aid increased state and local independence from federal control, but they did at least hold subnational authorities to certain broadly defined objectives like community development or increased employment. Under the Carter administration, federal direction of the block grant programs was strengthened, and funds that had been spread by formula across the country were concentrated by means of new "targeting" provisions in places where the need seemed greatest.[34] Such modest reassertions of national purpose ended shortly after the election of Ronald Reagan, but the consolidation of federal aid programs into generalized block grants continued.[35]

The movement toward decentralization was formidable, but it was sometimes constrained by unanticipated features of bureaucratic disaggregation. Revenue sharing and block grants, for example, reduced the programmatic controls imposed on local governments, but they still carried a variety of procedural restrictions that enjoined the recipients to provide assurances of nondiscrimination, to pay prevailing wage rates, to comply with federal audit or citizen participation requirements, and to meet a dozen or more other standards that applied to all users of federal funds, no matter what the purpose of the expenditures.[36] Furthermore, since block grants and revenue sharing funds were distributed more broadly than earlier grants-in-aid, these administrative regulations were imposed for the first time on many local jurisdictions that had not previously qualified for federal support. The paradoxical result was that the reduction of federal controls under the New Federalism was sometimes perceived instead as an extension of national bureaucratic intrusiveness. The effort to diminish federal red tape actually helped to fuel a new round of antibureaucratic complaints.

The New Federalism, of course, was itself an expression of antibureaucratic sentiment. Giving states and localities more authority over federal funds required a reduction in the authority of federal administrators. Subnational governments were not the only institutions likely to benefit from this weakening of the federal bureaucracy. Presidential control of national policy had often been frustrated by the resistance of specialized bureaucratic agencies. The same proposals that increased the administrative autonomy of states and localities might therefore be expected to enhance the political authority of the White House, strengthening what one former official of the Nixon administration called the "Administrative Presidency."[37] In this case at least, reversing the march of power to Washington seemed to lead, by a roundabout route, to the White House.

It may also have led to a further erosion of the intergovernmental bureaucracy that had grown so rapidly during the 1960s. With the balance of political power already tipping against bureaucratic institutions, additional restrictions on bureaucratic authority became progressively easier to impose. But the shifting political situation only created the opportunity to exploit a weakness that had long been present. The vulnerability of federal bureaucracies was inherent in the nature of the functions they performed, and in the twenty years following 1960, many of those functions had lost much of their substantive content. National domestic agencies had become less directly concerned with actually serving the public. They were operating more frequently as holding companies for a variety of organizations outside Washington that performed the government's work according to local preferences. Federal programs themselves often provided little more than the general framework for public policy; the substantive details were supplied in the field. What had emerged in Washington was a public bureaucracy alienated from its own grass-roots constituency and often unable to articulate distinct public purposes. Consequently it was ill-prepared to defend itself against proposals that would transfer its functions or its money to other institutions, both nonfederal and nonpublic.

One such proposal was advanced by the Reagan administration in 1982 as part of its own version of the New Federalism. The plan would have transferred a variety of federal functions to the states and distinguished more sharply between the responsibilities of national and subnational governments. The proposal was vaguely reminiscent of those suggested by President Eisenhower's Federal-State Action Commission (the Kestnbaum Commission), and it met much the same fate. States and localities were still skittish as a result of taxpayer revolts in the late 1970s. They were hesitant to shoulder responsibilities previously discharged by the federal government.

But federal functions could be dispersed in other directions — to the "market" rather than to subnational governments. In federal housing programs, for example, it might be possible to dismantle the bureaucratic structures needed to approve and subsidize low-income housing construction by distributing vouchers directly to prospective renters. The recipients of vouchers could then purchase low-income housing on the private market, and the government could withdraw from the business of supplying shelter for the poor. Stimulated by the vouchers of low-income households, the market would do on its own what mortgage guarantees, interest subsidies, loans, and direct public construction had once accomplished.[38]

Even more complete reliance on the market mechanism was proposed. Instead of encouraging urban economic development through direct intervention, the federal government might offer tax incentives tied to enterprise zones and permit the not-so-hidden hand of the market to generate jobs and business firms where they were needed. In this and a host of other ways, the Reagan administration looked to the private sector rather than to public bureaucracies as instruments to achieve public purposes.[39] Moreover, the tendency to substitute market arrangements for bureaucratic organizations enjoyed considerable popularity outside Republican circles.[40]

Bureaucracy, always an object of disfavor, had undergone a twenty-year process of disaggregation. Now it was being replaced. To some degree the new assault on bureaucratic institutions was an outgrowth of the old attack. Disaggregation had made for organizational disjointedness and inefficiency. It had created a need for complicated regulations as a means of coordination. It had obscured the public goals that might help to justify the existence of public organizations.

REFORMING THE BUREAUCRACY

As early as the 1970s, national bureaucracy had been embattled on two fronts. Efforts to disaggregate bureaucratic functions to states, localities, citizen activists, or the market mechanism all tended to break the hold of bureaucratic institutions at the grass roots, where government services were delivered directly to the public. At the same time, the federal bureaucracy was also coming under fire from the loftiest heights of the political system. The drive to establish presidential control over the executive branch challenged bureaucratic authority from the top, while administrative disaggregation eroded it from the bottom.

High-level opposition to bureaucracy had strong precedents, but this enmity had traditionally come from conservatives worried about government waste and inefficiency. In liberal circles support for an expanding government role in the domestic economy had heavily outweighed concerns about its cost. By the 1970s, however, liberals had also become highly critical of bureaucracy, not least because many of the domestic problems assigned to bureaucratic organizations remained unsolved. The cause of bureaucratic reform was now one around which enthusiastic support could be rallied from all segments of the political spectrum.

Presidential reorganization of the executive branch was one of the most important vehicles for this reform impulse. This mechanism, like the underlying dissatisfaction with bureaucracy, had antecedents at least as far back as President Harry S. Truman, who appointed the first of two Hoover Commissions in 1947. Thirty years later another Democratic president, Jimmy Carter, came to office promising to bring a new heaven and a new earth through government reorganization — a perspective critics contend led to an excessive preoccupation with reorganization.[41] That postwar Democratic presidents should play a leading role in promoting administrative reorganization is somewhat surprising, since these chief executives lived off the legacy of Franklin D. Roosevelt, whose addiction to untidy administration has been described and defended by a variety of observers.[42]

This anomaly notwithstanding, Democrats as well as Republicans launched major reorganization studies from the White House.[43] Perhaps the most far-reaching of all the proposals resulting from these studies came from the second Hoover Commission. Appointed by President Eisenhower in 1953, this commission did not confine itself to a search for ways of making government agencies operate more efficiently, as had earlier reorganization studies. Instead it sought to identify certain government activities that should be eliminated altogether.

For at least this one brief moment, reorganization thus revealed itself as not just a colorless attempt to enhance the government's efficiency, but a counterrevolutionary movement aimed at rolling back the tide of history and reversing the expansion of government activity that the New Deal had begun.[44] But this counterrevolutionary phase of reorganization was short-lived. Even in the relatively conservative climate of the 1950s, few politicians in high office were prepared to mount a crusade against the New Deal bureaucracy and the programs it administered. As Herbert Emmerich wrote of the second Hoover Commission: "Not a single major permanent program resulting from the years of depression, recovery, war, and reform was abolished as a result of this prodigious inquiry."[45]

It would be hard to show that the reorganization activities of any postwar presidents either saved the taxpayers substantial sums of money or greatly enhanced the efficiency of executive operations. These are the two chief bases on which reformers have traditionally sold the value of reorganization to the general public, especially to the business community on which it has long depended for political support. Throughout this period Congress made repeated efforts to require presidents to specify how much money would be saved by the reorganization plans they were proposing, but the White House proved unwilling or unable to do so.[46] What reorganization has accomplished in the postwar years is, however, certainly no less important. It has greatly increased the power of the president and his authority over the executive establishment. This is why the reorganization movement has had the staying power it has exhibited throughout this period. All postwar presidents have had a continuing interest in reorganization not because of their passion for government efficiency, but simply because they recognized the impact of reorganization in aggrandizing the power of the chief executive. A liberal Democrat in the White House could appreciate the value of reorganization in this respect no less than a conservative Republican.

During the earlier history of American bureaucracy, reorganization did not serve presidential interests to nearly the same degree. In the nineteenth century it was Congress rather than the president that took the lead in pressing for improved management practices within the executive branch. Writing in 1958 about these nineteenth-century efforts at reorganization, Dwight Waldo said, "The idea of the President, as Chief Administrator, is wholly almost absent from these first 'comprehensive' investigations," while on the other hand, "this idea has been the central organizing motif of the investigations of this generation."[47]

One major reorganization study undertaken in the nineteenth century was that of the Dockery-Cockrell Commission, which looked into executive operations between 1893 and 1895. Its report "strengthened the existing feeling held by Congress, the administration, and the public that Congress would from time to time step in and examine into and reorganize the executive branch. It was not expected or contemplated, however, that investigations to follow would be initiated by the President asserting that administration was accountable to the executive."[48]

Indeed, it was not until the report of the Keep Committee in 1905 that a reorganization study first introduced the idea of presidential supremacy over the activities of the executive branch.[49] Symptomatic of this new orientation was the fact that the Keep Committee reported directly to the White House rather than, as previous reorganization groups had done, to Congress. Since World War II, presidential leadership in executive reorganization has been widely accepted, although Congress has continued to keep a watchful and somewhat distrustful eye on the use of presidential power in this regard.

Budgeting is another area in which bureaucratic reform has contributed to presidential ascendancy in the postwar era. As was true of the reorganization movement, the main thrust of budgetary reform has been toward centralization, and as the process of making decisions on expenditures has been increasingly centralized, it has inevitably come under closer White House control.

Immediately after World War II, when Truman was president, it appeared that budgeting would be an avenue through which senior bureaucrats would exercise a high degree of influence over presidents, rather than merely serving as instruments of presidential control over bureaucracy. As it operated in the 1940s under both Roosevelt and Truman, the Bureau of the Budget, which had become part of the presidential entourage as a result of a 1939 reorganization plan, played a leading role in presidential decision making.[50] It had the power to allocate executive appropriations among competing administrative agencies, and — no less important — it reviewed every agency's policy proposals to Congress to ensure that they were in accord with the president's own program and priorities.[51]

At that time power in the bureau rested with its career staff — highly skilled professionals running an agency that symbolized the importance of bureaucratic expertise in making sound executive policy decisions. At the peak of their power, senior bureaucrats in the budget agency saw themselves as a cadre of permanent officials at the highest level of government who served the presidency as an institution rather than the individual presidents who happened to be occupying the White House at a particular time. Budget officials expected that their power would endure from one administration to another, and that presidents of both parties would defer to their professional judgment. In the extent of their influence over policy, the senior civil servants in the Bureau of the Budget in the late 1940s came very close to enjoying the preferred status and power of high-level European bureaucrats — a standing that American bureaucrats have hungered for but seldom attained.

This brand of dominance over a major area of executive decision making proved, however, to be short-lived. The 1960s saw a gradual attrition in the power of the budget agency professionals.[52] The president's own political appointees began to assume control over decisions that budget professionals had previously been making. During the Kennedy and Johnson administrations, White House staff members took over much of the policy development role that career bureaucrats in the budget agency had once controlled. Both these presidents made it clear that, when policy issues were involved, political rather than bureaucratic officials would exercise command.

In 1970 the Bureau of the Budget was transformed by President Nixon into the Office of Management and Budget. Its powers were more narrowly confined to administrative matters, and much of its policy role was shifted to a newly established Domestic Council that was dominated by the White House staff. At the same time the upper echelon of OMB was politicized by the addition of four new program assistant directors (PADs). As a result of these changes, an agency that had once been regarded as a citadel of bureaucratic expertise in government, or "neutral competence" as it is sometimes called, found itself being used to advance White House political objectives during the Nixon years. This politicizing trend in the budgetary process reached its culmination in the Reagan presidency when in 1981 a former congressman, David Stockman, was appointed to head OMB and serve as the administration's chief advocate of its economic policies before Congress.

Indicative also of the declining influence of bureaucratic expertise in the budgetary process during the postwar years is the fact that political leaders interested in making major changes in budgeting techniques sought in this endeavor help from experts outside the government. In 1961 the secretary of defense, Robert S. McNamara, began using a system known as PPBS (a planning-programming budgeting system) in developing his own budgetary projections. The aim of PPBS was to identify alternative ways of spending money to achieve defense objectives and to choose the most cost efficient of these alternatives in designing budgets.[53] In 1965 President Johnson extended the PPBS system to cover domestic as well as national security programs. Career bureaucrats were obliged to defer to White House leadership and take instruction from management experts drawn from the Rand Corporation and other nongovernment organizations in establishing the PPBS system throughout the government.

Three changes thus took place in budgeting that typified larger shifts occurring throughout the public bureaucracy in the postwar era: (1) the influence of career bureaucrats crested in the 1940s and 1950s and then began to recede; (2) power moved gradually but inexorably from the bureaucratic experts to the political appointees at the White House and the command posts of executive agencies; (3) experts from outside the government began to play an increasingly important role in executive decision making. As a result, senior career officials found themselves fighting a losing battle on two fronts. They were increasingly shunted aside by the president's men and women who came to power every four years, and they found their professional expertise challenged by the expanding role that experts drawn from outside the government began to play in policy development.

Changes in the process for selecting bureaucratic personnel came much more slowly in the postwar period than did changes in either organization or budgeting. Neither the president nor Congress wanted to give rise to any suspicion of tampering with the highly cherished merit system, although this nineteenth-century reform had come under increasing criticism after World War II. Chief among the complaints from both sides of the political aisle was the charge that the merit system extended so far into the upper ranks of bureaucracy and provided career civil servants with so much job security that government executives appointed by the president could not wield effective control over the work of their own organizations. The dissatisfaction of political executives with the operation of the merit principle was particularly strong when it required them to retain in high-level positions career bureaucrats whom they distrusted.

The election of Dwight Eisenhower in 1952 brought this discontent to a head. Eisenhower was the first Republican president since 1932. There was widespread fear in Republican ranks that a New Deal bureaucracy created and nurtured under Democratic presidents would have difficulty accepting Republican efforts to steer national policy in somewhat different directions. Hence Eisenhower introduced a new category of political appointees (schedule C) into the civil service system to reinforce political control over the career staff. Coincidentally, this Eisenhower innovation also served to mollify disgruntled Republicans, whose efforts to gain access to public employment after twenty years in the political wilderness were impeded by civil service regulations.[54]

When the next Republican president, Richard Nixon, came to the White House in 1969, he confronted not only the New Deal bureaucracy he had known during his eight-year service as vice-president under Eisenhower, but also a host of new programs and activities that President Lyndon Johnson had initiated between 1964 and 1968 in pursuit of his Great Society objectives. Nixon, whose suspicion of bureaucracy had occasionally surfaced during his vice-presidential years, found himself presiding over a bureaucratic establishment even more thoroughly "Democratized" than Eisenhower's had been.[55]

The Nixon White House adopted a two-fold strategy for dealing with a bureaucracy it regarded as having dubious loyalties. First, it centered control over major policy decisions in the White House rather than the executive departments. Even cabinet officials found themselves relegated to carrying out rather than initiating policy proposals in their own areas of administrative responsibility. Second, through General Revenue Sharing and in other ways, the administration shifted power from national agencies to their state and local counterparts. Nixon thus aimed to trim the role of the national bureaucracy through techniques of both centralization and decentralization.

As far as the civil service system itself was concerned, the Nixon White House both evaded and used its regulations to encourage the departure of civil servants it regarded as untrustworthy. This was the legendary "Malik plan" for dealing with troublesome civil servants who might oppose efforts by the Nixon White House to shape the direction of executive policy.[56] Although Nixon officials made no secret of their dislike for the way the merit system operated and their belief that it impeded the president's ability to carry out his election "mandate," the Republicans were too weak in Congress for Nixon to take any serious steps toward legislative reform of the procedures he found objectionable.

It was the election of a Democrat, Jimmy Carter, as president in 1976 that brought the postwar period's only comprehensive effort to reform the civil service system. Investing in this goal far more political capital than most presidents would have thought expedient, Carter finally succeeded in pushing through Congress the Civil Service Reform Act of 1978. A major purpose of this reform legislation was to enable agency executives to use financial sanctions as a means of increasing their control over subordinates in their own organizations.[57]

But the new law also had one characteristic in common with earlier attempts at both organizational and budgetary reform—it tended to make the bureaucracy a more pliable instrument of presidential power. One of the changes the new reform act wrought was the elimination of the three-member bipartisan Civil Service Commission that had run the merit system since its establishment in 1883. It was replaced by an Office of Personnel Management (OPM), whose director was appointed by the president.

When the Reagan administration took office in 1981, it was able to use OPM as a vehicle for asserting far more control over personnel policies than any previous administration had tried to achieve. The way this power was employed generated widespread resentment within the career civil service. When the one hundredth anniversary of the signing of the Pendleton Act dawned on 16 January 1983, its goal of establishing a career civil service system based on the merit principle was widely viewed as being in jeopardy. This was especially true among the union organizations representing government employees, which charged that under the guise of civil service reform politics was being reintroduced into personnel decisions.[58]

Up until World War II, one area of bureaucracy that had remained largely outside the presidential orbit was the territory occupied by the independent regulatory commissions. These commissions, which oversee the decisions of business firms in such strategic sectors of the American economy as energy, transportation, banking, and communications, had all been granted a highly autonomous status by statute, and their independence had been confirmed by a celebrated Supreme Court decision in 1935, overruling President Roosevelt's attempt to bring the Federal Trade Commission under tighter White House control.[59]

Not long after the Humphrey decision, the independent position of these regulatory bodies was denounced by the Brownlow Commission, a group of administrative experts appointed by Franklin

Roosevelt to study and make recommendations for improving the organization and management of the executive branch. Reporting in 1937, the Brownlow Commission charged that these independent regulatory agencies were "a headless 'fourth branch' of the government, a haphazard deposit of irresponsible agencies and uncoordinated powers."[60] Its chief remedy for the ills it described was to give the president greater influence over the policymaking functions of the independent regulatory agencies.

Congress did not take kindly to the Brownlow Commission's recommendations regarding regulatory agencies. In fact, it exempted many of these agencies from any reorganization plan drawn up by Roosevelt, when it granted him authority to carry out the recommendations of the Brownlow report.[61] In the years following World War II, however, the legislative mood changed. Congress began to approve presidentially initiated reorganization plans that greatly strengthened White House influence over these agencies. Noteworthy in this respect was a series of postwar reorganization plans that allowed the president to designate the chairmen of various commissions. Thereafter, these chairmen came to be regarded as the president's representatives on the commissions, and the officials to whom the other members looked for leadership. As a result, the policies of the commissions increasingly reflected White House needs and preferences. While retaining their independent legal status, the commissions certainly did not play the maverick role within the executive establishment in the postwar period that the Brownlow Commission had attributed to them in 1937.[62]

Since the 1970s other major developments have altered the status of the independent regulatory commissions to the president's advantage. With wide political support, deregulation has now become the order of the day in the federal government. Under Democrat Jimmy Carter and Republican Ronald Reagan strenuous efforts have been made to free many areas of economic activity from the administrative regulation to which they have long been subject. Competition in the marketplace is now expected to provide consumers with the low prices and efficient services that administrative regulation was once designed to achieve.[63]

The strongest initial thrust toward deregulation came in air transportation. Here, as in other areas where it has occurred, deregulation emerged as an issue on which liberals and conservatives could agree, though for quite different reasons. Liberals like Senator Edward Kennedy of Massachusetts saw deregulation in this sector of the economy as a means of lowering fares and increasing the availability of airline services for all travelers. Airline deregulation thus became a "consumer issue" for liberals, a reflection of their growing belief that a great deal of traditional regulation had actually served the interests of the industry being regulated rather than the consumers it was supposed to protect.

For conservatives, on the other hand, deregulation was more likely to be supported because it "got government off the back of business" and restored the integrity of the free enterprise system. In the case of the airline industry the net result of this unusual alliance was a removal of government controls over air fares, encouragement for new firms to enter the industry, and an opportunity for all airlines to provide transportation in whatever market areas they chose to fly. There has also been bipartisan support across ideological and partisan lines for deregulation in other areas of economic activity, including banking, telecommunications, and trucking transportation.

The political consensus that emerged to sustain the deregulatory movement was confined, however, to the sphere of economic regulation where the government supervised particular industries — sometimes, as in the case of telecommunications, at their own request. It had been pressure from the communications industry that led Congress to establish the Federal Radio Commission in 1925 and its successor agency, the Federal Communications Commission, in 1933.[64] Where such economic regulation did not come at the request of the industry targeted, critics nonetheless complained that the industry controlled the way regulation was carried on. The specter of the "captive agency" has loomed large in postwar criticism of the ineffectiveness of regulatory administration.

But even as a consensus has been formed in support of deregulation in the older spheres of government intervention in the economy, a widespread demand has also emerged in the postwar era for new forms of social regulation.[65] Regulatory agencies have been established to protect the environment, to prevent racial or other forms of discrimination, to safeguard the consumer from injurious foods or drugs, and to eliminate hazards to workers' health and safety. Political support for this newer kind of social regulation is almost as broad as that sustaining deregulation in the economic sector. Of course criticism has been leveled at the length to which such regulation is sometimes carried. Environmental protection groups, for example, have been charged with helping to raise prices and reduce employment in the automobile industry. The White House has made strong efforts, especially during the Reagan administration, to force all regulatory organizations to consider costs as well as benefits before putting new rules into effect.

But these reservations aside, support for such forms of social regulation as environmental and consumer protection runs strong and deep in American society—as Sam Hays made clear earlier in this book. Even the Reagan administration, which made fervent rhetorical and symbolic assaults on social regulation in the early days after it took office, was forced to retreat from this stance in 1983. The two Reagan officials environmental groups regarded as most hostile to their cause were both forced to resign—Secretary of the Interior James Watt and EPA administrator Anne Burford. Each was charged with following policies injurious to the environment. Public fear of the dangers posed by toxic waste or by accidents at nuclear power plants (as occurred at Three Mile Island in Pennsylvania during the Carter administration) provides a firm political underpinning for wide areas of social regulation. Any contemporary administration that takes this fear lightly does so at great risk to itself.

A political consensus has thus emerged in the Postwar period supporting two policies going in opposite directions in the regulatory field. It favors the deregulation of traditional areas of government economic intervention while remaining thoroughly committed to a strong network of newer kinds of social regulation. The deregulatory movement has weakened many of the old-line regulatory agencies that had long followed policies the White House found objectionable. These agencies often took a protective attitude toward the industries they regulated, awarding price increases to business firms under their jurisdiction even as the White House was making strenuous efforts to control an upward spiral in prices.

The arrival of social regulation has also strengthened White House influence in the regulatory field. Under arrangements initiated by President Ford and subsequently followed by Presidents Carter and Reagan, regulatory agencies are now required to clear all new rules with OMB before putting them into effect. As part of the clearance process, these agencies must show that the benefits of any proposed regulation will exceed its costs. This new White House monitoring system has extended presidential influence over administrative decision making into areas it had never before penetrated.[66]

The one regulatory agency that has best withstood White House encroachment into its sphere of authority is the Federal Reserve Board. Perhaps the chief reason it has done so is because the White House needs an instrumentality like the FRB to manage the money supply in ways that are certain to arouse strong political criticism, particularly when the board follows tight money policies that have a negative impact on credit dependent industries and unemployment begins to soar. Of course, as close observers of the board have long pointed out, the agency takes care to avoid policies that are grossly detrimental to presidential interests, especially during election years. This is a theme that Heywood Fleisig's essay in this volume has developed very fully. Ever since 1951, when the board escaped the domination of the Treasury Department, it has preserved its autonomy by following a strategy of "Finlandization" — doing nothing to which its powerful political neighbors in Congress and the White House might strongly object.[67]

The chief area in which presidents did not push for or benefit from bureaucratic reform in the postwar period was the field of disclosure of information about the government. As a matter of fact, in the decade after the war the White House did much to create the problem at which reform efforts were eventually to be directed. Presidents Truman and Eisenhower led the way in promoting a substantial expansion in government secrecy in the United States, although this country had historically prided itself on having a very "open" political system. This growth in secrecy was the product of a number of factors, not least the growth of government itself, which generated a need to protect the privacy of information that came into official custody about the people who worked for public agencies and the citizens they served or regulated.[68]

But the most striking development dictating an expansion in government secrecy in the postwar era was the explosive war-triggered growth of military secrets. The atomic bomb, a weapon born and built in secrecy, was a vivid symbol of both the necessity and the value of concealing military information. Beginning with President Truman, the White House developed an elaborate system for classifying and concealing defense-related materials in the hands of the government. President Eisenhower initiated the practice of claiming the shield of "executive privilege" for information regarding White House activities. The growth of secrecy in the postwar development of American national government was thus a product of pressure from presidential as well as bureaucratic sources.[69]

By the late 1950s, however, a backlash developed against the wide range of secretive practices that had emerged within the executive branch. Congress held lengthy hearings at which it was revealed that secrecy was often used to hide inefficient or illegal behavior on the part of executive officials. The media of communications, acting as a lobby for the "people's right to know," pressed very strongly for remedial legislation, and Congress eventually enacted a freedom of information law in 1965. This statute restricted the ability of executive officials to withhold information, although it still recognized that there were a number of situations in which executive secrecy might be justified. Certain categories of information, such as military or trade secrets, were given protection from disclosure under the new law.

As it was actually administered, the 1965 Freedom of Information Act came to be regarded by reformers in Congress and the media as a shield for secrecy rather than a weapon for promoting disclosure. The nine exemptions in the law permitting agencies to withhold information proved in fact to provide legal underpinning for a continuation of bureaucratic secrecy. Misgivings about the law's effectiveness were magnified during the Nixon administration, when the disclosure of the Pentagon papers revealed how much executive officials had concealed from the public about the conduct of the Vietnam War during Lyndon Johnson's presidency.

Thereafter, the Nixon administration brought the use of executive secrecy to a dramatic climax during the Watergate affair, when White House bureaucrats, and eventually the president himself, became entangled in the webs of intrigue they had secretly spun. One of the major consequences of Watergate was the enactment of a greatly strengthened freedom of information statute, which became law in 1974 after Congress had overridden President Ford's veto. The new law greatly broadened the availability of information in government files to ordinary citizens and simplified the procedures that had to be followed in order to obtain it.

Not all reform groups have been happy with the way the 1974 law works. Journalists, for example, complain that though they were at the forefront of the political coalition supporting this legislation, they have benefited very little from it. Pressed by deadlines, reporters need speedier access to stories than freedom of information legislation provides. Nevertheless, public interest groups have made good use of the statute in the constant surveillance they maintain over the activities of regulatory agencies. All agencies now carry on a substantial freedom of information operation, including some organizations that were at the forefront of opposition to the new legislation, like the FBI, the CIA, and the Pentagon. Tens of thousands of pages of material are released each year in response to freedom of information requests from business and nonprofit organizations as well as individual citizens.[70]

The presidents have had to be dragged along this particular path of reform. The original legislation in 1965 was kept as weak as it was because of the general understanding that a stronger law would be vetoed by President Johnson. Nixon was certainly the most vehement of all presidents in openly defending the practice of executive secrecy. He associated it with a major success in his administration — ending the Vietnam conflict and securing the release of the American prisoners of war. As noted earlier, Ford vetoed the 1974 act, and more recently Ronald Reagan has issued proposals for strengthening the protection afforded defense information by the classification system.

Clearly, therefore, information practices is one area of administration in which presidents have looked upon bureaucratic reform with a jaundiced eye. Yet in spite of this presidential resistance, a substantial amount of reform has actually taken place. Thus, although the White House has exerted enormous influence over bureaucratic developments since World War II, other forces have also had a substantial impact in bringing about the changes that have taken place in America's bureaucratic state.

The most important of these forces in the case of information practices has been the expanding power of the media in modern American politics—a power that presidents often regard as equal to their own. Open government has been a fundamental article of faith for the media, and the enactment of freedom of information legislation largely results from their commitment to this faith. Allied with the media in supporting "sunshine" laws have been the public interest groups that have also become an increasingly important force in American politics. Free access to government information is high on the agenda of groups like Common Cause and the Nader organization.[71]

The influence of this freedom of information lobby over bureaucratic change has been manifest not only during the administrations of weak presidents (as in 1974 when it induced Congress to override Gerald Ford's veto of a newly enacted disclosure law), but during the terms of strong presidents as well. In 1966 it put Lyndon Johnson in the position of having to sign a freedom of information law for which he personally had no enthusiasm. In 1984 its opposition forced Ronald Reagan to rescind a directive that would have bound executive officials handling defense information to secrecy not only during their government service but for years thereafter.

AMERICAN BUREAUCRACY IN 1984

It was when the Pendleton Act was passed by Congress and signed by the president in 1883 that America first embarked on the great experiment of creating a nonelected governing class of bureaucrats who would draw their power not from the outcome of popular elections but from their own expertise and professional training. The Pendleton Act did not, of course, create a bureaucracy where none had existed before. From the first days of the American republic, a growing number of permanent clerks had carried on the everyday tasks of the national government. However, the Pendleton Act gave legal recognition to the fact that the work of these employees required special skills and that the country Americans regarded as the world's greatest democracy would now be governed by many officials over whom the public had little direct control.[72]

Through the years the small sector of government covered by the original merit system requirements of the Pendleton Act steadily expanded in both size and influence. At the end of World War II nearly all employees of the federal government were hired, promoted, and fired under some variant of the merit system, and virtually no sector of American life was left untouched by the influence or the intrusion of this career bureaucracy. Political leaders from both major political parties vied with each other in proclaiming their devotion to the merit principle and their commitment to keeping politics out of the bureaucracy.

In the decades that have elapsed since World War II, significant changes have taken place in this government system. Before the war the push was all toward isolating the bureaucracy from the political sphere — allowing government agencies more and more autonomy and permitting individual bureaucrats to exercise a broad range of power on their own authority. Since the war, emphasis has been placed instead on maintaining or restoring political control over the bureaucracy. Both the presidents and Congress have made determined efforts to regain powers that they believe have either been ceded to or seized by the bureaucracy. The prewar movement toward depoliticizing the bureaucracy has been supplanted in the postwar years by a growing effort in the United States to recapture a bureaucratic apparatus that political leaders perceived as having spun completely out of control.

As noted earlier, the impetus for much of this shift in perspective came from the White House, which was eager to establish its own hegemony within the executive branch. The White House saw the independent position of many administrative agencies as a threat to its preeminence. From Truman to Reagan the trend is unmistakable. The number of political appointees at the top of each executive agency has grown substantially, while career bureaucrats have found themselves excluded more and more from major policy deliberations.

This change in the character of its relations with the bureaucracy has also been a source of change in the presidency itself. Increasingly, each president has found himself sharing power with other White House officials in ways that the Constitution certainly did not anticipate. The presidency has become virtually a collegial body — an institutional arrangement that the framers of the Constitution had considered and explicitly rejected. Of course, the need to control the bureaucracy was not the only factor bringing about this pluralization of the presidency. The lengthening policy agenda of the White House in the postwar years generated the need for a complex presidential advisory apparatus, which often dominated as much as it informed presidential decision making. But the responsibility for overseeing the myriad programs and activities of the executive branch was certainly a major force behind the growth of the White House staff and the transformation of the presidency into an office in which many men and women now share in the exercise of power.[73]

Similar trends have been visible in the case of Congress. Increasingly since World War II, legislators have sought in a variety of ways to augment their ability to monitor and control bureaucratic decision making. Inevitably this has led to a very substantial expansion in the size and influence of the legislative staff as Congress has sought help in its effort to play its oversight role effectively. Several permanent legislative staff organizations have been established, including the Congressional Research Service, the Congressional Budget Office, and the Office of Technology Assessment. The General Accounting Office has been modernized, and its review functions have become more sophisticated. The staffs of individual legislators and congressional committees have also been strengthened. As a result Congress, like the presidency, has found itself becoming bureaucratized by the necessity of dealing with a wide range of executive agencies whose programs it creates and whose activities it must thereafter police.[74]

Moreover, in a study of the increasing value of incumbency in congressional elections, Morris Fiorina traces the advantage of sitting legislators to the fact that an ever-expanding bureaucratic apparatus provides members of Congress with abundant opportunities to serve their constituents by intervening in their behalf with government agencies. Thus its interaction with the executive bureaucracy not only has had the effect of bureaucratizing Congress but has also helped to reduce legislative turnover and to make casework for constituents a constant legislative preoccupation. As Fiorina puts it: "The nice thing about case work is that it is mostly profit; one makes many more friends than enemies. In fact, some congressmen undoubtedly stimulate the demand for their bureaucratic fixit services."[75]

Thus in similar and significant ways both the presidency and Congress have been changed by the rise of a large and complex executive bureaucracy, and a persuasive argument can certainly be made that neither institution has actually lost any power to the bureaucracy during this period. What has happened instead is that each institution has used its interaction with the bureaucracy to augment its own power.

This resurgence of political control over bureaucracy has been a major development in the postwar period. These years have also seen a parallel trend in the legal sector as the courts have become increasingly involved in administrative decision making. Following the enactment of the Administrative Procedures Act of 1946, which settled some long-standing border disputes between the courts and bureaucracy, the judiciary accepted an arrangement under which judges would defer to the expertise of bureaucrats whenever their decisions came before the courts for review. This deference was based on the judicial presumption that agencies knew more about the subjects they dealt with than the courts, and as long as their decisions were not in violation of any well-established principle of law, the findings and conclusions of bureaucrats should be accorded judicial respect.

In recent years, however, the courts have shown a much greater willingness to challenge administrative decisions and to substitute their own judgment for that of bureaucrats. One factor contributing to this shift in perspective was a growing recognition by judges that bureaucratic expertise in many areas fell somewhere short of infallibility; the experts often disagreed, leaving the courts no option but to reconcile such disputes. Many judges also came to believe that judicial intervention was frequently necessary to protect the fundamental constitutional rights of individuals aggrieved by the rulings of some administrative body.

Judicial concern was particularly evident in the case of individuals who have been described as "captives of the administrative state" — inmates of prisons or mental institutions who, in the absence of judicial intervention, might be entirely at the mercy of some administrative agency.[76] Critics of this form of judicial intervention have sometimes charged the courts with being more arbitrary in the use of their power than the administrative agencies whose decisions they are overruling. In effect, it has been said, the courts have created a "jurocracy" every bit as overbearing in the use of its power as bureaucracy is traditionally alleged to be.[77]

Regardless of how one evaluates the "jurocracy," these developments provide abundant evidence that each of the traditional institutions of American government — the courts, the presidency, Congress — has taken strong and effective measures to contain the power of bureaucracy in postwar America. Yet fear of bureaucracy and antagonism toward it continued to grow, reaching a climax in the late 1970s. It was then that the deregulatory movement began its successful assault on the powers of regulatory agencies, and taxpayer revolts throughout the country, most notably the movement in support of Proposition 13 in California, signaled the depths of public dislike for bureaucracy and all its work.[78] Attacks on bureaucracy also played a prominent role in presidential campaigns at this time. Both Jimmy Carter in 1976 and Ronald Reagan in 1980 featured such attacks in their successful quests for the presidency.

Herbert Kaufman has described the fear of bureaucracy that prevailed during these years as a "raging pandemic."[79] Fear there certainly was, but there was also something else — a growing disrespect for the capacity of bureaucracy to achieve anything in the way of effective results. The traditionally negative attitude toward bureaucracy in Western societies had been based on the belief that it was too strong — that its power would soon override the limits imposed on any constitutional government. Now, increasingly, complaints came to be focused instead upon the weakness of bureaucracy, upon its inability to meet the expectations of citizens regarding many of the activities it carried on, especially the social programs inaugurated as part of Lyndon Johnson's War on Poverty in the 1960s. Neoconservatives, in particular, were relentless in criticizing these programs as incapable of achieving the results their sponsors had confidently promised.[80] For real expertise Americans tended more and more to look to the private rather than the public sector.

Moreover, organizations in the national bureaucracy were increasingly seen as captives of special interests — representing the few at the expense of the many. In the earlier part of this century, especially during the Progressive Era, executive agencies were commonly perceived as being established to promote the public interest — their mission was to protect the welfare of the disadvantaged majority (so to speak), which was being victimized by unscrupulous corporations or other predatory forces. Now, increasingly, such agencies are seen not as acting in behalf of the public at large, but as serving the selfish goals of powerful groups within American society. In the eyes of its critics, bureaucracy had become merely another embodiment of the spirit of faction against which James Madison had so eloquently warned in the *Federalist Papers*. Joseph Califano, who had served as President Carter's secretary of health, education, and welfare, complained about his service in bureaucracy in precisely these terms: "What's pernicious is that the Government, which should be weighing these special interests in light of the national interest, is not doing that. It has created a whole series of special interest bureaus. And that's bad for our society."[81]

But in spite of this criticism and disappointment, bureaucracy has continued its relentless growth in postwar America. This was true under presidents like Lyndon Johnson, whose Great Society goals could be realized only through government programs. It was also characteristic of the presidency of Richard M. Nixon, whose whole political career was marked by an antagonism toward government and particularly toward bureaucracy. Nixon's tenure in office saw the creation of such powerful new bureaucracies as the Environmental Protection Agency, the Occupational Safety and Health Administration, and in the White House itself, the Office of Telecommunications Policy.

Both the friends and the enemies of bureaucracy have thus contributed to its expansion. As noted earlier, this postwar growth of national bureaucracy would have been even greater save for the Johnson administration's strategy of using state and local agencies to carry out Great Society programs. So if postwar history suggests that there was little basis for earlier fears that the bureaucracy would become all powerful in the United States, it also testifies to the inevitability of this bureaucracy in modern America, no matter how far its popularity may sink or its power decline.

Notes

By Way of Introduction

1. Harold Seidman, "Crisis of Confidence in Government," *Political Quarterly* 43 (January-March 1972): 82–83.

2. Harvey C. Mansfield, "Federal Executive Reorganization: Thirty Years of Experience," *Public Administration Review* 29 (July-August 1969): 332–45; Harold Seidman, *Politics, Position and Power* (London: Oxford University Press, 1975); Ronald C. Moe, "The Two Hoover Commissions in Retrospect," *Congressional Research Service Report*, 82-14 Gov, 12 March 1982.

3. Peri Arnold, "The First Hoover Commission and the Managerial Presidency," *Journal of Politics* 38 (February 1976): 46–70.

4. Mansfield, "Federal Executive Reorganization"; Douglas M. Fox, "The President's Proposals for Executive Reorganization: A Critique," *Public Administration Review* 33 (September-October 1973): 401–6; see also Marver H. Bernstein, "The Presidency and Management Improvement," *Law and Contemporary Problems* 35 (1970): 505–18.

5. Richard P. Nathan, *The Plot That Failed: Nixon and the Administrative Presidency* (New York: John Wiley, 1975); Hugh Heclo, "OMB and the Presidency — the Problem of 'Neutral Competence,'" *Public Interest* 38 (Winter 1975): 80–98.

6. Hugh Heclo, "The State and America's Higher Civil Service," manuscript, 1982 (available from the author); see also the same author's *A Government of Strangers: Executive Politics in Washington* (Washington, D.C.: Brookings Institution, 1977), esp. pp. 240ff.

7. For convenient summaries see Martin Albro, *Bureaucracy* (New York: Praeger, 1970), and Francis E. Rourke, *Bureaucracy, Politics, and Public Policy*, 2d ed. (Boston: Little, Brown, 1976).

8. Steven Skowronek, *Building a New American State: The Expansion of National Administrative Capacities, 1877-1920* (New York: Cambridge University Press, 1982), pp. 19–46.

9. See, for instance, Robert D. Cuff, "American Historians and the 'Organizational Factor,'" *Canadian Review of American Studies* 4 (Spring 1973): 19–31; and Robert F. Beckhofer, Jr., "The Organizational Interpretation of American History: A New Synthesis," *Prospects* 4 (1979): 611–29. I have discussed the literature in Louis Galambos, "The Emerging Organizational Synthesis in Modern American History," *Business History Review* 44 (Autumn 1970): 279–90, and "Technology,

Political Economy, and Professionalization: Central Themes of the Organizational Synthesis," *Business History Review* 57 (Winter 1983): 471–93.

10. See Galambos, "Technology," pp. 485–91.

11. Lloyd Ulman, *The Rise of the National Trade Union*, 2d ed. (Cambridge: Harvard University Press, 1955).

12. See Robert E. Kohler, *From Medical Chemistry to Biochemistry: The Making of a Biochemical Discipline* (New York: Cambridge University Press, 1982).

13. See, for example, Alfred D. Chandler, Jr., *Strategy and Structure: Chapters in the History of the Industrial Enterprise* (Cambridge: MIT Press, 1962); and idem, *The Visible Hand: The Managerial Revolution in American Business* (Cambridge: Harvard University Press, 1977).

14. See, for illustration, Richard Hofstadter, *The Progressive Historians* (New York: Random House, 1970); Samuel P. Hays, "The Social Analysis of American Political History," *Political Science Quarterly* 80 (September 1965): 373–94; Allen J. Matusow, *The Unraveling of America: A History of Liberalism in the 1960s* (New York: Harper and Row, 1984).

15. See, for example, Ellis W. Hawley's work, including *Herbert Hoover as Secretary of Commerce, 1921–1928: Studies in New Era Thought and Practice* (Iowa City: University of Iowa Press, 1981), and his "Three Facets of Hooverian Associationalism: Lumber, Aviation, and Movies, 1921–1930," in *Regulation in Perspective: Historical Essays*, ed. Thomas K. McCraw (Cambridge: Harvard University Press, 1981), pp. 95–123. See also Guy Alchon, *The Invisible Hand of Planning: Capitalism, Social Science, and the State in the 1920s* (Princeton: Princeton University Press, 1985); and Robert Griffith, "Dwight D. Eisenhower and the Corporate Commonwealth," *American Historical Review* 87 (February 1982): 87–122.

16. Skowronek, *Building a New American State*.

17. I have discussed this theme in Louis Galambos and Barbara Spence, *The Public Image of Big Business in America, 1880–1940: A Quantitative Study in Social Change* (Baltimore: Johns Hopkins University Press, 1975).

18. Marver H. Bernstein, *Regulating Business by Independent Commission* (Princeton: Princeton University Press, 1955; reprinted Westport, Conn.: Greenwood, 1977).

19. See, Heclo, *Government of Strangers*, esp. pp. 116ff.; and Herbert Kaufman, *The Administrative Behavior of Federal Bureau Chiefs* (Washington D.C.: Brookings Institution, 1981), pp. 1–3.

20. Heclo, "State and America's Higher Civil Service."

21. See Carolyn L. Weaver, *The Crisis in Social Security: Economic and Political Origins* (Durham: Duke University Press, 1982); Brian Balogh, "Securing Support: The Emergence of the Social Security Board as a Political Actor, 1935–1939," manuscript, 1983 (available from the author).

22. Louis Galambos, *America at Middle Age: A New History of the United States in the Twentieth Century* (New York: McGraw-Hill, 1982), pp. 51–68.

23. Herbert Kaufman, *Are Government Organizations Immortal?* (Washington D.C.: Brookings Institution, 1976).

24. Hugh Heclo, "Issue Networks and the Executive Establishment," in *The New American Political System*, ed. Anthony King, (Washington, D.C.: American Enterprise, 1978), pp. 90–93.

25. Christopher L. Tomlins, *The State and the Unions: Labor Relations, Law and the Organized Labor Movement in America, 1880–1960* (New York: Cambridge University Press, 1985), pp. 148–281.

26. Heclo, "Issue Networks and the Executive Establishment."

27. This was particularly true in Congress; see Samuel C. Patterson, "The Semi-Sovereign Congress," in *The New American Political System*, ed. Anthony King, pp. 125–77.

28. This aspect of bureaucracy is critically examined in Anthony Downs, *Inside Bureaucracy* (Boston: Little, Brown, 1966).

29. Max Weber, *The Theory of Social and Economic Organization* (Glencoe, Ill.: Free Press, 1977), pp. 329–34.

30. Numerous studies have stressed the variability of bureaucratic behavior: see, for example, Peter Blau, *The Dynamics of Bureaucracy: A Study of Interpersonal Relations in Two Government Agencies*, 2d ed. (Chicago: University of Chicago Press, 1973); Seidman, *Politics, Position and Power*; and James Q. Wilson, ed., *The Politics of Regulation* (New York: Basic Books, 1980).

THE POLITICS OF ENVIRONMENTAL ADMINISTRATION

1. For a more extended version of this argument see Samuel P. Hays, "Political Choice in Regulatory Administration," in *Regulation in Perspective*, ed. Thomas K. McCraw (Cambridge: Harvard University Press, 1981), pp. 124–54. In the words of a recent analyst, "The bureaucracy and its organized clienteles are surely the most durable components of the policy process." See John Edward Chubb, "Interest Groups and the Bureaucracy: The Politics of Energy" (Ph.D. diss. University of Minnesota, 1979), p. 21.

2. This argument has been expressed most extensively by the concept of "corporate liberalism" in such works as Gabriel Kolko, *The Triumph of Conservatism: A Reinterpretation of American History, 1900–1916* (New York: Free Press, 1963), and James Weinstein, *The Corporate Ideal in the Liberal State, 1900–1918* (Boston: Beacon Press, 1968).

3. See, for example, Louis Galambos, *Competition and Cooperation: The Emergence of a National Trade Association* (Baltimore: Johns Hopkins University Press, 1966).

4. For an account of the way the corporate model was followed in early twentieth-century municipal government reform see Samuel P. Hays, "The Politics of Reform in Municipal Government in the Progressive Era," *Pacific Northwest Quarterly* 55 (1964): 157–69.

5. Two studies that elaborate this process in detail are Michael E. Parrish, *Securities Regulation and the New Deal* (New Haven: Yale University Press, 1970), and Stanley P. Caine, *The Myth of a Progressive Reform: Railroad Regulation in Wisconsin, 1903–1910* (Madison: State Historical Society of Wisconsin, 1970).

6. For an extended argument in this vein see Samuel P. Hays, "The Structure of Environmental Politics since World War II," *Journal of Social History* 14, no. 4 (1981): 719–38.

7. A more elaborate analysis of value change and environmental affairs is Samuel P. Hays, "From Conservation to Environment: Environmental Politics in the United States since World War Two," *Environmental Review* 6, no. 2 (1982): 14–41.

8. For two specialized studies see Stephen R. Kellert, *American Attitudes, Knowledge and Behaviors toward Wildlife and Natural Habitats* (Washington, D.C.: U.S. Fish and Wildlife Service, 1978–80), and Opinion Research Corporation, *The Public's Participation in Outdoor Activities and Attitudes toward Na-*

tional Wilderness Areas (Princeton: Opinion Research Corporation, Caravan Surveys, 1977). A more recent study is Continental Group, *Toward Responsible Growth: Economic and Environmental Concern in the Balance* (Stamford, Conn.: Continental Group, 1982).

9. Two items pertaining to evolving consumption patterns in the 1930s are the number of households with radio sets, which rose between 1929 and 1939 from 10,250,000 to 27,500,000, and the growth of visits to national parks during the same decade, which rose from 3,248,000 to 15,531,000. See U.S. Department of Commerce, Bureau of the Census, *Historical Statistics of the United States* (Washington, D.C.: Government Printing Office, 1975), ser. H 808, R104.

10. For a more extended account see items in notes 1 and 7.

11. Marver H. Bernstein, *Regulating Business by Independent Commission* (Princeton: Princeton University Press, 1955; reprinted Westport, Conn.: Greenwood, 1977).

12. The best-known writings are by the Nader group. See James S. Turner, *The Chemical Feast* (New York: Viking Press, 1970); Edward Finch Cox, *The Nader Report on the Federal Trade Commission* (New York: R. W. Baron, 1969); Ralph Nader, *Unsafe at Any Speed* (New York: Grossman, 1965); Ralph Nader, comp., *The Consumer and Corporate Accountability* (New York: Harcourt, Brace, 1973).

13. Michael Frome, *The Forest Service* (New York: Praeger, 1971); Harold K. Steen, *The U.S. Forest Service* (Seattle: University of Washington Press, 1976).

14. D. Harper Simms, *The Soil Conservation Service* (New York: Praeger, 1970).

15. Marion Clawson, *The Bureau of Land Management* (New York: Praeger, 1971); William Voigt, Jr., *Public Grazing Lands: Use and Misuse by Industry and Government* (New Brunswick, N.J.: Rutgers University Press, 1976); Phillip O. Foss, *Politics and Grass: The Administration of Grazing on the Public Domain* (Seattle: University of Washington Press, 1960; reprinted Westport, Conn.: Greenwood, 1975).

16. This theme is developed further in Samuel P. Hays, *Conservation and the Gospel of Efficiency* (Cambridge: Harvard University Press, 1959).

17. A recent account of the wilderness movement is Craig W. Allin, *The Politics of Wilderness Preservation* (Westport, Conn.: Greenwood, 1982).

18. The attack on stream channelization can be followed most fully in U.S. House of Representatives, Committee on Government Operations, *Stream Channelization* (4 parts), 92d Cong., 1st sess. (Washington, D.C.: Government Printing Office, 1971).

19. A running account of land use issues within the Bureau of Land Management from an environmental point of view can be found in *PLI Newsletter*, published by the Public Lands Institute (Denver, and Washington, D.C., 1978–).

20. For a running account of such issues see *American Rivers*, quarterly publication of the American Rivers Conservation Council (Washington D.C.; 1973-).

21. William Ashworth, *Hells Canyon: The Deepest Gorge on Earth* (New York: Hawthorne Books, 1977).

22. The best account of this "response" involves a study of the U.S. Forest Service; see Ben W. Twight, *Organizational Values and Political Power: The Forest Service versus the Olympic National Park* (University Park: Pennsylvania State University Press, 1983).

23. See William C. Everhart, *The National Park Service* (New York: Praeger, 1972); Alfred Runte, *National Parks: The American Experience* (Lincoln University of Nebraska Press, 1979).

24. For accounts of air quality policy see John C. Esposito, *Vanishing Air* (New York: Center for Responsive Law, 1970), and Richard J. Tobin, *The Social Gamble* (Lexington, Mass.: Lexington Books, 1979). For water quality see Harvey Lieber, *Federalism and Clean Waters* (Lexington, Mass.: Lexington Books, 1975). A useful introduction to both is Barbara S. Davies and J. Clarence Davies III, *The Politics of Pollution*, 2d ed. (New York: Pegasus, 1975).

25. For a general review of occupation health problems, including administrative agencies, see Nicholas A. Ashford, *Crisis in the Workplace: Occupational Disease and Injury* (Cambridge: MIT Press, 1976). The work of the Occupational Safety and Health Administration can be followed best in the two newsletters, *Occupational Health and Safety Letter* (Washington, D.C., 1970–), published by Gerson W. Fishbein, and *Occupational Health and Safety Recorder* (Washington, D.C., 1970–), published by the Bureau of National Affairs.

26. Coastal zone management has spawned an enormous literature, largely because of the extensive funds available for planning. Relevant affairs can be followed in *Coastal Zone Management Journal* (New York, 1974–) and the weekly newsletter, *Coastal Zone Management* (Washington, D.C., 1970–), published by Nautilus Press.

27. A major episode in this process was the dispute between the Office of Surface Mining and the Council of Economic Advisors concerning the economic impact of the new regulations. For CEA concerns, expressed via its Council on Wage and Price Stability, see "Report of the Regulatory Analysis Review Group Submitted by the Council on Wage and Price Stability, November 27, 1978, concerning Proposed Surface Coal Mining and Reclamation" (author file) and the resulting documents submitted for the record by the CEA indicating considerable reliance by the CEA on the regulated industry for the formulation of its views; these documents were submitted under the title "Compilation of Conversations and Correspondence on the Permanent Regulatory Program Implementing Section 501(b) of the Surface Mining Control and Reclamation Act of 1977" (author file). Events in the evolution of the surface mining program can be followed in *Environment Reporter*, 5 May, 1 and 15 September, 1978: *Washington Post*, 24 September 1978, 6, 7, 13, and 25 January 1979; *New York Times*, 4 December 1978, 7, 8, 14, and 31 January 1979; *Wall Street Journal*, 2 and 31 January 1979. See also author interview with William Eichbaum, former assistant solicitor, Department of the Interior, in charge of surface mining regulations, 22 May 1980. For an account of implementation from an environmental viewpoint see Carolyn R. Johnson, David S. May, and George W. Pring, *Stripping the Law on Coal: A Study of the Surface Mining Control and Reclamation Act by the U.S. Office of Surface Mining and the State Agencies in Colorado, New Mexico, North Dakota, Utah and Wyoming*, Public Lands Institute Report (Denver: Public Lands Institute, 1980).

28. Solar energy issues can be followed in *Solar Age* (Harrisville, N.H., 1976–), and *Solar Energy Intelligence Report* (Washington, D.C., 1976–).

29. Two convenient sources of information on this issue are *The New Farm* (Emmaus, Pa., 1979–) and *Organic Gardening and Farming* (Emmaus, Pa., 1942–). For the relevant official document see U.S. Department of Agriculture, "Report and Recommendations on Organic Agriculture," July 1980. Some insight into the political forces involved with reference to research strategies is in Don F. Hadwiger, *The Politics of Agricultural Research* (Lincoln: University of Nebraska Press, 1982).

30. These activities can be followed in several citizen group newsletters; for example, "International Report," published by the Sierra Club (San Francisco, 1973–83).

31. See Council on Environmental Quality, *Environmental Quality,* annual report published in 1971 and annually thereafter.

32. Theory involves influences from without and within the agencies. The former have dominated debate with arguments emphasizing crucial or limited influences of "interest groups." See Paul Culhane, *Public Land Politics* (Baltimore: Johns Hopkins University Press, 1981). The alternative view is well expressed by Twight, *Organizational Values and Political Power* (note 22 above).

33. Richard A. Liroff, *A National Policy for the Environment: NEPA and Its Aftermath* (Bloomington: Indiana University Press, 1976).

34. One, "208" planning under the 1972 Water Quality Act, can be followed in a volume especially prepared for citizens who sought to participate in the process. See Conservation Foundation, *Toward Clean Water: A Guide To Citizen Action* (Washington, D.C.: Conservation Foundation, 1976). Another, the "principles and standards" in national water planning, can be followed in Water Resources Council, "Water and Related Land Resources: Establishment of Principles and Standards for Planning," in *Federal Register,* 38–174, 10 September 1973, part 3.

35. Documents cited in note 27, "Compilation of Conversations and Correspondence," issued by the Council of Economic Advisors, represented a particularly crucial case in that they pertained to decision making in the Executive Office of the President (EOP) after the close of the administrative proceeding record in the Department of the Interior. While the documents in this particular case were made public, legal proceedings intended to extend that practice from the agency to the EOP level did not succeed. For a discussion of this problem see Gregory S. Wetstone, ed., "Meeting Record from Resolution of Scientific Issues and the Judicial Process: *Ethyl Corporation v. EPA,*" 21 October 1977, held under the auspices of the Environmental Law Institute (Washington, D.C., 1981), discussion on pp. 84ff., and especially discussion between Judges Skelly Wright and Harold Leventhal of the U.S. Court of Appeals, District of Columbia.

36. Andrew C. Gordon and John P. Heinz, eds., *Public Access to Information* (New Brunswick, N.J.: Transaction Books, 1973), esp. pp. 184–222.

37. Lettie M. Wenner, *The Environmental Decade in Court* (Bloomington: Indiana University Press, 1982); Frederick R. Anderson and Robert H. Daniels, *NEPA in the Courts: A Legal Analysis of the National Environmental Policy Act* (Baltimore: Johns Hopkins University Press, 1973). For activities of environmental groups see publications of the Sierra Club, *National News Report,* the Natural Resources Defense Council, *Newsletter,* and Environmental Defense Fund, *EDF Letter.*

38. This is my conclusion, drawn impressionistically rather than systematically, from reading a considerable number of environmental impact analyses, concerning especially forest, range, and national park management, water resources, and coal leasing.

39. See, for example, the dialogue between the parties in the dispute over EPA regulation of lead, in which all affirmed the importance of their own freedom to participate in decision making, in Wetstone, "Meeting Record from Resolution of Scientific Issues" (note 35).

40. For some general remarks on the useful role of the public in environmental administration, see reflections on his tenure as administrator of EPA by Russell Train, in *Conservation Foundation Letter* (Washington, D.C., January 1977). Train remarked, "I think it is clear that the citizen environmental movement has made possible the statutory authorities we now have and it is absolutely essential to keep a fire lit under the administrative agencies at all levels of government" (p. 8).

41. While public participation took place in many instances, one comprehensive example was water planning under section 208 of the 1972 Clean Water Act. In this planning in Pennsylvania, for example, carried out within ten regions of the state, there was a "public participation" coordinator at both state and regional levels, from whom planning documents could be readily secured. Environmental agencies often drew upon League of Women Voters staff for these positions.

42. See opposition of EPA, as well as other agencies to an expanded federal citizen suit bill in 1971; U.S. Senate, Committee on Commerce, *Environmental Protection Act of 1971*, hearings, 15–16 April 1971 (Washington, D.C.: Government Printing Office, 1971).

43. Industry reactions can be obtained from the pages of *Environment Reporter* during the months of late 1976 and early 1977 when the Carter appointments were being made; even more pointed are responses in trade magazines such as *Chemical Week, Coal Age,* and *Waterways Journal.*

44. For the evolution of regulatory politics during the Carter administration see "Regulatory Controversy: The Case of Health and Safety," conference with proceedings, 7–8 March 1980, Washington, D.C., cosponsored by the Progressive Alliance, the Environmental Law Institute, and the National Center for Policy Alternatives. An account of similar events during the Reagan administration is Robert Nelson, "A World of Preference: Business Access to Reagan's Regulators," Democracy Project Reports no. 5 (New York: Democracy Project, 1983).

45. Little has been written on the crucial "standards of proof" controversy. Some flavor of the issue within a comparative United Kingdom-United States context is Brendan Gillespie, Dave Eva, and Ron Johnston, "Carcinogenic Risk Assessment in the USA and the UK: The Case of Aldrin/Dieldrin," in *Science in Context,* ed. Barry Barnes and David Edge (Milton Keynes, U.K.,: Open University Press, 1982), pp. 303–35. A telling early case of dispute was the initial version of the sulfur oxides criteria document and the different scientists drawn upon for this and the final version; the second version required far higher levels of proof than did the first. See John C. Esposito, *Vanishing Air* (New York: Center for Responsive Law, 1970), pp. 280–87. For most of the question of shifting and varied scientific assessments one must go to original rather than secondary sources, such as accounts in *Environmental Science and Technology, Journal of the Air Pollution Control Association, Conservation Foundation Letter,* and the hearings held on air quality criteria in 1967 and 1968 by the Senate Committee on Public Works.

46. A good account of the politics of cost-benefit analysis is Mark Green and Normal Waitzman, *Business War on the Law* (Washington, D.C., 1981).

47. A classic case was the controversy over wilderness candidate areas, those that would be selected for study for their potential as wilderness areas. Developmental groups such as timber, mining, and livestock interests continually sought to restrict the selection of candidate areas as well as to restrict the final choices for wilderness designation among candidate areas. Hence the struggle over RARE II, the process by which wilderness candidate areas were decided during the Carter administration. For a general review of wilderness politics see Allin, *Politics of Wilderness Preservation* (note 17).

48. See statement in Benjamin G. Ferris, Jr., and Frank E. Speizer, "Criteria for Establishing Standards for Air Pollutants," in *The Business Roundtable Air Quality Project,* vol. 1 (Cambridge: Harvard School of Public Health, Division of Applied Science, Harvard University, 1980): "We define an adverse effect as medically significant physiologic or pathologic changes generally evidenced by permanent damage or incapacitating illness to the individual." The state of Montana, on the other

hand, when it revised its air quality regulations in 1980, included the provision that the program's objective was to prevent air pollution that "interfere[s] with normal daily activities" and specifically identified lower lung function in school children as an "adverse effect" that should be prevented. See clippings on this issue in the *Missoulian* (Missoula, Mont.) (author file); *Down to Earth* Montana Environmental Information Center (Helena, Mont.), March/April, May/June, and September/October 1980.

49. Two programs that relied heavily on "baseline" monitoring in order to determine changes from that level that might be due to pollution were the Prevention of Significant Deterioration program, which received statutory provision in the Clean Air Act of 1977, and the water quality provisions of the Surface Mining Act of 1977. Industry objected strenuously to being required to gather such data, and in both cases the effort to measure environmental change from polluting activities was seriously weakened.

50. In the industrial wastewater treatment program, EPA sought to set up general industrial categories within which the same technology standards would apply; although industry objected strenuously to this approach, the courts upheld EPA's strategy. In chemical regulation, however, efforts by OSHA to establish a generic regulation for determining carcinogenicity were successfully thwarted by industry in preference for a "case-by-case" approach in which carcinogenicity would be determined for each chemical separately and presumably by different methods.

51. The proceeding in the case of the herbicide 2,4,5-T is a case in point. The issue can be followed in *Chemical Regulation Reporter, Chemical Week*, an industry source, and *NCAP News* (Eugene, Ore.), an environmental source, during 1979–81). See especially *Chemical Week*, 9 April 1980, pp. 32–33.

52. A case in point was the Montana Environmental Quality Council, which in its early years in the early 1970s served as a major advocate of environment objectives and produced some rather striking annual reports to that end. By 1981 its appointments had changed so that it had become completely neutralized, was unable to act, and became a "political football." Environmental legislators urged that it be abolished. See, for example, the *Missoulian* (Missoula, Mont.), 18 February 1981.

53. Relevant examples were the discovery of liver cancer among workers exposed to polyvinyl chloride; discovery of elevated cancer rates in New Orleans as background for the Safe Drinking Water Act of 1974; the kepone incident and others as providing impetus for the Toxic Substances Control Act in 1976; the various hazardous waste incidents such as Love Canal for the 1980 Superfund Act. A similar incident, it is useful to recall, involving the deaths of over one hundred people from an untested sulfanilamide drug, led to passage of the 1938 Pure Food and Drug Act and the requirement that newly marketed drugs be tested for health effects. See Charles O. Jackson, *Food and Drug Legislation in the New Deal* (Princeton: Princeton University Press, 1970).

54. Statement by John Middleton, head of the National Air Pollution Control Administration in U.S. Senate, Committee on Public Works, *Air Pollution, 1968*, 90th Cong., 2d sess., hearings on air quality criteria, 29–31 July 1968 (Washington, D.C.: Government Printing Office, 1968).

55. See items in note 45 pertaining to sulfur oxides criteria document.

56. For a brief account of this issue see two items, Stanton Coerr, "EPA's Air Standard for Lead," and David Schoenbrod, "Why Regulation of Lead Has Failed,"

in *Low Level Lead Exposure: The Clinical Implications of Current Research,* ed. Herbert L. Neddleman (New York: Raven, 1980), 253–57 and 258–66. See Gregory S. Wetstone and Jan Goldman, "Chronology of Events Surrounding the *Ethyl* Decision" (draft), Environmental Law Institute, Washington, D.C., 1981.

57. Wetstone, "Meeting Record," p. 145 (note 35).

58. Useful summaries of these changes for two agencies are Wilderness Society, *The Watt Record: Bureau of Land Management Lands* (Washington, D.C.: Wilderness Society, 1983), and idem, *The Watt Record: The National Park System* (Washington, D.C.: Wilderness Society, 1983). For a review of direct regulator-regulated contacts during the Reagan administration see Robert Nelson, *A World of Preference: Business Access to Reagan's Regulators,* Democracy Project Report no. 5, (New York: Democracy Project, 1983).

59. A useful account of these changes described from the viewpoint of environmental opponents is "The Environmental Activists," *Chemical Week,* 19 October 1983, pp. 48–50, 52, 54, 56.

60. Relevant events can be followed in the newsletters of environmental groups such as the Sierra Clubs *National News Report,* issued weekly during sessions of Congress, or with less detail in *Environment Reporter,* during the years of the Reagan administration.

61. Details pertaining to the controversies concerning James Watt and the Department of the Interior and Anne Burford and the Environmental Protection Agency can be followed in the *New York Times,* the *Washington Post, Newsweek, Time,* and especially *Environment Reporter,* 1981–83 (author file).

62. By early 1984 a "dead center" policy had been reached in EPA but was not contemplated for the Department of the Interior.

63. Fish and Wildlife Service objections to developmental proposals in the 1960s can be followed in National Wildlife Federation, *Conservation Report,* 1966, 27 May (geothermal steam leases), 28 July (pollution of estuaries), 30 September (thermal pollution of waters), 7 October (highway transportation).

64. Congressman John Dingell, who became chair of the Subcommittee on Fisheries and Wildlife Conservation in the House of Representatives in 1966, spoke out frequently on behalf of the Fish and Wildlife Service. See several hearings on the protection of estuarine areas: U.S. House of Representatives, Subcommittee on Fisheries and Wildlife Conservation, *Estuarine and Wetlands Legislation,* 89th Cong., 1st sess. (Washington, D.C.: Government Printing Office, 1966) and *Estuarine Areas,* 90th Cong., 1st sess. (Washington, D.C.: Government Printing Office, 1967).

65. William G. Wing, "The Concrete Juggernaut," part 2, *Audubon Magazine,* August 1966, for an example of highway construction through the Wheeler National Wildlife Refuge in Alabama.

66. U.S. Senate, Public Works Committee, *Thermal Pollution,* 90th Cong., 2d sess., hearings on the extent to which environmental factors are considered in selecting power-plant sites with particular emphasis on ecological effects of discharge of waste heat into rivers, lakes, estuaries, and coastal waters (Washington, D.C.: Government Printing Office, 1968, 1969).

67. National Wildlife Federation, *Conservation Report,* 13 May 1966, 23 September 1966, 30 September 1966.

68. Subcommittee on Fisheries and Wildlife Conservation, *Estuarine Areas,* pp. 189–207 (note 66).

69. The range of Fish and Wildlife Service concerns can be observed in the

scientific research undertaken by its Office of Biological Services to undergird its impact analyses. See U.S. Department of the Interior, Fish and Wildlife Service, *Biological Services Program* (fiscal years 1975ff.).

70. One should recall that the first serious proposal in the legislative history of the EIS was introduced by John Dingell from the Committee on Merchant Marine and Fisheries of the House of Representatives on 23 March 1967. The bill reflected that committee's perennial concern for developmental impacts on fish and wildlife. It is also not without interest that when the House committee reported on a similar measure in the next Congress its legislative form was an amendment to the Fish and Wildlife Coordination Act. The bill written by Senator Jackson was then substituted for the House bill and later passed as the National Environmental Policy Act of 1969. To follow details see National Wildlife Federation, *Conservation Report*, 2 and 9 May, 6 June, 4, 11, and 18 July 1969.

71. The environmental impact reports were to "accompany the proposal through existing agency review processes." Tim Atkeson, legal officer of the Council on Environmental Quality, said: "As we read the law and the legislative history, the public's involvement comes by disclosure of the thing [report] at the end of the process. The public gets a retrospective look, and their impact comes largely as some comment about the same decision in the future." See *Water Resources Newsletter* 5–6 December 1970; 4.

72. National Wildlife Federation, *Conservation Report*, 10 March 1967, 13 October 1967.

73. *Farm Chemicals*, December 1970, pp. 22–23; the article concluded, "Dismayed by USDA's relinquishing of power in pesticide matters and thwarted by the 'closed door' attitude, industry is looking for ways to renew the attitude of partnership that has always characterised its relationship with government."

74. For an analysis of this influence with respect to the Nixon-appointed National Industrial Pollution Control Council, and especially the role of the Department of Commerce, see Richard H. K. Vietor, *Environmental Politics and the Coal Coalition* (College Station: Texas A & M Press, 1980), pp. 168–78.

75. In the 1977 Clean Air Act the EPA was instructed to consider several additional pollutants for regulation: radioactive pollutants, cadmium, arsenic, and polycyclic organic matter; environmentalists chose to specify these because the EPA had been unwilling to take them up on its own initiative.

76. A major statement critical of prescriptive legislation in air pollution is Bruce A. Ackerman and William T. Hassler, *Clean Coal/Dirty Air* (New Haven: Yale University Press, 1981). Ackerman argues in favor of the view that agencies be given considerable leeway to make their own choices; his argument, however, seems to be influenced heavily by his belief that the substantive decision to require mandatory percentage reduction for SO2 emissions required by the 1977 Clean Air Act was undesirable.

77. U.S. House of Representatives, Committee on Government Operations, Natural Resources and Power Subcommittee, House Report 1579, 90th Cong., 2d sess. (Washington, D.C.: Government Printing Office, 1980). This committee report was given renewed publicity, with more extended analysis, by Senator Metcalf in his investigations of advisory committees in 1970.

78. See, for example, U.S. House of Representatives, Subcommittee on Investigations and Oversight, Committee on Science and Technology, *Formaldehyde: Review of Scientific Basis of EPA's Carcinogenic Risk Assessment*, 97th Cong., 2d sess., 20 May 1982 (Washington, D.C.: Government Printing Office, 1983).

79. See the statement of John E. Daniel, chief of staff of EPA administrator

Anne Burford, in testimony to the House Energy and Commerce Committee, as reported in *Environment Reporter,* 30 September 1983, pp. 927–28. See also the dispute over alleged improper influence by the OMB in EPA regulatory action in *Chemical Regulation Reporter,* 18 November 1983, p. 1252; 25 November 1983, pp. 1268–69.

80. This is my conclusion drawn from following a considerable number of issues with accompanying EIS statements, especially with respect to the public lands.

81. See data compiled in Wenner, *Environmental Decade in Court* (note 37). Wenner analyzed federal court cases in the 1970s. Out of 1,125 plaintiffs, 636 were environmentalists (p. 41), and in air quality cases out of 233 plaintiffs 81 were environmentalists and 93 came from industry (p. 66).

82. Ross Sandler, "Citizen Suit Litigation," *Environment,* March 1981, pp. 38–39. In a two-year period, January 1979 to January 1981, 19 cases were brought under citizen suit provisions and decided in the federal courts. Of these 12 were brought by environmental groups, 4 by industries, and 3 by state and local governments.

83. Jethro K. Lieberman, *The Litigious Society* (New York: Basic Books, 1981) discusses the varied types of litigation in the federal courts. Of 168,789 civil suits filed between 1 July 1979 and 30 June 1980, 39,810 were initiated by the U.S. government, 49,000 were private contract suits, 22,000 were personal injury claims, 9,000 were social security cases, 23,000 were prisoner petitions, 13,000 were civil rights cases, and 7,755 were product liability cases. There were so few environmental cases that they were not listed.

84. See Wenner, *Environmental Decade in Court,* table, p. 66 (note 81). The strong emphasis on the high level of environmental litigation was expressed primarily by those promoting environmental mediation who sought to contrast the undesirability of litigation with the desirability of mediation; in so arguing they greatly overemphasized the actual role of litigation. See Center for Environmental Conflict Resolution, *Environmental Mediation: An Effective Alternative?* (Palo Alto, Calif., 1978), esp. pp. v–vi, for the heavy focus on litigation as the main problem.

85. The Reagan environmental revolution was brought about almost exclusively through changes in administrative personnel and policy.

86. See details about local "right to know" ordinances in California in *Chemical Week,* 28 September 1983, pp. 29, 32. In New York, on the other hand, a state appeals court ruled that local governments could not regulate pesticides, which were exclusively the province of state action; *New York Times,* 28 December 1983.

87. In Minnesota the air pollution statute provides that "no local government unit shall set standards of air quality which are more stringent than those set by the pollution control agency." *Nucleonics Week,* 26 February 1970.

88. In Illinois the mayor of Catlin, near Danville, objecting to a proposed 6,000-acre strip mine by Amax Coal Company on prime agricultural land in his township, complained: "The state pre-empted our rights" to regulate coal mining locally. Reported by Harold Henderson, "Caving in on Coal," *Illinois Times,* 5–11 September 1980, p. 81.

89. In 1980 Connecticut established a Hazardous Waste Facility Siting Board with power to override local zoning laws. *Environmental Science and Technology,* August 1980, p. 894.

90. In 1980 the Wisconsin Department of Natural Resources revised its wetlands regulation, NR 115, with legislative approval, prohibiting counties from

forming regulations stricter than those of the state. *Our Wetlands*, published by the Wisconsin Wetlands Association, August–September 1980.

91. A survey by Gladwin Hill of industry representation on state air and water pollution control commissions was reported in the *New York Times*, 7 December 1970. For concern about this problem see statement by Dr. John T. Middleton of the air pollution division of the EPA, *Environment Reporter* 1, no. 37 (8 January 1971).

92. In the years after passage of the 1970 federal Clean Air Act, industry representatives attempted to persuade states that previously adopted more stringent standards should be relaxed to the federal level. Usually they were successful. But even by the time of the 1977 amendments seven states still had lower allowable limits of sulfur dioxide than the federal standard.

93. For Pennsylvania standards under the 1967 act see *Journal of the Air Pollution Control Association* 17, no. 7 (July 1967): 474 and 17, no. 11 (November 1967): 762. For citizen group action in forcing modification of the standards see *Conservation Foundation Letter*, November 1969.

94. The *Conservation Foundation Letter*, November 1969, reported that citizen successes in setting strict standards had been so striking that "there are indications that some industries are wondering if they might not fare better under federal standards rather than state standards." For the reaction of industry to state standards and a report on testimony at Senate hearings by Fred E. Tucker, manager of pollution control services for National Steel Corporation, favoring national air quality standards, see *Environmental Science and Technology*, May 1970, pp. 4–5. Tucker was critical of "the people who appear to be playing a numbers game with air quality standards, by setting lower and lower allowable pollutant levels in state standards."

95. Coastal zone issues can be followed in greatest detail in the weekly newsletter, *Coastal Zone Management* (Washington, D.C., 1970–).

96. For the California case see *Coastal Zone Management*, 2 January 1980, p. 1.

97. Events can be followed in *Coastal Zone Management*, 2 January 1980, p. 2; 25 February 1981, p. 1; 6 May 1981, p. 1; 15 July 1981, p. 1; 5 August 1981, p. 1; 12 August 1981, p. 2; 16 September 1981, pp. 1–2; 23 September 1981, pp. 4–5; and 7 October 1981, p. 102.

98. For a succinct statement of the conflict inherent in these "two conflicting governance philosophies," see the statement by David Morris before the National Association of Counties County Energy Action Conference, May 1981, as reported in *Energy Information and Energy Planning Report*, 5, no. 1 (25 May 1981): 1, 5.

99. For a general discussion of a wide range of nuclear issues involving federal preemption of state authority see *Groundswell* 4–5 (September/October 1981): 1–3; a listing of state laws subject to potential preemption is on pages 5–11 of this issue.

100. Early in 1981 congressional staff defined the issue: "Industry generally supports federal noise regulations as preferable to myriad local rules, which would differ from place to place. But local governments . . . want the authority to establish rules that are stricter than the federal regulations. Currently the noise act preempts stricter state and local noise regulations." See Environmental Study Conference, U.S. Congress, *Weekly Bulletin*, 23 February 1981, p. C7.

101. Industry sought a preemption provision in the 1972 extension of the federal pesticide law but failed. See *Farm Chemicals*, October 1970, p. 70, November 1971, p. 12, December 1971, p. 12. For environmental opposition to preemption

see U.S. Senate, Subcommittee on Environment, hearings on the 1972 pesticide act, testimony of Cynthia Wilson, pp. 130–31.

102. This issue can be followed in detail in 1981 and 1982 in Environmental Study Conference, *Weekly Bulletin*, 25 May, 15 June, 14 and 21 September, and 2 November 1981; 1 February, 22 and 29 March, 3 May, 21 June, and 20 September 1982 and in the ESC annual report, "Environmental, Energy and Natural Resources Legislation in the 97th Congress," p. 6.

103. For this campaign in the late 1940s see Voigt, *Public Grazing Lands* (note 15).

104. The most recent study to distinguish among regions with respect to environmental values sorts out attitudes on a four-point scale from "resource utilization" on one end to "resource preservation" on the other. In terms of the percentage of respondents expressing the strongest "resource preservation" attitudes, the Rocky Mountain states ranked highest with 35 percent, followed by New England 32 percent, the Pacific Coast 28 percent, Middle Atlantic 28 percent, North Central 26 percent, Middle West 20 percent, West South Central 20 percent, South Atlantic 18 percent and Middle South 17 percent. See Continental Group, *Toward Responsible Growth* (note 8). This regional variation is consistent with other environmental attitude studies that provide regional comparisons.

105. Protests against oil drilling in wilderness areas in Montana and Wyoming came from within those states. For a running account of the issue in Montana see the *Missoulian* (Missoula, Mont.), beginning with the 16 November 1979 issue, news item, "Company Wants to Explore for Gas, Oil inside Wilderness." An early statement of reaction to drilling from Congressman Pat Williams of western Montana is in the *Missoulian*, 22 April 1981 "March Dedicated to Preservation of Bob Marshall." For Wyoming see release from office of Senator Malcolm Wallop of Wyoming, "Speech before the Rocky Mountain Oil and Gas Association, Denver, Colorado, Oct. 8, 1981." See also account of Wallop's view in *Jackson Hole News*, 15 October 1981, "Wallop Hits Wilderness Leases."

106. Out of this circumstance came drives in several states, especially Idaho and Utah, for changes in state land policies to permit "multiple use."

107. By early October 1983, 50 percent of respondents in a *Deseret News*/KSL poll of residents of Utah approved the view that Secretary James Watt should resign; 33 percent opposed his resignation. See LaVarr Webb, "Half of Utahns Say Watt Should Go," *Deseret News*, 7 October 1983.

108. See items by Esposito, Tobin, Lieber, and Davies (note 24).

109. Joseph T. O'Connor, "The Automobile Controversy — Federal Control of Vehicular Emission," *Ecology Law Quarterly*, 4, no. 3 (1975): 661–92, and Luke J. Danielson, "Control of Complex Emission Course — Step toward Land Use Planning," *Ecology Law Quarterly* 4, no. 3 (1975): 693–737.

110. Thomas M. Disselhorst, "Sierra Club v. Ruckelshaus: 'On a Clear Day . . . ,'" *Ecology Law Quarterly* 4, no. 3 (1975): 739–80.

111. There were some exceptions. California conducted considerable research on its own, thereby enabling it to take a somewhat independent position in many environmental matters. Montana undertook some crucial research, financed by proceeds from its coal severance tax, to undergird its new air quality regulations proposed in 1980. And a number of states took up their own research on the acid rain issue. See, for example, *Proceedings, Acid Precipitation Research Needs Conference* (Syracuse, N.Y.: College of Environmental Science and Forestry, State University of New York, 1982); California Air Resources Board, *California Sympo-*

sium on Acid Precipitation (San Francisco: California Air Resources Board, 1981); Wisconsin Department of Natural Resources, *Wisconsin Interpretive Assessment Document on Acid Deposition* (Wisconsin Department of Natural Resources, 1983); Vermont Department of Water Resources and Environmental Engineering, *Vermont Acid Precipitation Program: Long-Term Monitoring, 1981-1982* (Montpelier: Department of Water Resources and Environmental Engineering, 1983).

112. Differences in research strategies by federal, state, and private sponsors on the issue of acid rain can be observed in Keystone Center, *Report on the Acid Precipitation Research Coordination Workshop* (Keystone, Colo.: Keystone Center, 1982).

113. For research undertaken by the electric power industry through the Electric Power Research Institute, see its periodical, *EPRI Journal* (Palo Alto, Calif., 1976-); for work of the Chemical Industry Institute of Toxicology see its *Annual Report* (Research Triangle Park, N.C., 1978-).

114. One such issue was research in indoor air pollution, which the Reagan administration sought to eliminate. For accounts of the controversy see *Science*, 6 November 1981, p. 639; the administration argued that it had no authority to deal with indoor air. See also *Environmental Health Letter*, 1 November 1981.

115. The best account of the history of the lead issue is Wetstone and Goldman, "Chronology of Events" (note 56). However, this account is still quite limited, and the conclusion here is drawn from many items in varied sources such as *Science, Environmental Science and Technology, Journal of the Air Pollution Control Association*, assessments by the National Academy of Sciences, and Herbert L. Needleman, ed., *Low Level Exposure* (New York: Raven, 1980). The issue has yet to receive satisfactory historical analysis.

116. It is often argued that economic effects were never considered in the early history of pollution control. Yet economic analyses were made as the program evolved. The Federal Water Pollution Control Act of 1966, for example, required that the Federal Water Pollution Control Administration assess federal costs. See its report, *Water Pollution Control, 1970-1974: The Federal Costs* (Washington, D.C.: Department of the Interior, Federal Water Pollution Control Administration, 1969).

117. For a case study of a "battle of the models" with reference to the impact of electric power generation on the Hudson River striped bass population, see L. W. Barnhouse et all., "Population Biology in the Courtroom: The Hudson River Controversy," *BioScience* 34, no. 1 (January 1984): 14-19.

118. Dr. Herbert Needleman, a prominent frontier researcher on the health effects of lead, was the subject of persistent criticism from the lead industry. See the description of him as representing "what is at best a minority view that adverse health effects occur at blood-lead levels below $\mu g/dl$" in U.S. Congress, House of Representatives, Subcommittee on Health and the Environment, *Oversight — Clean Air Act Amendments of 1977*, 96th Cong., 1st sess. (Washington, D.C.: Government Printing Office, 1980), testimony of Jerome Cole of the International Lead Zinc Research Organization, p. 344.

119. A host of issues involve confidentiality. They can be observed, for example, in the first round of premanufacture notices for chemical registration under the 1976 Toxic Substances Control Act and the development of regulations pertaining to section 5 of that act. See *Chemical Regulation Reporter*, 27 April 1979, p. 82; 11 May 1979, pp. 147-49; and 18 May 1979, pp. 218-19.

120. For a review of state legislation to that time see *Chemical Week*, 26 May 1982, pp. 13-14.

121. See, for example, Jan M. Newton, *An Economic Analysis of Herbicide Use for Intensive Forestry Management* (Eugene, Oreg.: Oregon Public Interest Research Group, 1979).

122. These issues can be followed in *Forest Management* (Eugene, Oreg., 1980–), an environmental journal that seeks to help citizen groups understand the complexities of U.S. Forest Service policy. See its specialized publications such as Randal O'Toole, *The Citizens' Guide to FORPLAN* (Eugene, Oreg.: Cascade Holistic Economic Consultants, 1983).

123. Much of this debate focused ultimately on the alternatives between a "threshold-margin of safety" versus a "risk-assessment" made of establishing an appropriate health objective. For a defense of the latter approach, which came to exercise more influence after the mid-1970s, see *The Business Roundtable Air Quality Project*, vol. 1 (Cambridge: Harvard School of Public Health, Division of Applied Science, Harvard University, 1980).

124. Both business and environmentalists were quite aware of the significance of choices of scientific advisors. The entire issue obtained more concerted focus when in the spring of 1983 a list was uncovered from EPA files concerning acceptable and unacceptable scientists. See *Environmental Health Letter*, 15 March 1983, p. 3. For changes in Reagan appointments to the Cancer Advisory Board, which involved a similar issue, see letter to the editor by Janet D. Rowley et al., *Science*, 20 January 1984, p. 236.

125. For examples of technical information services developed by environmentalists see Nuclear Information and Resource Service, *Groundswell* (Washington, D.C., 1978–); Environmental Law Institute, *National Wetlands Newsletter* (Washington, D.C., 1979–); *Forest Management* (Eugene, Oreg., 1980–); Environmental Action Foundation, *Exposure* (Washington, D.C., 1980–).

126. *Chemical Week*, a persistent chemical industry critic of environmentalists, title an article about environmental activity "The Environmental Activists, They've Grown in Competence and They're Working Together," *Chemical Week*, 19 October 1983, pp. 48–50, 52, 54, 56.

127. The EPA criteria document on lead illustrates this process. Through the efforts of David Schoenbrud, attorney for the Natural Resources Defense Council, which brought the legal action to force EPA to adopt an ambient lead standard, lead researchers Herbert Needleman and Sergio Piomelli were brought into the criteria document proceedings. For this purpose NRDC, in cooperation with the National Air Conservation Commission of the American Lung Association, persuaded Needleman and Piomelli to publish a summary of frontier findings, "The Effects of Low-Level Lead Exposure," which was incorporated into proceedings on the criteria document. The issue can be followed in *Environment Reporter*, 1977–78; see especially 7 July 1978, pp. 427–28. Needleman later testified in the House Subcommittee on Health and the Environment, *Oversight–Clean Air Act Amendments of 1977*, pp. 272–86 (note 118).

128. The role of the media in the Love Canal case is reflected extensively in Michael Brown, *Laying Waste: The Poisoning of America by Toxic Chemicals* (New York: Washington Square Press, 1979), pp. 3–96. For a report prepared by EPA highly critical of the role of the media in toxic chemical cases with four case studies of kepone, lead (Dallas), Love Canal, and dioxin, see *Inside EPA, Weekly Report*, 13 January 1984, pp. 12–14.

129. A useful case study in this type of strategy involved the "Seven cities" lead study, carried out under the auspices of the joint industry-government Lead Liaison Committee early in the 1970s. The project was undertaken with the agreement

that data would not be made available until the study was completed. But the project director, known to be close to the lead industry, released some data to bolster the industry position in proceedings over the California lead standard. See Wetstone and Goldman, "Chronology of Events" (note 56).

130. Appointments to and activities of the EPA Science Advisory Board, which can be followed in *Environment Reporter*, seemed to be a result of a deliberate policy to make scientific decisions more open. Under the Reagan administration that policy was reversed. See, for example, the formaldehyde case in House of Representatives, Subcommittee on Investigations and Oversight, Committee on Science and Technology, *Formaldehyde: Review of Scientific Basis of EPA's Carcinogenic Risk Assessment*, 97th Cong., 2d sess., 20 May 1982 (Washington, D.C.: Government Printing Office, 1983). A more open policy was established with the appointment of William Ruckelshaus as EPA administrator.

131. For an analysis of water policy in these terms see Laurence H. Tribe, Corinne S. Schelling, and John Voss, eds., *When Values Conflict: Essays on Environmental Analysis, Discourse and Decision* (Cambridge, Mass.: Ballinger, 1976).

132. For Britain see Howard Hill, *Freedom to Roam: The Struggle for Access to Britain's Moors and Mountains* (Ashbourne, Derbyshire: Moorland, 1980).

133. For an urban political drive to clean up toxic waste dumps in a working-class neighborhood, see Janice Weiss, "How People Take Power," *Exposure* 34–35 (September–October 1983): 1, 4–6.

134. Fred Hirsch, *Social Limits to Growth* (Cambridge: Harvard University Press, 1976).

135. Louis Harris and Associates, *Risk in a Complex Society: A Marsh and McLennan Public Opinion Survey* (March and McLennan, 1980).

THE SOCIAL SECURITY BUREAUCRACY IN TRIUMPH AND IN CRISIS

1. In regard to the bureaucracy, see Francis E. Rourke, ed., *Bureaucratic Power in National Politics*, 2d ed. (Boston: Little, Brown, 1972).

2. This theme is developed more fully in Carolyn L. Weaver, *The Crisis in Social Security: Economic and Political Origins* (Durham, N.C.: Duke University Press, 1982). For other works endeavoring to explain social security policymaking from an economic and political perspective, see Martha Derthick, *Policymaking for Social Security* (Washington, D.C.: Brookings Institution, 1979); Edgar Browning, "Why the Social Insurance Budget Is Too Large in a Democracy," *Economic Inquiry* 13 (September 1975): 373–88; William Mitchell, *The Popularity of Social Security* (Washington, D.C.: American Enterprise Institute, 1977); and F. A. Hayek, *The Constitution of Liberty* (Chicago: University of Chicago Press, 1960), pp. 285–305.

3. See Richard Posner, "Theories of Economic Regulation," *Bell Journal of Economics and Management Science* 2 (Autumn 1974): 335–58. See also James M. Buchanan, "Why Does Government Grow?" in *Budgets and Bureaucrats: The Sources of Government Growth*, ed. Thomas E. Brocherding (Durham, N.C.: Duke University Press, 1977), pp. 3–18.

4. See, for example, Thomas E. Borcherding and Robert T. Deacon, "The Demand for the Services of Non-federal Governments," *American Economic Review* 62 (December 1972): 891–901; and Theordore C. Bergstrom and Robert P. Goodman, "Private Demands for Public Goods," *American Economic Review* 63 (June 1973): 280–96. See also Edgar Browning, "Social Insurance and Intergenerational

Transfers," *Journal of Law and Economics* 16 (October 1973): 215–37, and idem, "Why the Social Insurance Budget Is Too Large."

5. See George Stigler, "The Theory of Economic Regulation," *Bell Journal of Economics and Management Science* 2 (Spring 1971): 3–21; Posner, "Theories of Economic Regulation," pp. 335–58; and Sam Peltzman, "Toward a More General Theory of Regulation," *Journal of Law and Economics* 19 (August 1976): 211–40; and Robert McCormick and Robert Tollison, *Politicians, Legislation, and the Economy: An Inquiry into the Interest-Group Theory of Government* (The Hague: Martinus Nijhoff, 1981).

6. See, for instance, Posner, "Theories of Economic Regulation," p. 337; Isaac Ehrlich and Richard Posner, "An Economic Analysis of Legal Rule Making," *Journal of Legal Studies* 111 (January 1974): 257–86; and Peltzman, "Toward a More General Theory of Regulation."

7. See C. M. Hardin, K. A. Shepsle, and B. R. Weingast, *Public Policy Excesses: Government by Congressional Subcommittees*, Formal Publication no. 50 (Saint Louis: Washington University Center for Study of American Business, 1982), and B. R. Weingast and M. J. Moran, "The Myth of Runaway Bureaucracy: The Case of the FTC," *Regulation*, May/June 1982, pp. 31–36.

8. See Gordon Tullock, *The Politics of Bureaucracy* (Washington, D.C.: Public Affairs Press, 1965); William A. Niskanen, *Bureaucracy and Representative Government* (New York: Adline Atherton, 1971); and Ludwig von Mises, *Bureaucracy* (New Rochelle, N.Y.: Arlington House, 1969). See also E. G. West, "The Political Economy of American Public School Legislation," *Journal of Law and Economics* 10 (October 1967): 101–28; and Robert Mackay and Joseph Reid, "On Understanding the Birth and Evolution of the SEC," in *Regulatory Reform in an Atmosphere of Crisis: Current-Day Implications of the Roosevelt Years*, ed. G. Walton (New York: Academic Press, 1979).

9. Lawrence C. Dodd and Richard L. Schott, *Congress and the Administrative State* (New York: John Wiley, 1979), p. 2.

10. See Niskanen, *Bureaucracy and Representative Government*; Richard E. Wagner, "Supply Side Aspects of the Theory of Local Government: Owners, Managers, and Take-Over Bids," mimeographed, Virginia Polytechnic Institute and State University, 1975; and Jack A. Stockfish, "Analysis of Bureaucratic Behavior: The Ill-Defined Production Process," Working Paper, Rand Corporation, Santa Monica, Calif., 1975.

11. The Social Security Act, PL 271, 74th Congress (H.R. 7260), Approved 14 August 1935. For further development, see Weaver, *Crisis in Social Security*, pp. 92–94, 96–99, and 115–24.

12. In addition, there were provisions for lump-sum refunds equal to 3.5 percent of covered wages for workers who retired without gaining eligibility for benefits and for the estates of workers who died before receiving at least this amount. These payments were eliminated in 1939.

13. Fund reserves were expected to grow to the point that by 1980, interest would cover 40 percent of benefit payments. Current tax levies would have met the balance. See Edwin Witte, "Old-Age Security in the Social Security Act," in *Social Security Perspectives: Essays by Edwin Witte*, ed. Robert Lampman (Madison: University of Wisconsin Press, 1962), pp. 128–29; Robert J. Myers, *Social Security* (Homewood, Ill.: Richard D. Irwin, 1975), pp. 135–44; and Hearings before the Committee on Ways and Means on H.R. 4120, U.S. House of Representatives, 74th Cong., 1st sess., p. 903.

14. "Social Security Act Amendments of 1939," *U.S. Statutes at Large*, 76th Cong., 1st sess., vol. 53, part 2, pp. 1360–1402.

15. Social Security Administration, *Social Security Bulletin: Annual Statistical Supplement, 1981*, p. 79, and for the CPI series used throughout, see *Economic Report of the President*, 98th Cong., 1st sess., House Document 98-2 (February 1983), p. 221.

16. The reserve fund projected for 1980 was cut from $50 billion to $20 billion. See Witte, "Old-Age Security in the Social Security Act," pp. 128–29, and Myers, *Social Security*, pp. 143–45.

17. This is developed more fully in Weaver, *Crisis in Social Security*, 93–96, 115–24. See also Carolyn L. Weaver, *Understanding the Sources and Dimensions of Crisis in Social Security: A First Step toward Meaningful Reform* (Washington, D.C.: Fiscal Policy Council, 1981).

18. Hayek focuses on the importance of intragenerational redistribution as a source of program growth in Hayek, *Constitution of Liberty*, pp. 285–305.

19. For more on information control in the public sector, see Randall Bartlett, *Economic Foundations of Political Power* (New York: Free Press, 1973); Gordon Tullock, *Toward a Mathematics of Politics* (Ann Arbor: University of Michigan Press, 1967), pp. 100–132.

20. On the important role played over the years by SSA's Office of the Actuary, see Derthick, *Policymaking for Social Security*, pp. 170–82.

21. "Social Security Amendments of 1955," Hearings before the Committee in Finance, U.S. Senate, 84th Cong., 2d sess., on H.R. 7225, 25–27, 31 January, 1, 2, 8–9 February 1956, p. 1237.

22. "Social Security Amendments of 1967," Hearings before the Committee on Finance, U.S. Senate, 90th Cong., 1st sess., on H.R. 12080, part I, 22–23 August 1967, pp. 244–45.

23. Robert J. Myers, *Expansionism in Social Insurance* (Westminster: Institute of Economic Affairs, 1970), p. 29.

24. Derthick, *Policymaking for Social Security*, p. 23.

25. See "Social Security Benefits and Eligibility," Hearings before the Committee on Finance, U.S. Senate, 87th Cong., 1st sess., in H.R. 6027, 25–26 May 1961, p. 67; "Social Security Amendments of 1967," pp. 223–24; and "Social Security Amendments of 1971," Hearings before the Committee on Finance, U.S. Senate 92d Cong., 1st sess., on H.R. 1, 27–29 July, 2–3 August 1971, p. 30.

26. For a detailed account of the staffing of the Social Security Board, see Charles McKinley and Robert Frase, *Launching Social Security: A Capture-and-Record Account, 1935–1937* (Madison: University of Wisconsin Press, 1970).

27. On political ignorance as a rational response to costly and imperfect information, see Anthony Downs, *An Economic Theory of Democracy* (New York: Harper, 1957), pp. 207–59; and Tullock, *Toward a Mathematics of Politics*, pp. 100–114. On the impact of uncertainty on information manipulation by public suppliers, see Tullock, *Toward a Mathematics of Politics*, pp. 100–132; and Bartlett, *Economic Foundations of Political Power*, pp. 70–75.

28. Arthur Altmeyer, "Federal Old-Age Security Program" (NBC radio program, 6 November 1936), printed in "Addresses by A. J. Altmeyer" (unpublished manuscript, Department of Health, Education, and Welfare).

Echoing this theme, in 1939 President Roosevelt likened social security taxpayers to the "policyholders of a private insurance company," and in the 1960s HEW secretary Anthony Celebrezze, hoping to marshal support for the new medicare proposal, said, "The social security system, in a broad sense, gives you a policy

. . . it is merely established on the same principles as a normal insurance policy." See text of President Roosevelt's message to Congress, 16 January 1939, in "Congress Looks at Social Security," *Congressional Digest* (1935), and "Medicare Care for the Aged," Hearings before the Committee on Ways and Means, House of Representatives, 88th Cong., 1st and 2d sess., on H.R. 3920, 18–22 November 1963, and 20–24 January 1964, p. 53.

29. "Social Security Benefits and Eligibility," pp. 90–91. See also "Social Security After 18 Years," Staff Report for the Committee on Ways and Means, House of Representatives, 83d Cong., 2d sess., 1954, in which SSA is identified as the source of misunderstanding on the part of the public.

30. Witte, "Old-Age Security in the Social Security Act," p. 310. For more on the politics of pay-as-you-go systems and the incentives for growth, see Browning, "Why the Social Insurance Budget Is Too Large."

31. Derthick, *Policymaking for Social Security*, p. 33.

32. See statement by Secretary Celebrezze, "Medical Care for the Aged," p. 27.

33. Ellen Woodward, "Social Security Today and Tomorrow," address before the Mississippi Conference of Social Workers, 29 April 1943 (unpublished addresses by members of the Social Security Boards, Library, U.S. Department of Health, Education, and Welfare), p. 2. See also Arthur J. Altmeyer, *The Formative Years in Social Security* (Madison: University of Wisconsin Press, 1968), in which Altmeyer chronicles the history and administration of the program through 1954.

34. *Report of the Social Security Board for 1943: Social Security during and after the War*, reprinted in *Statutory History of the United States: Income Security*, ed. Robert B. Stevens (New York: Chelsea House, 1970), pp. 267–68.

35. *Annual Report of the Federal Security Agency, 1945* reprinted in *Statutory History of the United States*, ed. Stevens, pp. 300–302.

36. Social Security Administration, *Social Security Bulletin* 46, no. 6 (June 1983): 33, and U.S. Department of Commerce, *Historical Statistics of the United States: From Colonial Times to 1970* (Washington, D.C.: Government Printing Office, 1976), part 1, p. 10.

37. Congress twice overrode presidential vetoes to restrict compulsory coverage by a half-million workers. Newspapers and magazine vendors were excluded from coverage, and a narrower definition of "employee" was introduced. See *Statutory History of the U.S.*, ed. Stevens, pp. 318–19, and Altmeyer, *Formative Years*, pp. 152–68.

38. See, for example, Edwin Witte, "Social Security and Free Enterprise," an address at the Kansas State Teachers' College, 13 April 1950 (unpublished addresses, Library, U.S. Department of Health, Education, and Welfare), and Altmeyer, *Formative Years*, pp. 169–70. In his address, Witte said that during the past two years a "great outcry has been raised that the quest for social security is undermining our economy of free enterprise and threatens freedom itself." This complaint, he said, had never been more strongly advanced.

39. $42 as compared to $25. Altmeyer, *Formative Years*, pp. 169–70.

40. Daniel Holland, *Private Pension Funds: Projected Growth* (New York: National Bureau of Economic Research, 1966), p. 19.

41. Witte, "Social Security and Free Enterprise," p. 8.

42. *Social Security Bulletin* 46, no. 6 (June 1983): 33.

43. Social Security Administration, *Social Security Bulletin, Annual Statistical Supplement: 1981*, p. 79.

44. See Weaver, *Crisis in Social Security*, pp. 126–31, for a more thorough discussion of the politics of coverage expansion. See also *Congressional Quarterly*

Almanac 6 (1950): 140, and 10 (1954): 188, and Social Security Administration, *History of the Provisions of OASDHI, 1934–1981*, SSA Pub. no. 11-11515, January 1982, p. 1.

45. See "Local Withdrawals Raise Social Security Threat," *Washington Post*, 15 January 1983; "Hospitals Leading Trend to Drop out of Social Security," *Washington Post*, 23 April 1983; and "Drop Outs: Many Leave Ailing System," *Los Angeles Times*, 20 May 1982.

46. U.S. Advisory Council on Social Security, *Final Report of the Advisory Council on Social Security: 1948* (Washington, D.C.: Federal Security Administration, 1948), p. 6.

47. These are states in U.S. Social Security Board, *Annual Report: 1935–1936*, p. 14.

48. Robert J. Myers, *Social Security and Allied Government Programs* (Homewood, Ill.: Richard D. Irwin, 1975), pp. 140–41. For the individual with average earnings retiring in 1940, combined employee-employer tax payments would have purchased a private annuity yielding $6.50 per year. The annual benefit for a sixty-five-year-old male retiring under social security was $271. See Donald Parsons and Douglas Munro, "Intergenerational Transfers in Social Security," in *The Crisis in Social Security: Problems and Prospects*, ed. Michael Boskin (San Francisco: Institute for Contemporary Studies, 1978), pp. 74–75.

49. This was the case with federal government employees, who were covered (new hires only) in 1983.

50. See *Social Security Bulletin, Annual Statistical Supplement: 1981*, p. 10, for a historical summary of coverage provisions. See also Federal Security Administration, *Annual Report: 1951* (Washington, D.C.: Federal Security Administration, 1952), *Congressional Quarterly Almanac* 6 (1950): 161, and *Congressional Quarterly Almanac* 12 (1956): 392–93.

51. Federal Security Administration, *Annual Report: 1950* (Washington, D.C.: Federal Security Administration, 1950), p. 15.

52. For instance, nearly 100,000 old-age assistance recipients became eligible for social security upon enactment of the 1950 amendments. *Annual Report of the Federal Security Administration: 1951*, pp. 4, 23; and Social Security Administration, *Social Security Bulletin: Annual Statistical Supplement: 1973*, p. 157. See also *History of the Provisions of OASDHI; Social Security Bulletin, Annual Statistical Supplement: 1981*, pp. 8–32, and *Staff Data and Materials Related to Social Security Financing*, Committee on Finance, U.S. Senate, 97th Cong., 2d sess. (December 1982), pp. 46–47.

53. Lewis Meriam, Karl T. Schlotterbeck, and Mildred Maroney, *The Cost of Financing Social Security* (Washington, D.C.: Brookings Institution, 1950), pp. 19–20. For a summary of the debates and congressional action on the 1956 amendments, see *Congressional Quarterly Almanac* 12 (1956): 392–97. See also Derthick, *Policymaking for Social Security*, pp. 295–338.

54. Derthick, *Policymaking for Social Security*, p. 304.

55. See Myers, *Social Insurance Expansionism*, on "incrementalism" as a key method used by the bureaucracy to expand the basic program. See also Derthick, *Policymaking for Social Security*, pp. 23–26, 308–13.

56. "Social Security revisions," pp. 27, 51.

57. Robert Myers, *Expansionism in Social Insurance*, pp. 29–30.

58. Charles Schottland, "Social Security Amendments of 1956: A Legislative History," *Social Security Bulletin* 19 (September 1956): 3–15, and *Congressional Quarterly Almanac* 12 (1956): 392–93.

59. *Social Security Bulletin, Annual Statistical Supplement: 1981,* pp. 27–28; *Issues Related to Social Security Act Disability Programs,* Committee on Finance, U.S. Senate, 96th Cong., 1st sess. (1979); and *Staff Data and Materials Related to the Social Security Disability Insurance Program,* Committee on Finance, U.S. Senate, 97th Cong., 2d sess. (August 1982).

60. *Congressional Record,* 17 November 1983, pp. S16549–50.

61. *Social Security Financing,* p. 45.

62. See Weaver, *Crisis in Social Security,* pp. 142–43.

63. "Medical Care for the Aged," p. 27.

64. *Historical Statistics,* p. 10; *1983 Annual Report of the Board of Trustees of the Federal OASDI Trust Funds,* p. 87; and *Social Security Bulletin* 46, no. 6 (1983): 33.

65. Social Security Administration, *Social Security Bulletin, Annual Statistical Supplement: 1977–79,* pp. 80–81.

66. The proportion of the elderly on old-age assistance, a program financed by matching grants to the states, fell continuously, from 22 percent in 1940 to 9 percent in 1973. *Social Security Bulletin, Annual Statistical Supplement: 1975,* p. 57.

67. Cohen began his career in social security in 1934, when he served on the staff of the Committee on Economic Security. Ball joined SSA in 1939. Derthick, *Policymaking for Social Security,* pp. 52–55.

68. See *History of Provisions of OASDHI;* Weaver, *Crisis in Social Security,* pp. 144–72; and Derthick, *Policymaking for Social Security,* pp. 316–68.

69. *Social Security Financing,* pp. 46, 50.

70. "Medical Care for the Aged," p. 49. See *Congressional Quarterly Almanac* 20 (1964): 231–37, 21 (1965): 54; *Congressional Quarterly Weekly Report,* 20 July 1965, p. 1493; Theodore Marmor, *The Politics of Medicare* (Chicago: Aldine, 1970); and Eugene Feingold, *Medicare: Policy and Politics* (San Francisco: Chandler, 1966).

71. On the subsidizing of demand and other related issues, see Rita Ricardo-Campbell, *The Economics and Politics of Health* (Chapel Hill: University of North Carolina Press, 1982).

72. Marmor, *Politics of Medicare,* and Derthick, *Policymaking for Social Security,* pp. 316–38.

73. "Medicare Care for the Aged," pp. 166–68.

74. See *History of the Provisions of OASDHI.*

75. Judith M. Feder, *Medicare: The Politics of Federal Hospital Insurance* (Lexington, Mass.: Lexington Books, 1977), p. 111, "Medicare and Medicaid: Problems, Issues, and Alternatives," Committee on Finance, U.S. Senate, 91st Cong., 1st sess. (February 1970); *Social Security Bulletin, Annual Statistical Supplement: 1981,* p. 28; *Social Security Financing,* p. 45; *Historical Statistics,* p. 10; *Social Security Bulletin* 46, no. 6 (1983): 29; and *1983 Economic Report of the President,* p. 248.

76. For an interesting political analysis of this period, see Derthick, *Policymaking for Social Security,* pp. 339–68.

77. American Enterprise Institute, *The Pending Social Security Amendments of 1970,* Reprint of Legislative Analysis no. 14 (Washington, D.C.: American Enterprise Institute, 1970), pp. 21–22/

78. *Social Security Financing,* p. 46.

79. See comments by Wilbur Mills in *Congressional Record,* 21 May 1970, p. 4669.

80. Wages had to grow by about twice the rate of inflation. In fact, real wages in covered employment fell in 1974 and 1975 and again in the late 1970s. Over the decade, real wage growth averaged close to zero. On the problems with the 1972 adjustment, see *Social Security Financing,* Committee on Finance, U.S. Senate, 95th Cong., 1st sess. (June 1977).

81. See Colin D. Campbell, *Over-Indexed Benefits: The Decoupling Proposals for Social Security,* Domestic Affairs Study no. 46 (Washington, D.C.: American Enterprise Institute, May 1976); "Propping up Social Security," *Business Week,* 19 July 1976, p. 36; Alicia H. Munnell, *The Future of Social Security,* Brookings Studies in Social Economics (Washington, D.C.: Brookings Institution, 1977), pp. 32–40; and Robert Kaplan, *Indexing Social Security* (Washington, D.C.: American Enterprise Institute, 1977).

82. As recommended by a subcommittee of actuaries and economists to the 1971 Advisory Council on Social Security, SSA actuaries abandoned the "level-wage" assumption previously used for estimating program costs, adopting instead the assumption of rising average covered wages. The old method consistently produced surpluses. See 1971 Advisory Council on Social Security, *Reports on OASDI and Medicare* (Washington, D.C.: Government Printing Office, 1971), pp. 91–92, 124–33.

83. *Social Security Financing,* p. 50.

84. Ibid., p. 51.

85. Ibid., p. 51, and *1983 Economic Report,* p. 221.

86. By 1976, the seventy-five-year costs were projected to average 28.6 percent of payroll (excluding HI). This implied that under the actuaries' intermediate forecasts, the combined employee and employer tax would have to have averaged nearly 29 percent to finance OASI and DI benefits alone, with no net accumulation of reserves. The long-term tax in the law was less than half of that, at a combined rate of 11.9 percent. Fully 60 percent of scheduled benefits could not have been met. See Munnell, *Future of Social Security,* p. 100.

87. In November 1982 the retirement fund was technically insolvent, unable to pay a full month's benefits on time. In the course of just two months, $17.5 billion was transferred from the DI and HI trust funds to the OASI fund in order to allow benefits to be paid through June 1983 (under the authority of PL 97-123, which would have expired in June). Without the 1983 amendments, it was expected that even if interfund borrowing were reauthorized, the borrowing demands of OASI would have been so great as to render the entire system insolvent by the end of 1983. The long-term situation was even more grave. See *Social Security Financing,* pp. 11–34, and Eli N. Conkar, "Estimated Operations of the Oasi, DI and HI Trust Funds under Present Law on the Basis of 1983 Alternative II-B and III Assumptions," 28 February 1983 (unpublished memo, Office of the Actuary, Social Security Administration).

For several informative sources on the development of the financial crisis in social security, see Robert S. Kaplan, *Financial Crisis in the Social Security System* (Washington, D.C.: American Enterprise Institute, 1976); J. W. Van Gorkom, *Social Security — the Long-Term Deficit* (Washington, D.C.: American Enterprise Institute, 1976); Edward Cowan, "Background and History: The Crisis in Public Finance and Social Security," in *Crisis in Social Security,* ed. Boskin, pp. 1–15; and Munnell, *Future of Social Security.*

88. Jack S. Futterman, "Unburdening the Administration of the Social Security Programs of Short-Term Commissions" (unpublished paper presented at sympo-

sium, McCahan Foundation for Research in Economic Security, Bryn Mawr, Pa., 29 October 1982), p. 12.

89. See, for example, *Congressional Record,* 13 May 1981, pp. H2170–74, H2206–07; 14 May 1981, pp. H2217–23, H2231–33; 19 May 1981, pp. S5200, H2293, H2315, H2323; 20 May 1981, pp. S5262–66, S5275–5309; 31 July 1981, p. S9074; and 14 October 1981, pp. S11368–72. See also statements of Senators Armstrong and Moynihan in "Social Security Financing and Options for the Future," hearings before the Social Security Subcommittee, U.S. Senate, part 1, 97th Cong., 1st sess. (July 1981), pp. 4–19; "Social Security in 1982, 1984 and 2020," *New York Times,* 20 May 1982; "Senate Unanimously Rebuffs President on Social Security," *Washington Post,* 21 May 1982; "Social Security Stew Simmers," *New York Times,* 30 October 1982; "Social Security Issue Splits Reagan, Public," *Los Angeles Times,* 21 November 1982; "Post-Election Politics on Social Security Flares Up," *Washington Post,* 5 November 1982; and "Still Making Hay on Social Security," *Washington Post,* 2 February 1983. See also fundraising letters of Republican and Democratic National Committees of October and December 1982.

90. The Social Security Amendments of 1977 (PL 95–216) reduced long-range benefits by modifying the indexing provisions. Earnings as well as the benefit formula used for determining initial benefits became indexed, and the basis was changed from price to wage inflation. (Benefits for people on the rolls remained price indexed.) Costs were reduced relative to the flawed price-indexed system, but they were permanently increased relative to a fully price-indexed system. The 1977 amendments also introduced a dollar-for-dollar offset of social security dependents' benefits for people who also receive public retirement pensions.

The Disability Amendments of 1980 (PL 96–265) applied a tighter cap on family benefits in disability cases, reduced the number of years of earnings that could be dropped in computing benefits for younger workers, and, in a series of administrative changes, instituted a minimum three-year eligibility review requirement for people on the DI rolls.

In 1981 the Omnibus Budget Reconciliation Act (PL 97–35) phased out the social security student benefit, eliminated the minimum benefit for present and future recipients (subsequently restored for current recipients), restricted the payment of lump-sum death benefits, limited payments for vocational rehabilitation, reduced the period over which young widow(er)s with children could draw benefits, tightened the offset of disability benefits on account of other disability payments, and deliberalized the retirement-earnings test.

Finally, the Social Security Amendments of 1983 (PL 98–21) delayed the annual COLA from July to January, made up to half of social security benefits taxable for higher-income beneficiaries, reduced the windfalls accruing to people receiving social security and another public pension from noncovered work, raised the age at which full retirement benefits are payable in the next century from sixty-five to sixty-seven, and provided for a triggered modification of the COLA (based on the lower of wage or price increases) when trust fund reserves are criticially low.

On net, the 1977–83 legislation reduced the growth of benefits already scheduled in the law but at the same time increased considerably the commitment of the nation's resources to social security.

91. Futterman, "Unburdening the Administration," pp. 1–2, and Derthick, *Policymaking for Social Security,* p. 19.

92. Futterman, "Unburdening the Administration," pp. 2–3.

93. Simply providing the COLA each year requires changing six hundred com-

puter programs and takes twenty thousand hours of processing time, day and night, for four months. For the agency to discover that a beneficiary has moved, died, or worked and earned a higher benefit may take years. Quite literally, "SSA is only marginally capable of performing critical program functions (the issuance of monthly checks)," SSA is now in the process of undertaking a five-year modernization plan. See "SSA Systems Modernization Plan: From Survival to State of the Art," Executive Summary (Social Security Administration, February 1982), pp. iv and v; and Statement of John A. Svahn, commissioner of Social Security, before Subcommittee on Oversight and Subcommittee on Social Security of the Committee on Ways and Means, U.S. House of Representatives, 22 May 1981.

94. See Jane Bryant Quinn, "Social Security Computers Are Wreaking Havoc," *Washington Post*, 31 May 1982; Sylvia Porter, "Social Security's Ailing Computers," *Washington Post*, 20 April 1982; and "Social Security goes Abroad to Dead People," *Washington Post*, 20 August 1981.

95. This is elaborated in Carolyn L. Weaver, "The Long-Term Outlook for Social Security — Continued Political Turmoil," in *Checks and Balances on Social Security: Symposium in Honor of Robert Myers* (Washington, D.C.: University Press of America, forthcoming).

96. Although estimates vary depending on methodology and time frame, all show the average cost-benefit ratio to have been very low or, conversely, the real rate of return to have been high relative to that available on private investments. Colin Campbell, for instance, estimated that the cost-benefit ratio for couples retiring in the 1960s was 15 to 20 percent. In a more recent study, Frieden, Leimer, and Hoffman found that the average real rate of return (the interest rate that equates the present value of taxes with the present value of benefits), for workers retiring between 1967 and 1970 exceeded 14 percent, with the low-average earners receiving a real rate of return some 70 percent higher. Hurd and Shoven estimate the median internal rate of return (the interest rate that equates the present value of taxes with the present value of benefits, both discounted at 3 percent) to have averaged 9.76 percent for married couples in 1975. See Colin D. Campbell, "Social Insurance in the United States: A Program in Search of an Explanation," *Journal of Law and Economics* 12 (October 1969): 252–54; Alan Frieden, Dean Leimer, and Ronald Hoffman, "Internal Rates of Return to Retired Worker-Only Beneficiaries under Social Security, 1967–1970," *Studies in Income Distribution*, HEW Publication no. (SSA) 77-11776 (Washington, D.C.: Government Printing Office, 1977), pp. 16–20; and Michael D. Hurd and John B. Shoven, "The Distributional Impact of Social Security," National Bureau of Economic Research Working Paper no. 1155, June 1983. See also James R. Capra, Peter D. Skaperdas, and Roger M. Kubarych, "Social Security: An Analysis of Its Problems," *Federal Reserve Bank of New York Quarterly Review*, Autumn 1982, pp. 1–17.

97. Robert Ball, *Social Security: Today and Tomorrow* (New York: Columbia University Press, 1978), p. 333.

98. Myers, *Social Security*, p. 210.

99. Martin Feldstein, "The Social Security Fund and National Capital Accumulation," in *Funding Pensions: Issue and Implications for Financial Markets*, Conference Series no. 16 (Boston: Federal Reserve Bank of Boston, 1976), p. 43.

100. As indicated earlier, rate of return estimates vary, but all empirical estimates show a long-term decline in returns for future retirees (even those developed before the 1983 amendments). Hurd and Shoven's simulations, for example, show rates of return declining by more than 50 percent for couples reaching sixty-five in the year 2000 relative to those attaining that age in 1970. For married couples now

middle aged or younger, the internal rate of return is projected (pre-1983 amendments) to be close to zero or negative, with the poorest returns being provided to
younger, higher-income workers. According to SSA estimates, the unmarried
worker with high earnings just entering the system at age twenty-two to forty-
seven is not expected to receive back the value of his tax payments (not even the
employee's half). The same worker with very low earnings may receive benefits of
up to two and a half times the value of combined employee and employer tax
payments. See Hurd and Shoven, "Distributional Impact of Social Security," and
Orlo R. Nichols and Richard G. Schreitmueller, "Some Comparison of the Value of
a Worker's Social Security Taxes and Benefits," Actuarial Note no. 95, HEW Pub.
no. (SSA) 78-11500 (April 1978).

The 1983 amendments reduced returns for future retirees, particularly those
with high earnings, by increasing taxes and by delaying and taxing benefits.

101. In 1977 and 1983, reductions in future benefits were mandated and steps
were taken to stabilize financing by linking the determinants of income and outgo.
The revision of indexing procedures in 1977 slowed benefit growth and in some
measure enhanced financial stability. The 1983 legislation increased the retirement
age and explicitly linked income and outgo through a provision that bases the
COLA on the lower of the increase in wages or prices when reserves are critically
low — a provision that typifies risk sharing between the generations. Whereas the
1977 bill imposed 90 percent of the financing burden on workers through revenue
measures, the 1983 bill imposed 60 percent (considering the taxation of benefits an
implicit benefit reduction). See *Social Security Financing*, pp. 35–36, and Richard
S. Foster, "Short-Range Financial Status of the Social Security Program under the
Social Security Amendments of 1983" (unpublished memo, Office of the Actuary,
Social Security Administration, 6 April 1983).

102. Foster, "Short-Range Status."

103. For an interesting account of the role played by advisory councils, see
Derthick, *Policymaking for Social Security*, pp. 89–109.

104. The 1983 amendments include provisions to: (1) mandate an implementation study on making SSA an independent agency; (2) require separate accounting
for social security in the federal budget beginning in 1983 and remove social security from the unified budget in 1993; (3) prevent the opting out of state and local
governments and, as of 1 January 1984, extend mandatory coverage to high-level
federal executives, federal judges, employees of nonprofit organizations, and
newly hired federal workers; and (4) require the SSA actuaries to certify the rea-
sonableness of the assumptions (noneconomic) and methodology underlying the
Board of Trustees' reports. See "Social Security amendments of 1983," PL 98-21, 20
April 1983.

105. Robert Ball, "Take Social Security out of the Budget," *Washington Post*, 22
May 1982.

THE RISE OF THE NATIONAL SECURITY BUREAUCRACY

1. Mira Wilkins, *The Emergence of Multinational Enterprise: American Business Abroad from the Colonial Era to 1914* (Cambridge: Harvard University Press,
1970), pp. 199–217; Robert H. Wiebe, *The Search for Order, 1877–1920* (New
York: Hill and Wang, 1967), pp. 224–36.

2. Richard A. Johnson, *The Administration of United States Foreign Policy*
(Austin: University of Texas Press, 1971), pp. 71–76.

3. Charles E. Neu, *The Troubled Encounter: The United States and Japan* (New York: John Wiley, 1975), pp. 70–71; Richard Hume Werking, *The Master Architects: Building the United States Foreign Service, 1890–1913* (Lexington: University Press of Kentucky, 1977), pp. 143–70.

4. Robert D. Schulzinger, *The Making of the Diplomatic Mind: The Training, Outlook, and Style of United States Foreign Service Officers, 1908–1931* (Middletown, Conn.: Wesleyan University Press, 1975), pp. 99–104, 134–40; Neu, *Troubled Encounter*, pp. 120–21, 146–47.

5. Waldo H. Heinrichs, Jr., "Bureaucracy and Professionalism in the Development of American Career Diplomacy," in *Twentieth-Century American Foreign Policy*, ed. John Braeman, Robert H. Bremner, and David Brody (Columbus: Ohio State University Press, 1971), pp. 198–200; Johnson, *Administration of United States Foreign Policy*, pp. 61, 195.

6. Martin Weil, *A Pretty Good Club: The Founding Fathers of the U.S. Foreign Service* (New York: W. W. Norton, 1978), pp. 82–108; Richard J. Barnet, *Roots of War* (New York: Atheneum, 1972), pp. 24–29.

7. Robert Dallek, *Franklin D. Roosevelt and American Foreign Policy, 1932–1945* (New York: Oxford University Press, 1979), pp. 529–38; Robert A. Divine, *Roosevelt and World War II* (Baltimore: Johns Hopkins Press, 1969), pp. 96–98.

8. Johnson, *Administration of United States Foreign Policy*, pp. 73–79; Dean Acheson, *Present at the Creation: My Years in the State Department* (New York: W. W. Norton, 1969), p. 47.

9. Weil, *Pretty Good Club*, pp. 220–27; Acheson, *Present at the Creation*, pp. 213–16, 733–37; Gaddis Smith, *Dean Acheson* (New York: Cooper Square, 1972), pp. 391–403.

10. Harry S. Truman, *Memoirs*, vol. 2, *Years of Trial and Hope* (Garden City, N.Y.: Doubleday, 1956), pp. 46–60; Richard F. Haynes, *The Awesome Power: Harry S. Truman as Commander in Chief* (Baton Rouge: Louisiana State University Press, 1973), pp. 93–115.

11. Anna Kasten Nelson, "National Security I: Inventing a Process (1945–1960)," in *The Illusion of Presidential Government*, ed. Hugh Heclo and Lester M. Salamon (Boulder, Colo.: Westview Press, 1981), pp. 241–42; Robert J. Donovan, *Tumultuous Years: The Presidency of Harry S. Truman, 1949–1953* (New York: W. W. Norton, 1982), pp. 53–65, 105–13.

12. Johnson, *Administration of United States Foreign Policy*, pp. 87–92.

13. Robert Griffith, "Dwight D. Eisenhower and the Corporate Commonwealth," *American Historical Review* 87 (February 1982): 87–122; Dwight D. Eisenhower, *The White House Years: Waging Peace, 1956–1961* (Garden City, N.Y.: Doubleday, 1963), pp. 87–88, 114–35.

14. Nelson, "National Security I," pp. 245–56; Fred I. Greenstein, *The Hidden-Hand Presidency: Eisenhower as Leader* (New York: Basic Books, 1982), pp. 100–151.

15. Robert A. Divine, *Eisenhower and the Cold War* (New York: Oxford University Press, 1981), p. 154; Keith C. Clark and Laurence J. Legere, eds., *The President and the Management of National Security: A Report by the Institute for Defense Analysis* (New York: Frederick A. Praeger, 1969), pp. 220–28.

16. Nelson, "National Security I," pp. 252–55; Louis Galambos, *America at Middle Age: A New History of the United States in the Twentieth Century* (New York: McGraw-Hill, 1983), pp. 103–4.

17. Townsend Hoopes, *The Devil and John Foster Dulles* (Boston: Little,

Brown, 1973), pp. 141–60; Johnson, *Administration of United States Foreign Policy*, pp. 87–114.

18. David Caute, *The Great Fear: The Anti-Communist Purge under Truman and Eisenhower* (New York: Simon and Schuster, 1978), pp. 303–24; George F. Kennan, *Memoirs, 1950–1963* (Boston: Little, Brown, 1972), pp. 190–228, 274–75; Arthur M. Schlesinger, Jr., *A Thousand Days: John F. Kennedy in the White House* (Boston: Houghton Mifflin, 1965), p. 412.

19. Richard H. Immerman, *The CIA in Guatemala: The Foreign Policy of Intervention* (Austin: University of Texas Press, 1982), pp. 16–18; Ray S. Cline, *Secrets, Spies and Scholars: Blueprint of the Essential CIA* (Washington, D.C.: Acropolis Books, 1976), pp. 199, 151–55, 183–84.

20. Cline, *Secrets, Spies and Scholars*, pp. 119–84.

21. William Colby, *Honorable Men: My Life in the CIA* (New York: Simon and Schuster, 1978), p. 180.

22. Arthur M. Schlesinger, Jr., *Robert Kennedy and His Times*, 2 vols. (Boston: Houghton Mifflin, 1978), 1:435–61; Theodore C. Sorenson, *Kennedy* (New York: Harper and Row, 1965), p. 509.

23. Bernard Bailyn, David Brion Davis, David Herbert Donald, John L. Thomas, Robert H. Wiebe, and Gordon S. Wood, *The Great Republic: A History of the American People*, 2 vols. (Lexington, Mass.: D. C. Heath, 1981), 2:841–53, 880; Hugh Heclo, "Introduction: The Presidential Illusion," in *The Illusion of Presidential Government*, ed. Hugh Heclo and Lester M. Salamon, (Boulder, Colo.: Westview Press) pp. 1–16; Robert H. Wiebe, *The Segmented Society: An Introduction to the Meaning of America* (New York: Oxford University Press, 1975), pp. 188–205.

24. Douglas Kinnard, *The Secretary of Defense* (Lexington: University Press of Kentucky, 1980), pp. 72–90; Warren I. Cohen, *Dean Rusk* (Totowa, N.J.: Cooper Square, 1980), p. 94.

25. Sorenson, *Kennedy*, pp. 281–85; Cohen, *Rusk*, pp. 100–102; Maxwell D. Taylor, *Swords and Plowshares* (New York: W. W. Norton, 1972), pp. 198–200.

26. Herbert S. Parmet, *JFK: The Presidency of John F. Kennedy* (New York: Dial Press, 1983), pp. 158–60; Peter Wyden, *Bay of Pigs: The Untold Story* (New York: Simon and Schuster, 1979), pp. 93–102, 139–72, 305–10; Schlesinger, *Robert Kennedy*, 1:472.

27. George C. Herring, *America's Longest War: The United States and Vietnam, 1950–1975* (New York: John Wiley, 1979), p. 82; Sorenson, *Kennedy*, pp. 295–309.

28. Graham Allison and Peter Szanton, *Remaking Foreign Policy: The Organizational Connection* (New York: Basic Books, 1976), x.

29. Stephen Hess, *Organizing the Presidency* (Washington, D.C.: Brookings Institution, 1976), pp. 78–80, 84; Sorenson, *Kennedy*, p. 281; Richard M. Nixon, *Memoirs* (New York: Grosset and Dunlap, 1978), p. 234.

30. Gary Wills, *The Kennedy Imprisonment: A Meditation on Power* (Boston: Little, Brown, 1982), pp. 163–74, 199–206; Hess, *Organizing the Presidency*, p. 87.

31. Schlesinger, *Thousand Days*, pp. 406–36; Cohen, *Rusk*, pp. 94–107; Barry Rubin, *Secrets of State: The State Department and the Struggle over U.S. Foreign Policy* (New York: Oxford University Press, 1985), pp. 98–122.

32. Ernest R. May, *"Lesson" of the Past: The Use and Misuse of History in American Foreign Policy* (New York: Oxford University Press, 1973), pp. 163–65, 176–77; John Ensor Harr, *The Professional Diplomat* (Princeton: Princeton University Press, 1969), p. 301; This overseas orientation may be changing. After becom-

ing secretary of state, Cyrus Vance worried about "the growing reluctance of Foreign Service officers to serve abroad." Cyrus Vance, *Hard Choices: Critical Years in America's Foreign Policy* (New York: Simon and Schuster, 1983), pp. 43–44.

33. Kennan, *Memoirs, 1950–1963*, pp. 322–23.

34. I. M. Destler, *Presidents, Bureaucrats, and Foreign Policy: The Politics of Organizational Reform* (Princeton: Princeton University Press, 1972), pp. 162–67.

35. Donald P. Warwick, *A Theory of Public Bureaucracy: Politics, Personality, and Organization in the State Department* (Cambridge: Harvard University Press, 1975), p. 9.

36. John Franklin Campbell, *The Foreign Affairs Fudge Factory* (New York: Basic Books, 1971), p. 6; Henry S. Villard, *Affairs at State* (New York: Thomas Y. Crowell, 1965), p. 22; Charles E. Bohlen, *Witness to History, 1929–1969* (New York: W. W. Norton, 1973), p. 8; John Kenneth Galbraith, *Ambassador's Journal: A Personal Account of the Kennedy Years* (Boston: Houghton Mifflin, 1969), pp. 192, 272.

37. Warwick, *Theory of Public Bureaucracy*, pp. 205–15.

38. Campbell, *Foreign Affairs Fudge Factory*, pp. 128–36; Warwick, *Theory of Public Bureaucracy*, pp. 114–18; Henry Kissinger, *Years of Upheaval* (Boston: Little, Brown, 1982), pp. 439–40.

39. Harr, *Professional Diplomat*, pp. 35–40, 191–234.

40. Destler, *Presidents, Bureaucrats, and Foreign Policy*, pp. 159–61.

41. Ibid., pp. 161, 228–30; John Stockwell, *In Search of Enemies: A CIA Story* (New York: W. W. Norton, 1978), p. 63; Campbell, *Foreign Affairs Fudge Factory*, pp. 152–59.

42. Ibid., pp. 15–18, 191–96; Johnson, *Administration of United States Foreign Policy*, pp. 205–6; Morton H. Halperin, *Bureaucratic Politics and Foreign Policy* (Washington, D.C.: Brookings Institution, 1974), pp. 262–63.

43. Destler, *Presidents, Bureaucrats, and Foreign Policy*, pp. 16–42; Allison and Szanton, *Remaking Foreign Policy*, pp. 120–21; Warwick, *Theory of Public Bureaucracy*, pp. 9–10, 37–58, 186–88, 205–15.

44. Ernest R. May, *The Truman Administration and China, 1945–1949* (Philadelphia: J. B. Lippincott, 1975), pp. 40–41; Johnson, *Administration of United States Foreign Policy*, pp. 41–44; Halperin, *Bureaucratic Politics and Foreign Policy*, pp. 235–78.

45. Kenneth J. Meir, *Politics and the Bureaucracy: Policymaking in the Fourth Branch of Government* (North Scituate, Mass.: Duxbury Press, 1979), pp. xvii, 50–51; Johnson, *Administration of United States Foreign Policy*, pp. 26–27.

46. Kissinger, *White House Years*, p. 47; I. M. Destler, "National Security II: The Rise of the Assistant (1961–1981)," in *The Illusion of Presidential Government*, ed. Hugh Heclo and Lester M. Salamon (Boulder, Colo.: Westview Press, 1981) pp. 266–70; for an analysis of the growth of the White House staff and of the Executive Office of the President, with all its accompanying problems, see Hess, *Organizing the Presidency*, pp. 6–10, 125, 150–60.

47. Cohen, *Rusk*, pp. 96–99, 218–22; Emmette S. Redford and Marlan Blissett, *Organizing the Executive Branch: The Johnson Presidency* (Chicago: University of Chicago Press, 1981), pp. 219–20; Doris Kearns, *Lyndon Johnson and the American Dream* (New York: Harper and Row, 1976), pp. 216–19, 238–40.

48. Nixon, *Memoirs*, pp. 337–56, 825; Richard P. Nathan, *The Plot That Failed: Nixon and the Administrative Presidency* (New York: John Wiley, 1975), pp. 82–83.

49. Kissinger, *White House Years*, pp. 11–48; Henry Kissinger, *Years of Upheaval* (Boston: Little, Brown, 1982), pp. 414–15.

50. Destler, *Presidents, Bureaucrats, and Foreign Policy*, pp. 298–99; Kissinger, *White House Years*, pp. 39, 40–42; Nixon, *Memoirs*, p. 343.

51. Allison and Szanton, *Remaking Foreign Policy*, pp. 74–75; John G. Stoessinger, *Henry Kissinger: The Anguish of Power* (New York: W. W. Norton, 1976), pp. 210–12.

52. Allison and Szanton, *Remaking Foreign Policy*, pp. 74–75; Destler, *Presidents, Bureaucrats, and Foreign Policy*, pp. 141–53, 298–319.

53. Destler, *Presidents, Bureaucrats, and Foreign Policy*, pp. 308–14; Herring, *America's Longest War*, pp. 217–20; Kissinger, *Years of Upheaval*, p. 434.

54. Lawrence J. Korb, *The Fall and Rise of the Pentagon: American Defense Policies in the 1970s* (Westport, Conn.: Greenwood Press, 1979), pp. 4–7; Barnet, *Roots of War*, pp. 29–30, 33–37; Ernest R. May, "The Military Influence within the Executive Branch," in *The Military Establishment: Its Impact on American Society*, ed. Adam Yarmolinsky (New York: Harper and Row, 1971), pp, 32–34.

55. Kinnard, *Secretary of Defense*, pp. 2–3, 83–90; John C. Ries, *The Management of Defense: Organization and Control of the United States Armed Services* (Baltimore: Johns Hopkins University Press, 1964), pp. xvii–xxii, 161–67, 188–96, 204–8.

56. Korb, *Fall and Rise of the Pentagon*, pp. 112–16; Lawrence J. Korb, *The Joint Chiefs of Staff: The First Twenty-five Years* (Bloomington: Indiana University Press, 1976), pp. 8–9, 24–25, 118–20, 163–72, 180–81.

57. Samuel P. Huntington, "The Soldier and the State in the 1970s," in *The Changing World of the American Military*, ed. Franklin D. Margiotta (Boulder, Colo.: Westview Press, 1978), pp. 21–24; Korb, *Fall and Rise of the Pentagon*, pp. 26–78, 83–94; James Fallows, *National Defense* (New York: Random House, 1981), Andrew Cockburn, *The Threat: Inside the Soviet Military Machine* (New York: Random House, 1983), and Edward N. Luttwak, *The Pentagon and the Art of War: The Question of Military Reform* (New York: Institute for Contemporary Studies/ Simon and Schuster, 1984), express many of these doubts.

58. Thomas Powers, *The Man Who Kept the Secrets: Richard Helms and the CIA* (New York: Alfred A. Knopf, 1979), pp. 157, 181, 189–93, 202, 228–36, 401; Cline, *Secrets, Spies, and Scholars*, p. 216.

59. Cline, *Secrets, Spies, and Scholars*, pp. 88–89, 149–275; Colby, *Honorable Men*, pp. 294–302.

60. Colby, *Honorable Men*, pp. 329–447; Powers, *Man Who Kept the Secrets*, pp. 276–356; Stansfield Turner, *Secrecy and Democracy: The CIA in Transition* (New York: Harper and Row, 1985), pp. 39–47, 75–89.

61. James Bamford, *The Puzzle Palace: A Report on America's Most Secret Agency* (Boston: Houghton Mifflin, 1982), pp. 1–4, 56–101, 376–78; Thomas Powers, "The Ears of America," *New York Review of Books*, 3 February 1983, p. 14.

62. Thomas M. Franck and Edward Weisband, *Foreign Policy by Congress* (New York: Oxford University Press, 1979), pp. 3–154, 227–57; Michael Malbin, *Unelected Representatives: Congressional Staff and the Future of Representative Government* (New York: Basic Books, 1979), pp. 4–16.

63. Malbin, *Unelected Representatives*, pp. 239–51; James Sundquist, *The Decline and Resurgence of Congress* (Washington, D.C.: Brookings Institution, 1981), pp. 301–6, 367–414; Vance, *Hard Choices*, p. 14.

64. Charles W. Whalen, Jr., *The House and Foreign Policy: The Irony of Congressional Reform* (Chapel Hill: University of North Carolina Press, 1982), pp. 8–9, 70–77, 84–128, 150–72; J. William Fulbright, "The Legislator as Educator," *Foreign Affairs* 57 (Spring 1979): 727.

65. Sundquist, *Decline and Resurgence of Congress*, pp. 461–62, 482–83; *New York Times*, 24 June 1983.

66. Kissinger, *Years of Upheaval*, pp. 440–41.

67. Destler, "National Security II," pp. 263–64, 272–73; Wills, *Kennedy Imprisonment*, pp. 194–98.

68. Jimmy Carter, *Keeping Faith: Memoirs of a President* (New York: Bantam Books, 1982), pp. 52, 89–90; Zbigniew Brzezinski, *Power and Principle: Memoirs of the National Security Adviser, 1977–1981* (New York: Farrar, Straus, and Giroux, 1983), pp. 4–11, 18–22, 238, 288, 521–27.

69. James Fallows, "For Old Times' Sake," *New York Review of Books*, 16 December 1982, p. 10; Carter, *Keeping Faith*, pp. 53–55, 450; Brzezinski, *Power and Principle*, pp. 514, 523–24; Vance, *Hard Choices*, pp. 30–38, 92, 130, 328, 394–95, 409–11.

70. Lou Cannon, *Reagan* (New York: G.P. Putnam's Sons, 1982), pp. 373–75, 386–401; Laurence I. Barrett, *Gambling with History: Ronald Reagan in the White House* (Garden City, N.Y.: Doubleday, 1983), pp. 217–51; Alexander M. Haig, Jr., *Caveat: Realism, Reagan, and Foreign Policy* (New York: Macmillan, 1984), pp. 80–86.

71. Steven R. Weisman, "The Influence of William Clark: Setting a Hard Line in Foreign Policy," *New York Times Magazine*, 14 August 1983; I. M. Destler, "The Evolution of Reagan Foreign Policy," in *The Reagan Presidency: An Early Assessment*, ed. Fred I. Greenstein (Baltimore: Johns Hopkins University Press, 1983), pp. 117–58.

72. David C. Jones, "What's Wrong with Our Defense Establishment," *New York Times Magazine*, 7 November 1982, p. 38; Samuel P. Huntington, "The Defense Policy of the Reagan Administration," in *The Reagan Presidency*, ed. Fred I. Greenstein (Baltimore: Johns Hopkins University Press, 1983), p. 89, argues that the Reagan administration has the same strategy for a military buildup as the Carter administration but refuses to admit it for political reasons.

73. Philip Taubman, "Casey and His C.I.A. on the Rebound," *New York Times Magazine*, 16 January 1983; *New York Times*, 5 August 1983; John Ranelagh, *The Agency: The Rise and Decline of the CIA* (New York: Simon and Schuster, 1986), pp. 656–75.

74. Allison and Szanton, *Remaking Foreign Policy*, pp. 211–14; Stephen Skowronek, *Building a New American State: The Expansion of National Administrative Capacities, 1877–1920* (Cambridge: Cambridge University Press, 1982), pp. vii–ix, 288–92; the most recent analysis of the breakdown of American foreign policy, which ranges far beyond organizational failure, is I. M. Destler, Leslie H. Gelb, and Anthony Lake, *Our Own Worst Enemy: The Unmaking of American Foreign Policy* (New York: Simon and Schuster, 1984).

75. Wills, *Kennedy Imprisonment*, p. 206.

BUREAUCRACY AND THE POLITICAL PROCESS:
THE MONETARY AND FISCAL BALANCE

The views expressed in this chapter are those of the author and do not necessarily represent those of the World Bank or of other members of its staff. Each of the following people contributed something valuable to the essay, though to be candid each also disagrees with something in it. Readers may entertain themselves with the possible implications of that disagreement. Mark Connell and Eric Luftman provided excellent research assistance. These readers helped me immensely: Ralph Bryant, Ben Crain, Louis Galambos, Lance Girton, Catharine Hill, Robert Kilpatrick, Perry Quick, Justine Rodriguez, Joanne Salop, and Donald Tucker.

1. Paul A. Volcker, "The Dilemmas of Monetary Policy," Federal Reserve Bank of New York, *Monthly Review*, December 1975, p. 278, discussed the dual role of the Federal Reserve System.

2. Arthur F. Burns, "The Independence of the Federal Reserve System," *Federal Reserve Bulletin* 62 (June 1976): 494. One important difference between the Federal Reserve and other agencies, though, is that the Federal Reserve is financed from its own earnings and, therefore, is not subject to the same budgetary pressures as other agencies. Too much should not be made of this, however. Although the Federal Reserve "voluntarily" turns over "excess earnings" to the U.S. Treasury, clearly were it to "choose" instead to retain these earnings, the "right" to retain them would be taken away. Board salaries and expenses, most easily observed by Congress and the administration, are set with a close eye on comparable practices in the rest of the government.

The Federal Reserve, after all, holds about $150 billion in federal securities, representing about 10 percent of the federal debt outstanding. At current interest rates, were the Federal Reserve to spend its entire gross income, its expenditures would range in the neighborhood of entire budgets of the Department of Agriculture, Commerce, or Transportation. Obviously something other than outside earning limitation puts a cap on Federal Reserve expenditures.

3. William P. Yohe, "A Study of Federal Open Market Committee Voting, 1955–64," *Southern Economic Journal* 32 (April 1966): 396–405, for analysis of FOMC voting patterns between 1955 and 1964, when Chairman William M. Martin was in the majority on every vote. In one important exception in June 1978, when Chairman William Miller voted with the minority in opposing an increase in the discount rate, several commentators remarked on the unusual event. A. F. Ehrbar, "Bill Miller Is a Faint-Hearted Inflation Fighter," *Fortune*, 21 December 1978, p. 40; Lindley H. Clark, Jr., "Miller's Sixteen Months," *Wall Street Journal*, 24 July 1979, p. 20.

4. One author cites an instance where Chairman Miller was thought to have sided with the majority simply to avoid being outvoted. The author makes clear his view, though, that in general the chairman has the power to command. See Richard J. Levine, "Independent Force: Fed Chairman Miller Wins Power by Seizing on the Inflation Issues," *Wall Street Journal*, 21 June 1978, p. 35.

5. "The Reclusive Power Behind Fed Policy," *Business Week*, 5 March 1979, p. 51, describes the influence of Stephen Axilrod, staff director for monetary affairs under Miller and Burns. Axilrod's critics claimed he manipulated Fed decisions by controlling the range of options offered to the FOMC, but he argued that he simply knew what options would be acceptable to its members.

6. James A. Meigs, "Campaigning for Monetary Reform: The Federal Reserve Bank of St. Louis in 1959 and 1960," *Journal of Monetary Economics* 2 (November 1976): 439–53, describes the attempt of the Federal Reserve Bank of Saint Louis in 1959 and 1960, under bank president Delos C. Johns, to introduce a monetarist Federal Reserve policy. Meigs concludes that Chairman William McC. Martin ultimately made only minor concessions to Johns, and these he made chiefly for political reasons of his own (pp. 451–52). The monthly review of the Federal

Reserve Bank of Saint Louis has often been used as a forum for criticism of the Federal Reserve. Milton Friedman, "Letter on Monetary Policy to Senator William Proxmire," *Federal Reserve Bank of St. Louis* 56 (March 1974): 20–23; Darryl R. Francis, "How and Why Fiscal Actions Matter to a Monetarist," *Federal Reserve Bank of St. Louis* 56 (May 1974): 2–7.

7. "Reclusive Power Behind Fed Policy," 51–52. Indeed, one account claimed that six top Federal Reserve staff members resigned under Chairman Arthur Burns because their advice was ignored.

8. During a series of more than two dozen congressional hearings before the Monetary Policy Oversight Committee during 1975–77, attendance was twice as high on the days when Chairman Burns testified as when other witnesses were present. Steven M. Roberts, "Congressional Oversight of Monetary Policy," *Journal of Monetary Economics* 4 (August 1978): 545, on Banking Committee attendance during 1975–77.

9. Leon H. Keyserling, "The Council of Economic Advisers since 1946: Its Contributions and Failures," *Atlantic Economic Journal*, March 1978, pp. 17–35, for a view on the changing role of the Council of Economic Advisers.

10. James M. Hildreth, "Who Holds Power Now on Reagan Economic Team," *U.S. News and World Report*, 30 November 1981, pp. 26–27, has some general observations on the key players on Reagan's economic policy team. In particular, he suggests that Donald Regan has greatest influence because he knows how to make policy recommendations that mesh most closely with Reagan's own economic views. The article "Economic Advisers: Divided and Discounted," *Economist*, 13 March 1982, pp. 20, 23, supplements this, showing how the opinion of each of the president's advisers has been ignored at some point.

11. Mark Toma, "Inflationary Bias of the Federal Reserve System," *Journal of Monetary Economics* 10 (1982): 163–64, 188–89, argues that the Federal Reserve has an inflationary bias because it finances itself through the profits on its security portfolio, and like any bureaucracy, seeks to maximize its budget.

12. James N. Wetzel, "The Federal Role in the Economy," *Current History* 69 (November 1975): 181, believes that neither monetary nor fiscal policy was used as a macroeconomic stabilization tool between 1965 and 1975. Mace Broide, "The Congressional Budget Process — a Description of How it Works," *Staff* (a congressional staff magazine), no. 1 (January 1979); 1–2, on the other hand, portrays fiscal control as an overriding priority in Congress's tax and expenditure decisions, especially as a result of the formation of the House and Senate Budget Committees in 1974.

13. Although Burns, in a letter to the Joint Economic Committee, expresses the view that "it is important for Congress to put an end to fragmented consideration of expenditures," and pursue a coherent fiscal policy. Arthur F. Burns, "Money Supply in the Conduct of Monetary Policy" (Letter to Sen. Proxmire), in *Federal Reserve Bulletin* 59 (November 1973): 798.

14. William McC. Martin, Jr., "The Federal Reserve's Role in the Economy," *Federal Reserve Bulletin* 51 (December 1965): 1673, clearly states, "It is monetary policy that most adapt itself to the hard facts of the budget — and not the other way 'round." This is not something his successors would have said.

15. See Sheila Tschinkel and John S. Hill, "The Strategy of Monetary Control," *Federal Reserve Bank of New York, Monthly Review*, May 1976, pp. 124–35, for general discussion of how the Fed sets its operational strategies.

16. For example, Franco Modigliani, in Joint Economic Committee, "Financial Aspects of the Budget Deficit," hearing before the Joint Economic Committee, 24

April 1985, criticized the Fed for thwarting the administration's expansionary fiscal policy.

17. Arthur F. Burns, statement before House Budget Committee, *Federal Reserve Bulletin* 60 (October 1974): 403–4; statement before Senate Committee on the Budget, *Federal Reserve Bulletin* 61 (October 1975): 747; statement before Joint Economic Committee, *Federal Reserve Bulletin* 56 (March 1970): 254. Burns in effect told Congress that its lack of a tight fiscal policy undermined the anti-inflationary policy that the Federal Reserve was trying to pursue, shifting the blame onto their shoulders.

18. Arthur F. Burns, statements before Subcommittee on Financial Institutions Supervision, Regulation and Insurance of the Committee on Banking, Currency, and Housing, *Federal Reserve Bulletin* 62 (February 1976): 95, makes the point that while the Federal Reserve does adjust monetary policy to respond to the fiscal actions of Congress and the administration, it resists pressure that it be *required* to condition its own actions to the budget.

19. Brimmer, in Joint Economic Committee, "Financial Aspects of the Budget Deficit," hearing before the Joint Economic Committee, 24 April 1975, pp. 20–21, states that "during each of the last three post–World War II recessions, the Federal Reserve has absorbed one-fifth to two-fifths of the increase in the Federal Government's net borrowing from the public." Ehrbar, "Bill Miller Is a Faint-Hearted Inflation Fighter," hearings before the Joint Economic Committee, 24 April 1975, pp. 42–43, supports the argument that the Federal Reserve responds closely to the desires of the administration. In particular, he shows how Miller worked in tandem with Blumenthal and members of the White House staff, notably in a decision of 1 November 1978, when Blumenthal — not Miller — announced that the Federal Reserve would hike the discount rate and increase bank reserve requirements. Miller, for his part, lobbied for several items in Carter's fiscal program.

20. Arthur Burns, "The Anguish of Central Banking" (International Monetary Fund Per Jacobsson Lecture, Belgrade, Yugoslavia, 20 September 1979), pp. 15–18. Burns argues that since the mid-1960s the Federal Reserve System has been circumscribed in its efforts to control inflation by the necessity for accommodating the pressures imposed on the marketplace by "a Congress that was intent on providing additional services to the electorate and on assuring that jobs and incomes were maintained, particularly in the short run." Volcker concurs, stating that the Federal Reserve cannot control inflation by simply refusing to provide enough money to finance an expansionary fiscal policy without running the risk of pushing the system to collapse. Paul A. Volcker, "The Contribution and Limits of 'Monetary' Analysis," Federal Reserve Bank of New York, *Review,* October 1976, pp. 251–56.

21. Alternatively, the president may attempt to "pack" the Board with his appointees. The appointment of Preston Martin as vice chairman of the Federal Reserve Board was interpreted in this fashion by Ehrbar and by Bacon. A. F. Ehrbar, "The Reaganites vs. the Fed," *Fortune* 103 (4 May 1981): 296; K. H. Bacon, "Fed in a Fix: Reserve Board Faces an Agonizing Choice, amid White House Ire," *Wall Street Journal,* 22 January 1982, p. 1, 18.

22. "Has Jimmy Carter Got a Monetary Policy, and If So, What Is It?" Interview with Beryl Sprinkel, *Euromoney,* January 1977, pp. 60, 61. Sprinkel predicted that in his first two years in office Carter would be unable to loosen monetary growth as much as he would have liked, because Chairman Burns would not go along with it. (But Burns resigned shortly thereafter, anyway.)

23. Jonathan Fuerbringer, "Central Bank Rejects Ideas under Study," *New York Times,* 20 September 1982, p. D14, shows that since the Federal Reserve's creation

in 1913 the degree of political control exerted on it has varied considerably. Harvey M. Segal, "The Politics of Inflation of the Inflation of Politics," *Business Economics* 10 (January 1975): 33, believes that the shift toward monetarist views among members of the FOMC during the mid-1960s was initiated by pressure from Congress, especially Proxmire, Reuss, and Patman (but Segal has little evidence for this).

24. Jonathan Fuerbringer, "Central Bank Rejects Ideas under Study," *New York Times*, 20 September 1982, pp. D1, D14, discusses Federal Reserve independence and suggests that the fact that so many members of Congress are dissatisfied with the Federal Reserve's status and have sought to make the Fed more accountable to Congress or the administration challenges the belief that the Federal Reserve actually does what the administration wants. William McC. Martin, Jr., "Statement on Proposed Changes in Federal Reserve Act," *Federal Reserve Bulletin* 50 (February 1964): 151, had to defend the Federal Reserve in 1964 against a proposed amendment to the Federal Reserve Act that would have placed it directly under the control of the Treasury Department, comparable to the relationship between Bank of England and the Exchequer.

25. Lance Girton pointed this out to me.

26. See Burns, statement before Subcommittee on Financial Institutions Supervision, Regulation and Insurance, pp. 90–91, where he discusses the ultimate authority of Congress over the Federal Reserve.

27. There is probably an economic solution to this problem, but the political considerations above would probably dominate it.

28. See Ross Evans, "Fed's Tight Monetary Policy Provokes Harsh Hill Rhetoric but Little Legislative Threat," *Congressional Quarterly Weekly Reports* 39, 7 November 1981: 1; and Edward J. Kane, "New Congressional Restraints and Federal Reserve Independence," *Challenge*, November-December 1975, p. 42, and "Politics and Fed Policymaking," *Journal of Monetary Economics* 6 (1980): 203. There Evans, pp. 2159–63, recounts congressional unhappiness over the monetary policy being pursued by Chairman Volcker in the fall of 1981. One representative went so far as to introduce a resolution calling for the impeachment of the entire Federal Reserve Board of Governors. Kane (1975, p. 42, and 1980, p. 203) maintains that a major function of the Federal Reserve's independent status is to serve as a scapegoat for congressmen.

29. Robert Samuelson, "The Man of the Year is Not the Computer," *Washington Post*, 28 December 1982, p. D9, concurs, blaming Volcker for the ill effects of recent monetary policy but concluding that despite its reputed independence the Federal Reserve must operate "within the broad limits of consensus." James Tobin, "The Wrong Mix for Recovery," *Challenge*, May-June 1982, p. 23, argues that the Federal Reserve really is capable of meeting its money-supply targets and is more independent than its leaders would have us believe.

30. Edward J. Kane, "New Congressional Restraints and Federal Reserve Independence," *Challenge*, November-December 1975, p. 43. Kane alleges that the Federal Reserve pursued "even keeling" at the cost of effective countercyclical policy.

31. Richard J. Levine, "Reserve's Resolve," *Wall Street Journal*, 20 November 1979, p. 35, describes the emergency meeting that Volcker called in October 1979 upon returning from the International Monetary Fund conference in Belgrade. The conversations he held there convinced him of the need to take drastic monetary policy steps. On the other hand, during this episode Volcker was considered by a fellow member of the board to have been "more of an initiator than many times" in the past, which suggest that he was not necessarily completely in control of the

board before then. See also Lindley H. Clark, Jr., "Monetary Puzzle," *Wall Street Journal,* 23 February 1982, p. 1 on Volcker's emergency meeting.

32. John M. Berry, "Fed, Nearing Key Decision, Faces Pressure and Puzzles," *Washington Post,* 30 May 1982, p. F1, mentions the housing industry, in passing, as a lobbyist in monetary policy.

33. Edward J. Kane, "New Congressional Restraints and Federal Reserve Independence," *Challenge,* November-December 1975, p. 41. Sanford Rose, "Why the Fed Is a Flop at Managing Money," *Fortune,* 23 October 1978, p. 56, who writes that Chairman Miller used to present his quarterly reports to Congress in such a way that he usually left them "shrouded in an intellectual fog." But he interprets this as a case in which many congressmen chose to ignore, for political reasons, what they knew to be an overexpansive monetary policy in 1976. The Federal Reserve then was a handy scapegoat.

34. Lindley H. Clark, Jr., "Miller's Sixteen Months," *Wall Street Journal,* 23 July 1979, p. 20, though, says that one of Miller's greatest faults was that he was not secretive *enough.*

35. Paul A. Volcker, "The Dilemmas of Monetary Policy," *Federal Reserve Bank of New York, Monthly Review,* December 1975, p. 275, describes how the business community nowadays tries to second-guess the Federal Reserve.

36. Sherman J. Maisel, "Managing the Dollar," *Bankers Magazine* (Boston) 157 (Spring 1974): 45–46. In the view of former Governor Maisel, economists cannot agree because there are too many things they are uncertain about. Maisel makes the point that uncertainty pervades Federal Reserve decisions. And if the Federal Reserve does not really know how policy affects money supply and interest rates, how can the public?

By Way of Conclusion: American Bureaucracy since World War II

1. James Burnham, *The Managerial Revolution* (New York: John Day, 1941).

2. Frank H. Gervasi, *Big Government: The Meaning and Purpose of the Hoover Commission Report* (New York: Whittlesley House, 1949), p. 5.

3. *The Hoover Commission Report on Organization of the Executive Branch of Government* (New York: McGraw-Hill, 1949), p. 21.

4. Harold Seidman, *Politics, Position, and Power: The Dynamics of Federal Reorganization,* 3d ed. (New York: Oxford University Press, 1980), pp. 4–5.

5. *Hoover Commission Report,* pp. 3–4.

6. See James Q. Wilson, "The Rise of the Bureaucratic State," *Public Interest* 41 (Fall 1975): 97. Stephen Skowronek, *Building a New American State: The Expansion of National Administrative Capacities, 1877–1920* (New York: Cambridge University Press, 1982), pp. 168–76.

7. I. M. Destler, *Presidents, Bureaucrats, and Foreign Policy: The Politics of Organizational Reform* (Princeton: Princeton University Press, 1972), pp. 192–93. For a history of the relationship between presidents and the NSC see Anna Kasten Nelson, "National Security I: Inventing the Process (1945–1960)," in *The Illusion of Presidential Government,* ed. Hugh Heclo and Lester Salamon, pp. 229–62 (Boulder, Colo.: Westview Press, 1981).

8. James L. Pinick et al., eds., *The Politics of American Science, 1939 to the Present* (Chicago: Rand McNally, 1972), p. 135. For other discussions of Truman's problems with the structural arrangements originally proposed for the NSF, see Don K. Price, *Government and Science* (New York: New York University Press,

1954), pp. 32–64, and Nelson W. Polsby, *Political Innovation in America* (New Haven: Yale University Press, 1984), pp. 35–55.

9. See Samuel P. Huntington, *The Soldier and the State: The Theory and Politics of Civil-Military Relations* (Cambrige, Mass.: Belknap Press, 1957).

10. James Katz, *Presidential Politics and Science Policy* (New York: Praeger, 1978), pp. 39–40.

11. Leonard White, *The States and the Nation* (Baton Rouge: Louisiana State University Press, 1953), pp. 24–25.

12. Diel Wright, *Understanding Intergovernmental Relations*, 2d ed. (Monterey, Calif.: Brooks/Cole, 1982), pp. 53–55.

13. U.S. Department of Commerce, Bureau of the Census, *Historical Statistics of the United States: Colonial Times to 1970* (Washington, D.C.: Government Printing Office, 1975), pp. 228, 1116.

14. Hugh Heclo, "Issue Networks and the Executive Establishment," in *The New American Political System*, ed. Anthony King (Washington, D.C.: American Enterprise Institute, 1979), p. 13.

15. Samuel Huntington, "The Democratic Distemper," *Public Interest* 41 (Fall 1975): 13.

16. Heclo, "Issue Networks and the Executive Establishment."

17. Michael D. Reagan and John G. Sanzone, *The New Federalism*, 2d ed. (New York: Oxford University Press, 1981), p. 56.

18. Theodore Lowi, *The End of Liberalism: The Second Republic of the United States*, 2d ed. (New York: W. W. Norton, 1979), pp. 212–16.

19. See Wright, *Understanding Intergovernmental Relations*, p. 200.

20. J. Clarence Davies III and Barbara S. Davies, *The Politics of Pollution* (Indianapolis: Pegasus, 1975), p. 33.

21. Wright, *Understanding Intergovernmental Relations*, p. 57.

22. John G. Wofford, "The Politics of Local Responsibility: Administration of the Community Action Program, 1964–1966," in *On Fighting Poverty*, ed. James Sundquist (New York: Basic Books, 1969), p. 70.

23. For a different view, see Daniel P. Moynihan, *Maximum Feasible Misunderstanding* (New York: Free Press, 1969), p. 24.

24. Terry L. Christensen, "The Urban Bias of the Poverty Program," in *Analyzing Poverty Policy*, ed. Dorothy Buckton James (Lexington, Mass.: Lexington Books, 1975), p. 146; see also J. David Greenstone and Paul E. Peterson, "Racial Change and Citizen Participation: The Mobilization of Low Income Communities through Community Action," in *A Decade of Federal Antipoverty Programs*, ed. Robert Haveman (New York: Academic Press, 1977), pp. 241–78.

25. Moynihan, *Maximum Feasible Misunderstanding*, p. 84.

26. See Howard Hallman, "The Community Action Program: An Interpretive Analysis," in *Power, Poverty, and Urban Policy*, ed. Warner Bloomberg and Henry J. Schmandt (Beverly Hills, Calif.: Sage Publications, 1968), pp. 285–311.

27. See James Q. Wilson, "The Bureaucracy Problem," *Public Interest* 6 (Winter 1967): 3–9.

28. Bernard Frieden and Marshall Kaplan, *The Politics of Neglect: Urban Aid from Model Cities to Revenue Sharing* (Cambridge: MIT Press, 1975), pp. 78–79.

29. James Sundquist and David Davis, *Making Federalism Work: A Study of Program Coordination at the Community Level* (Washington, D.C.: Brookings Institution, 1969).

30. Frieden and Kaplan, *Politics of Neglect*, pp. 209–12.

31. See Robert Wiebe, *The Search for Order, 1877–1920* (New York: Hill and Wang, 1972): Skowronek, *Building a New American State*.

32. On the design and passage of the revenue sharing program, see Donald Haider, *When Governments Come to Washington: Governors, Mayors, and Intergovernmental Lobbying* (New York: Free Press, 1974), pp. 257–82.

33. Richard P. Nathan, Allen D. Manvel, and Susannah E. Calkins, *Monitoring Revenue Sharing* (Washington, D.C.: Brookings Institution, 1975), p. 5.

34. U.S. Department of Housing and Urban Development, *President's National Urban Policy Report, 1980* (Washington, D.C.: Government Printing Office, 1980), chap. 13.

35. Richard P. Nathan, "The Reagan Presidency in Domestic Affairs," in *The Reagan Presidency: An Early Assessment*, ed. Fred Greenstein (Baltimore: Johns Hopkins University Press, 1983), pp. 48–81; George E. Peterson, "The State and Local Sector," in *The Reagan Experiment*, ed. John Palmer and Isabel Sawhill (Washington, D.C.: Urban Institute, 1982), pp. 157–98.

36. Wright, *Understanding Intergovernmental Relations*, p. 98.

37. Richard P. Nathan, *The Plot That Failed: Nixon and the Administrative Presidency* (New York: John Wiley, 1975).

38. United States, President's Commission on Housing, *Report of the President's Commission on Housing* (Washington, D.C.: Government Printing Office, pp. 17–19.

39. E. S. Savas, *Privatizing the Public Sector: How to Shrink Government* (Chatham, N.J.: Chatham House, 1982).

40. See Charles Schultze, *The Public Use of Private Interest* (Washington, D.C.: Brookings Institution, 1977).

41. See Harold Seidman, *Politics, Position, and Power: The Dynamics of Federal Organization*, 3d ed. (New York: Oxford University Press, 1980), pp. 125–32.

42. See Arthur M. Schlesinger, Jr., *The Age of Roosevelt: The Coming of the New Deal* (Boston: Houghton Mifflin, 1959), chaps. 32, 33; Richard E. Neustadt, *Presidential Power: The Politics of Leadership from FDR to Carter* (New York: John Wiley, 1980), pp. 115–16; James MacGregor Burns, *Roosevelt: The Lion and the Fox* (New York: Harcourt Brace and World, 1956), pp. 370–75.

43. For a recent survey of reorganization commissions and studies, see James G. March and Johan P. Olson, "Organizing Political Life: What Administrative Reorganization Tells Us about Government," *American Political Science Review* 77 (June 1983): 281–96. A comprehensive study of administrative reorganization in the national government during the twentieth century may be found in Peri E. Arnold, *Making the Managerial Presidency: Comprehensive Reorganization Planning, 1905–1980* (Princeton: Princeton University Press, 1986).

44. See the description of the work of the second Hoover Commission in Herbert Emmerich, *Federal Organization and Administrative Management* (University: University of Alabama Press, 1971), pp. 101–28.

45. Ibid., p. 127.

46. See Seidman, *Politics, Position and Power*, pp. 10–13.

47. See Waldo's "Foreword" in Oscar Kraines, *Congress and the Challenge of Big Government* (New York: Bookman Associates, 1958), p. 7.

48. Kraines, *Congress and the Challenge of Big Government*, p. 107.

49. See Oscar Kraines, "The President versus Congress: The Keep Commission, 1905–1909, First Comprehensive Presidential Inquiry into Administration," *Western Political Quarterly* 23 (March 1970): 5–54.

50. For a history of the Budget Bureau (later OMB) in the postwar period see Larry Berman, *The Office of Management and Budget and the Presidency, 1921–1979* (Princeton: Princeton University Press, 1979).

51. See Richard E. Neustadt, "Presidency and Legislation: The Growth of Central Clearance," *American Political Science Review* 48 (September 1954): 641–71, and Stephen J. Wayne, *The Legislative Presidency* (New York: Harper and Row, 1978), pp. 70–100.

52. The best analyses of the rise and fall of the budget agency in the postwar era may be found in Hugh Heclo, "OMB and the Presidency: The Problem of Neutral Competence," *Public Interest* 38 (Winter 1970): 5–54, and Allen Schick, "The Budget Bureau That Was: Thoughts on the Rise, Decline and Future of a Presidential Agency," *Law and Contemporary Problems* 35 (Summer 1970): 519–39.

53. Aaron Wildavsky has written extensively on the role of PPBS in the budgetary process. See most recently, *The Politics of the Budgetary Process*, 4th ed. (Boston: Little, Brown, 1984), pp. 186–202.

54. U.S. Commission on Organization of the Executive Branch of the Government, *Task Force Report on Personnel and Civil Service* (Washington, D.C.: Government Printing Office, 1955), pp. 190–92, and 35–38; and Paul P. Van Riper, *History of the United States Civil Service* (Evanston, Ill.: Row, Peterson, 1958), pp. 495–96.

55. Richard P. Nathan, *The Administrative Presidency* (New York: John Wiley, 1983).

56. "Federal Political Personnel Manual: The 'Malek Manual,'" *Bureaucrat* 4 (January 1976): 429–508.

57. Mark W. Huddleston, "The Carter Civil Service Reforms: Some Implications for Political Theory and Public Administration," *Political Science Quarterly* 96 (Winter 1981–82): 607–21.

58. Dick Kirschten, "Administration Using Carter-Era Reform to Manipulate the Levers of Government," *National Journal* 9 (April 1983): 732–36.

59. *Humphrey's Executor vs. United States*, 295 U.S. 602 (1935).

60. President's Committee on Administrative Management, *Report of the Committee with Studies of Administrative Management in the Federal Government* (Washington, D.C.: Government Printing Office, 1937), p. 40.

61. 53 Stat. 561 (1933).

62. David M. Welborn, *Governance of Federal Regulatory Agencies* (Knoxville: University of Tennessee Press, 1977), pp. 31–49.

63. See, in this connection, Susan J. Tolchin and Martin Tolchin, *Dismantling America: The Rush to Deregulate* (Boston: Houghton Mifflin, 1983); and Barry M. Mitnick, *The Political Economy of Regulation: Creating, Designing and Removing Regulatory Forms* (New York: Columbia University Press, 1980).

64. Erwin G. Krasnow, Lawrence D. Longley, and Herbert A. Terry, *The Politics of Broadcast Regulation*, 3d ed. (New York: St. Martin's Press, 1982), pp. 10–16.

65. David Vogel, "The 'New' Social Regulation in Historical and Comparative Perspective," in *Regulation in Perspective: Historical Essays*, ed. Thomas K. McCraw (Cambridge: Harvard University Press, 1981).

66. George C. Eads and Michael Fix, "Regulatory Policy," in *The Reagan Experiment: An Examination of Economic and Social Policies under the Reagan Administration*, ed. John L. Palmer and Isabel V. Sawhill (Washington, D.C.: Urban Institute Press, 1982), pp. 129–53; and Lester M. Salamon, "Federal Regulation: A New Arena for Presidential Power?" in *The Illusion of Presidential Government*, ed.

Hugh Heclo and Lester M. Salamon (Boulder, Colo.: Westview Press, 1981), pp. 147–73.

67. Nathaniel Beck, "Presidential Influence on the Federal Reserve in the 1970s," *American Journal of Political Science* 26 (August 1982): 415–45; John T. Woolley, *Monetary Politics* (Cambridge: Cambridge University Press, 1984); and Donald F. Kettl, *Leadership of the Fed* (New Haven: Yale University Press, 1986).

68. For an analysis of the growth of secrecy in American and other democratic political systems, see Itzhak Galnoor, ed., *Government Secrecy in Democracies* (New York: Harper and Row, 1977).

69. The president's role with regard to this and other information practices is examined in Harold C. Relyea, *The Presidency and Information Policy* (New York: Center for the Study of the Presidency, 1981), esp. chap. 1.

70. See Evan Hendricks, *Former Secrets* (Washington, D.C.: Campaign for Political Rights, 1982).

71. The impact of the media on government information practices is described in Leon V. Sigal, *Reporters and Officials: The Organization and Politics of Newsmaking* (New York: D. C. Heath, 1973); for an analysis of the role of public interest groups in modern American politics see Jeffrey M. Berry, *Lobbying for the People: The Political Behavior of Public Interest Groups* (Princeton University Press, 1977); for recent bibliographical material on information policies and practices, see Elaine Tomchick and Harold C. Relyea, *Managing Official Information* (Wahington, D.C.: Congressional Research Service, 1980).

72. The development of the civil service system in the United States is traced in Van Riper, *History of the United States Civil Service*.

73. For a study of the use that recent presidents have made of their White House staffs, see Stephen Hess, *Organizing the Presidency* (Washington, D.C.: Brookings Institution, 1976).

74. On the growth of congressional staff, see Harrison W. Fox, Jr., and Susan W. Hammond, *Congressional Staff: The Invisible Force in American Lawmaking* (New York: Free Press, 1977), and Michael Malbin, *The Unelected Representatives* (New York: Basic Books, 1980).

75. Morris P. Fiorina, "The Case of the Vanishing Marginals: The Bureaucracy Did It," *American Political Science Review* 71 (March 1977): 180.

76. See David H. Rosenbloom, "The Judicial Response to the Rise of the American Administrative State," *American Review of Public Administration* 15 (Spring 1981): 29–51.

77. See Donald L. Horowitz, *The Jurocracy: Government Lawyers, Agency Programs and Judicial Decisions* (Lexington, Mass.: Lexington Books, 1977).

78. See, in this regard, David O. Sears and Jack Citrin, *Tax Revolt: Something for Nothing in California* (Cambridge: Harvard University Press, 1982).

79. Herbert Kaufman, "Fear of Bureaucracy: A Raging Pandemic," *Public Administration Review* 41 (January-February 1981): 1–9.

80. A very useful survey of neoconservative thought may be found in Peter Steinfels, *The Neoconservatives: The Men Who Are Changing America's Politics* (New York: Simon and Schuster, 1979).

81. *New York Times*, 18 September 1981, p. A 18.

Contributors

MATTHEW A. CRENSON is a professor in the department of political science at the Johns Hopkins University. His major publications include *The Un-Politics of Air Pollution: A Study of Non-Decision Making in the Cities; The Federal Machine: Beginnings of Bureaucracy in the Age of Jackson; Models in the Policy Process: Public Decision Making in the Computer Era* (coauthored); and, most recently, *Neighborhood Politics*.

HEYWOOD FLEISIG is an economist and economic historian with extensive experience in the federal government's fiscal and monetary bureaucracies. He worked for the Congressional Budget Office and the Federal Reserve Board before taking his current position in the World Bank. His numerous publications include articles in the *Journal of Economic History* and the *American Economic Review*, as well as *Long Term Capital Flows and the Great Depression: The Role of the United States, 1927–1933*.

LOUIS GALAMBOS is a professor of history and editor of *The Papers of Dwight David Eisenhower* at the Johns Hopkins University. His publications include *America at Middle Age: A New History of the U.S. in the Twentieth Century* and *The Public Image of Big Business in America, 1880–1940: A Quantitative Study in Social Change*. He is currently president of the Economic History Association.

SAMUEL P. HAYS, who recently served as Harmsworth Professor of American History, Oxford University, teaches in the department of history at the University of Pittsburgh. He recently published *The Politics of Health, Beauty, and Permanence: Shaping the Commons in the Environmental Era*. His many other books and articles include studies of urban, reform, and ethnic politics, as well as *American Political History as Social Analysis*.

CHARLES E. NEU teaches United States diplomatic history at Brown University. A former fellow at Harvard University's Charles Warren Center, Neu has recently conducted NEH seminars on the "Organizational Dimensions of American Foreign Policy." His books include *An Uncertain Friendship: Theodore Roosevelt and Japan, 1906–1909* and *The Troubled Encounter: The United States and Japan.*

FRANCIS E. ROURKE is a professor of political science at the Johns Hopkins University; he has also taught at Yale University and at the University of California at Berkeley. His major interest is public administration and in particular the role the federal bureaucracy has played in shaping public policy. His chief publications include *Secrecy and Publicity: Dilemmas of Democracy; Bureaucracy, Politics, and Public Policy;* and *Bureaucracy and Foreign Policy.*

CAROLYN A. WEAVER is an economist who has served on the staff of the U.S. Senate's Committee on Finance and as senior advisor to the National Commission on Social Security Reform. A former research fellow at the Hoover Institution, she is currently at the American Enterprise Institute in Washington, D.C. Her publications include *Understanding the Sources and Dimensions of Crisis in Social Security: A First Step Toward Meaningful Reform* and *Crisis in Social Security: Economic and Political Origins.* She is a member of the 1987 Social Security Disability Advisory Council.

Index

THE NEW AMERICAN STATE

Designed by Ann Walston.

Composed by Capitol Communication Systems, Inc.
in Paladium text and display type.

Printed by Thomson-Shore, Inc.
on 50-lb. S. D. Warren's Olde Style paper,
and bound by John H. Dekker and Sons, Inc.
in Holliston Roxite cloth.